When
Negroes
March

When Negroes March

THE MARCH ON WASHINGTON MOVEMENT
IN THE ORGANIZATIONAL POLITICS FOR FEPC

Herbert Garfinkel

WITH A NEW PREFACE BY LEWIS M. KILLIAN

Studies in American Negro Life / *August Meier, General Editor*

NEW YORK   *1969*   Atheneum

PUBLISHED BY ATHENEUM
COPYRIGHT © 1959 BY THE FREE PRESS
PREFACE COPYRIGHT © 1968 BY LEWIS M. KILLIAN
ALL RIGHTS RESERVED
LIBRARY OF CONGRESS CATALOGUE CARD NUMBER 69-15522
MANUFACTURED IN THE UNITED STATES OF AMERICA BY
KINGSPORT PRESS, INC., KINGSPORT, TENNESSEE
PUBLISHED IN CANADA BY MC CLELLAND & STEWART LTD.
FIRST ATHENEUM EDITION

To

Evelyn, Martin and Philip

On to Washington, ten thousand black Americans. . . . We shall not call upon our white friends to march with us. There are some things Negroes must do alone. This is our fight and we must see it through. If it costs money to finance a march on Washington, let Negroes pay for it. If any sacrifices are to be made for Negro rights in national defense, let Negroes make them. . . . Let the Negro masses speak!

—A. PHILIP RANDOLPH

PREFACE TO THE ATHENEUM EDITION

by Lewis M. Killian

WHEN HERBERT GARFINKEL'S case study of the March on Washington movement first appeared in 1959, there could be no question as to what "march" he meant. Although the event had been canceled, any student of Negro-white relations in the United States knew that "the March on Washington" was the mass demonstration planned under the leadership of A. Philip Randolph for July 1, 1941. The mere threat of this massive protest had led President Roosevelt to issue, on June 25, Executive Order 8802, establishing the first Fair Employment Practices Committee.

Since the first publication of this book, this original march on Washington has been overshadowed by two other marches, the convergence of over 200,000 Negro and white civil rights advocates on Washington in August 1963, and the Poor People's March of June 1968. The occurrence of such a movement three times in a quarter of a century does not, of course, signify that history repeats itself. Each movement developed out of a different setting, had its own distinctive characteristics, and produced different results. Yet examination of the current phase of the Negro revolution in the light of Garfinkel's history of an earlier phase reminds us that, to understand the present, we must know the past.

Although the passage of years and the turmoil of new developments in race relations warrant our classifying *When Negroes March* as history, the study was and is an excellent piece of sociological research. It is, first of all, an analysis of the dynamics of a social movement. It offers an incisive and detailed analysis of the problems of mobilization, organization, and strategy encountered by a movement which seeks to act through a mass organization. Secondly, it is a study of leadership. The successes and the setbacks experienced by A. Philip Randolph, the towering figure of the first March on Washington movement, can be understood only in the context of the ever shifting, always competitive array of individuals who constitute the ill-defined phenomenon called "Negro leadership." Finally, Garfinkel provides an in-depth analysis of one phase of the continuing interaction between the federal government and the Negro minority. Consideration of each of these three aspects of this study reminds us forcibly of the continuity to be found in the Negro people's struggle for equality, a continuity often obscured by the high drama and the apparent novelty of contemporary developments.

The eruption of the sit-ins in 1960 and the rapid rise to prominence of CORE, SCLC, and, later, SNCC underscored the dominant position of the NAACP in the preceding phases of the civil rights movement. The shift to the tactics of direct action was widely acclaimed as a revolt against the legalistic approach of the NAACP. That there were limits to the effectiveness of litigation, lobbying, and education, all part of a strategy of persuasion rather than of coercion, seemed to be a new insight given to a younger generation of Negroes disillusioned by the tortuous gradualism with which White America responded to the desegregation decision of 1954. A few years later the shock of the rejection of white allies by Black Power advocates gave rise to the myth that, ever since the demise of Marcus Garvey, Negro partisans had been eager to march shoulder to shoulder with white liberals in the pursuit of equality. The story of the 1941 March on Washington movement belies both of these impressions. This movement, appearing perhaps before its time, constituted the first use of what William Gamson has called "a strategy of constraints" by Negroes against the federal government.* What is remarkable is that in its first trial this strategy had as much success as it did.

In September 1940 a group of Negro leaders, including Walter White of the NAACP, had met with President Roosevelt to protest against segregation in the armed forces. Despite the massive Negro political support which had helped put Roosevelt in the White House for a second term, this conference produced only bitter disappointment for Negroes. The President reaffirmed the policy of segregation with a statement which implied that the Negro leaders had acquiesced in his decision. In the months that followed, the United States accelerated its military preparations but Negroes re-

* *Power and Discontent* (Homewood, Ill.: The Dorsey Press, 1968).

mained segregated in uniform and virtually excluded from the burgeoning defense industry. Negro discontent grew, but now the door to the White House was closed to Negro leaders. Not until a fortnight before the scheduled march of 100,000 Negroes on the capital was this door opened again. Only a week before the date of the march President Roosevelt issued the executive order establishing the President's Committee on Fair Employment Practices. There is no doubt that the threat of a massive display of Negro discontent accomplished what Negro votes and the good offices of older Negro organizations had not been able to achieve.

After the waning of Booker T. Washington's hegemony and the brief popularity of Marcus Garvey, Negro leadership had been virtually institutionalized in the top offices of the NAACP and the Urban League. There was no outstanding Negro leader such as Washington had been or Martin Luther King, Jr., was to become. But for a year and a half, from the inception of the March on Washington movement until the beginning of its decline and disintegration, A. Philip Randolph was *the* Negro leader in America. He was no longer merely the powerful head of the Brotherhood of Sleeping Car Porters; he was the personal symbol of a type of black lower-class militance which had not surfaced since Garveyism and was not to be seen again until the slogan "Black Power" echoed throughout the land. Ironically, Randolph is not identified with the Black Power movement of the 1960's but seems to fit more easily into the camp of those Negro leaders who advocate a strategy of coalition politics. Like his modern successors, this earlier Randolph recognized the importance of black-consciousness to the development of a movement which would involve the Negro masses. In trying to make the MOWM an all-black movement, however, he was also influenced by a consideration which does not concern contemporary Black Power leaders. Only a few years earlier Randolph, as president of the National Negro Congress, had been bitterly disillusioned by the ease with which white Communists had taken over the organization. He did not want the same thing to happen to the MOWM. Today it is the timorousness of white liberals, not the deviousness of white communists, that leads black leaders to distrust white allies.

It will never be known whether the original March on Washington could have been staged if it had not been canceled. The ability of Negroes to make the threat credible bears witness to the genius which Randolph displayed in stirring up widespread enthusiasm for the march with only halfhearted support from the NAACP and the Urban League, and in the face of opposition by the communists. His inability to sustain the enthusiasm or even to keep the movement alive bears witness to the significance of the factionalism which continues to plague Negro leadership. The story of Randolph's unsuccessful attempt to keep the MOWM alive and strong without the support of the older protest organizations provides valuable clues as to why the NAACP has been able to maintain its preeminence while other organizations have waxed and waned. Criticism of his attempts to launch a new campaign of civil disobedience in lieu of a new march, criticism based on the fear that the campaign would generate riots and severe repression, was an early manifestation of the fear of "white backlash" which hampers protest strategy today.

Studious attention to the reasons why Randolph felt that the MOWM was still needed after its initial victory might have saved many civil rights advocates from bitter disappointments in the years that followed. Like so many "victories" which have since been won by the Negro Revolution, Randolph's victory turned out to be more symbolic than real. The demand of the MOWM for an executive order was met; the price was the cancelation of the March. At this point the momentum of the movement was lost, just as two decades later the momentum of many campaigns of non-violent direct action was lost when white community leaders agreed to negotiate with Negro leaders in return for a moratorium on demonstrations. But FEPC did not produce quick results. During its first year it had to undertake a tremendous administrative task with a woefully small staff and a tiny budget. Then, just as the Committee seemed to be developing into an effective agency, it was subordinated to Paul McNutt's War Manpower Commission, a development which Negroes had feared from the beginning. The transfer, made because of pressure from Southern congressmen, removed the Committee from the direct control of the President and, at the same time, made it dependent upon Congress for its funds. The emasculation of FEPC was one consequence of President Roosevelt's transition from "Dr. New Deal" to "Dr. Win the War." Another generation of Negroes was to witness the same sort of betrayal of their high hopes when the Great Society was displaced by the Vietnam War as the first order of national business.

This volume has its greatest value today as a corrective to the prevalent and recurrent myth that Negroes have made great progress and won noteworthy concessions, particularly from the federal government, until the latest generation of leaders has "tried to go too fast." After all, it was almost thirty years ago that Randolph was able to rally Negroes to bring on the White House because of discrimination in employment. We can question just how much real progress has been made when, in 1968, Negroes still felt impelled to rally before the Lincoln Memorial to demand federal action to create more jobs. We must also ask, "How many more hollow victories will Negroes accept as the price for domestic peace before they abandon all faith in a society which promises so much and delivers so little?" The limits of their patience may be dangerously near.

Contents

Preface

PRESIDENT FRANKLIN D. ROOSEVELT, confronted with the prospect of thousands of Negroes demonstrating on the White House grounds, established the first Fair Employment Practice Committee (FEPC). He was told to his face that if he did not do so, 100,000 Negroes from across the country would "march on Washington" the first of July, 1941. That bold threat was made during the early stages of World War II when Negroes, after years of depression, sought to share in the defense-period prosperity. The intense bitterness and frustration which led the Negro community to rally around so desperate a scheme, created an intriguing episode in American political history. But there is more than interesting history here. These events of the recent past are continuous with the present situation in which civil rights is undoubtedly one of the nation's most pressing domestic problems.

Currently, much attention is directed to Negroes and to the dramatic events in civil rights politics. Most of the journalistic coverage has distorted the situation by sensational treatment of cases like that of Miss Autherine Lucy, "the Little Rock Nine," or other instances where violence or "personalities" have provided human-interest stories. Sober reporting has also suffered a kind of distortion by concentrating its analysis on the more obvious wielders of influential decisions—the Court, Congress, President, school administrators, etc. These formal levels of decision making, while vested with official authority, cannot be understood adequately apart from the group pressures which are brought to bear upon them. This may be a commonplace observation, but the lesson has been insufficiently applied to the Negro interests underlying the civil rights battle.

Behind the current agitation in the Negro community is a history of developing leadership and organization which requires intensive analysis if we are to understand the present. The defense period just prior to American entry into World War II is fundamental, because it was then that Negro political activity was forced into independent action. During the depression Negro politics was essentially New Deal politics. With the defense boom Negroes were left behind by the general white citizenry. Negroes remained unemployed and on relief in large numbers for some time after the general economic situation markedly improved, and former allies, the white liberal organizations, became preoccupied with the war crisis along with the Roosevelt Administration. It is true that following the war the Negro-white liberal alliance was reconstituted, but the earlier period of independent action profoundly altered the shape of the historic Negro protest.

To be sure, the March on Washington Movement (MOWM) was not the first example of independence or militancy in Negro history. Slave revolts were frequent enough to dispel as illusory the stereotypes of happy "Old Black Joe" and loyal "Uncle Tom." Free Negroes like Frederick Douglass were active abolitionists. The National Association for the Advancement of Colored People (NAACP) from its founding went considerably beyond the "accommodationist" policies of Booker T. Washington. But the NAACP had not succeeded in firing the imagination of Negroes as did the March on Washington Movement. What was new in the national defence period of the Forties was the spontaneous involvement of large masses of Negroes in a political protest without the collaboration of whites. Reluctantly supported by NAACP leaders, the MOWM captured the enthusiasm of lower-class Negroes as the interracial NAACP had never managed to do. Indeed the March, inspired by A. Philip Randolph (International President of the Brotherhood of Sleeping Car Porters), for a time loomed much larger than the NAACP. The present preeminence of the NAACP is a subsequent development, and its current sharpness of attack on racial discrimination is at least partly the result of lessons learned during the days when Negro militancy was synonymous with the March on Washington Movement.

Two forms of protest currently being utilized by Negroes were pioneered by Randolph's March. Twenty-five thousand Negroes in May of 1957 rallied in Washington before the Lincoln Monument to express demands for governmental action on civil rights. This "Prayer Pilgrimage for Freedom" revealed its MOWM heritage in the leadership provided by A. Philip Randolph who opened the giant meeting. A new and outstanding figure now involved is the Rev. Martin Luther King, Jr., of Montgomery, Alabama bus-boycott fame, who carries on the Gandhian "passive-resistance" strategy also foreshadowed by Randolph's MOWM.

Allied with the new movement is the NAACP and its capable and vigorous leader, Roy Wilkins, reflecting the unity of the Negro protest in its present phase. It is to the leadership of Dr. King and Mr. Wilkins that the future of the Negro protest belongs, but it is from Mr. Randolph that a great deal of their tactical conception of the struggle has stemmed.

This book relates the story of the dramatic movement which forced the FEPC from a reluctant President. What emerges is the natural history of a political issue and the organizational leadership which gave it life. Though but a single case-study, it has general import for understanding how new political issues may arise. Similarly, it is instructive concerning the life patterns of many successful social movements which blaze new political paths only to die as the issues they create are taken over by established groups and institutions.

The MOWM arose in a severe crisis which alienated and demoralized American Negroes. But that crisis was the source of greater cohesion among the Negro people and made possible the organization of a mass movement. Simultaneously, the political fermentation in a previously apathetic group provided the support for a new leadership. As traditional channels of influence were closed off to the established leaders, control over the program and strategy of the protest became fluid. The opportunity was seized by Randolph and, when his dramatic threat to "march on Washington" forced President Roosevelt to issue the FEPC order, the prestige of the MOWM and its sharp-tongued leader zoomed.

This preeminence was not long-lived, but the FEPC issue continued into the postwar period to become the major item in the civil rights proponents' programs. The circumstances which produced the decline of the March involved a complex of political, organizational and leadership-rivalry factors. These have been traced along with the gradual emergence of new priorities in the organizational strategy for extending civil rights.

My interest in Negro political organization began with an opportunity to observe at firsthand the 1951 campaign for a state FEPC law in Illinois. There the Negro community was astonishingly apathetic about FEPC. Negro organizations were, to be sure, officially a part of the proponent committee which led the campaign. However, they failed to raise money, organize meetings, send lobbyists to Springfield or even attend most meetings of the campaign steering commitee. White liberal, labor, Catholic, Protestant and, predominantly, Jewish groups provided the supporting base.

Although it was generally known that the FEPC issue had arisen with the March on Washington Movement, students of FEPC politics have passed over that organization with only sparse attention based on secondary sources. In stark contrast to the later FEPC advocates, exemplified in the Illinois situation, the MOWM was an all-Negro organization. This militant movement, which began with the exclusion of whites as a deliberate policy, gradually developed into a standard lobbying enterprise overwhelmingly dominated by white organizations. The desire to understand that transformation provided a challenge to political analysis and led to the research on which this book is based.

In brief, what follows is primarily the organizational history of the Negro March on Washington Movement in the genesis of FEPC politics; tracing its dramatic rise, its brilliant success, its inevitable decline and demise. An epilogue brings the analysis up to date, including some reflections on the implications of the study for the present situation in the ongoing struggle to promote racial justice in America.

Acknowledgments

Access to the files of the Brotherhood of Sleeping Car Porters was provided by its International President, Mr. A. Philip Randolph. There, without restriction, the records of the March on Washington Movement and the National Council for a Permanent FEPC were made available. Earlier, much primary data was obtained from the Illinois Fair Employment Practice Committee (the state-wide proponent organization) through the cooperation of its Executive Committee and the then Executive Secretary, Mr. Albert J. Weiss. The latter provided considerable insight into FEPC organizational politics.

Professors David Easton, Louis Wirth, Martin Diamond and Charles M. Hardin of the University of Chicago; Professor Avery Leiserson, of Vanderbilt University; Professor Philip Selznick of the University of California (Berkeley); and Mr. Oscar Tarcov of the Anti-Defamation League, all gave important advice and encouragement at different stages of the research and writing.

The National Opinion Research Center, through its Director, Dr. Clyde W. Hart, administered a grant from the Field Foundation which made it possible to spend considerable time as a participant-observer of the activities of the Illinois FEPC proponents, which took place during the 1951 campaign for a period of almost a full year. Dartmouth College, also, was generous with financial support and encouragement.

Many individuals (noted below) provided the benefit of their experiences in personal interviews, and I am very appreciative of their time and courtesy. A special acknowledgment is owed Miss Pauli

Murray who aided greatly with a voluminous correspondence concerning the March on Washington Movement and its leadership. Others who kindly wrote were Mr. C. L. Dellums, International Vice President of the Brotherhood of Sleeping Car Porters, Los Angeles, California; Mr. Eardlie John, attorney of New York City; and Mr. Frank R. Crosswaith, Chairman of the Negro Labor Committee, New York City.

The notes reveal other important documentary sources, particularly the Negro press and the files of the Schomburg Collection of the New York Public Library. I thank the librarians in charge of that collection as well as Miss Virginia Close and her reference department staff at Dartmouth College's Baker Library.

Considerable use of private correspondence and of published materials was made possible by generous persons and publishers who allowed me to quote them extensively. The *Free Press* of Glencoe, Illinois has been a most cooperative publisher tolerating many delays and revisions. I am grateful, too, to Miss Lucille Flanders who typed the manuscript.

No organizations or individuals other than the author are in any way reponsible for the interpretations and analyses made of their materials.

Interviews

Mr. Arnold Aronson, Staff, National Community Relations Advisory Council, New York, N.Y.

Mr. Russell Babcock, Executive Director, Illinois Interracial Commission.

Mr. Robert Bollard, Staff, Illinois CIO.

Mr. Theodore E. Brown, Educational Director, Brotherhood of Sleeping Car Porters, New York, N.Y.

Rev. Archibald Carey, Jr., Alderman, Chicago, Illinois.

Mr. Thomas Colgan, American Friends Service Committee, Chicago, Illinois.

Miss Angela De Gagne, Friendship House, Chicago, Illinois.

Mr. John Dreiske, Reporter, *Chicago Sun Times*.

Mr. Hy Fish, Labor Education Division, Roosevelt College, Chicago, Illinois.

Mr. Samuel Freifeld, Staff, Anti-Defamation League of B'nai B'rith, Chicago, Illinois.

Mr. F. Charles Gilmour, Manager, Personnel and Labor Relations, Illinois State Chamber of Commerce.

Mr. Max Goldman, Staff, Anti-Defamation League of B'nai B'rith.

Mr. Lester B. Granger, Executive Director, National Urban League.

Mr. Nat Gray, Staff, American Jewish Committee, Chicago, Illinois.

Mr. Nissen Gross, Staff, Anti-Defamation League of B'nai B'rith, Chicago, Illinois.

Mrs. Lillian Herstein, Field Representative, Jewish Labor Committee, Chicago, Illinois.

Dr. Homer Jack, Evanston, Illinois.

Rev. Robert Johnson, President, Illinois State National Association for the Advancement of Colored People.

Mr. Will Katz, Executive Secretary, American Jewish Committee, Chicago, Illinois.

Mr. Murray Klutch, Staff, Illinois Fair Employment Practice Committee.

Mr. Henry Kohn, Attorney and Illinois Fair Employment Practice Committee Leader.
Senator Roland V. Libonati, General Assembly, State of Illinois.
Mr. Hub Logan, Reporter, *Chicago Sun Times*.
Mr. Edward Marciniak, Editor, *Catholic Worker*, Chicago, Illinois.
Mr. Robert Marshall, Ann Arbor, Michigan.
Mr. Lewis Martin, Executive Editor, *Chicago Defender*.
Mr. Paul Mathias, General Counsel, Illinois Agricultural Association.
Mr. Frank McCallister, Director, Labor Education Division, Roosevelt College, Chicago, Illinois.
Mr. Henry McGee, National Association for the Advancement of Colored People, Chicago, Illinois.
Mr. Joseph Meek, President, Illinois Federation of Retail Associations.
Mr. Byron Miller, Executive Secretary, Chicago Branch, American Jewish Congress.
Mrs. Mary Moulton, Staff, Church Federation of Chicago.
Mr. Emanuel Muravchick, Jewish Labor Committee, New York, N.Y.
Miss Pauli Murray, writer and attorney, New York, N.Y.
Miss Ethel Polk, Staff, Michigan CIO, Lansing, Michigan.
Mr. A. Philip Randolph, International President, Brotherhood of Sleeping Car Porters, A.F.L., New York, N.Y.
Mr. Abbott Rosen, Executive Director, Anti-Defamation League of B'nai B'rith, Chicago, Illinois.
Mrs. Sonya Sapir, Staff, Commission on Human Relations, City of Chicago.
Rev. Waitsill Sharp, Executive Director, Chicago Council Against Racial and Religious Discrimination.
Mr. Elmer Shirrell, Member of Administrative Committee of Church Federation of Chicago, and Personnel Director of Curtis Candy Company.
Mr. Norman Thomas, Socialist leader and writer, New York, N.Y.
Mr. Willard S. Townsend, President, United Transport Service Employees of America, CIO.
Mr. Aldrich Turner, National Treasurer, March On Washington Movement.
Albert J. Weiss, Executive Director of Bureau on Jewish Employment Problems; formerly Executive Secretary, Illinois Fair Employment Practice Committee, Chicago, Illinois.
Mr. Walter White, Executive Secretary, National Association for the Advancement of Colored People, New York, N.Y.
Mr. Sidney Williams, Executive Secretary, National Urban League, Chicago, Illinois.
Mr. Nelson Willis, President, Chicago Branch NAACP.
Senator Christopher C. Wimbish, General Assembly, State of Illinois.
Mr. Thomas Wright, Executive Director, Commission on Human Relations, City of Chicago.
Mr. John Yancey, Staff, Chicago CIO.

chapter i

Negroes in the Defense Emergency

Probably the only person in political life during the late Thirties who was more popular with American Negroes than President Roosevelt was his wife Eleanor. The New Deal had received an overwhelming endorsement from lower class America, and the lower down one went into the strata of underprivileged citizenry the deeper that affection went. By 1936, that sentiment was overwhelming and had been translated into a deluge of supporting votes.[1]

The shift in Negro voting habits from the party of the Great Emancipator to a party also claimed by extreme white supremacists like Senator Bilbo, and Congressmen Rankin and Talmadge was an amazing Democratic achievement. True, along with a majority of other Americans, Negroes were grateful for the emergency work and relief programs of the New Deal. But the Rooseveltian popularity with Negroes went beyond economics.

For example, when the Daughters of the American Revolution refused to permit Marian Anderson to sing in Constitution Hall, Mrs. Roosevelt resigned from the DAR in public protest. The Department of Interior made the Lincoln Memorial available for a mammoth open-air concert by the famous Negro contralto and Secretary Harold L. Ickes presided. Later, Miss Anderson received the Spingarn medal from the hand of the First Lady at the 1940 conference of the National Association for the Advancement of Colored People

(NAACP). Mrs. Roosevelt was continually outspoken in favor of civil rights, and endeared herself and the Administration to the bulk of Negro voters.

Summing up "The Roosevelt Record" the 1940 election issue of *Crisis,* the NAACP's monthly organ, declared:

> Most important contribution of the Roosevelt Administration to the age-old color line problem in America has been its doctrine that Negroes are a part of the country as a whole. The inevitable discriminations notwithstanding, this thought has been driven home in thousands of communities by a thousand specific acts. For the first time in their lives, government has taken on meaning and substance for the Negro masses.[2]

We shall see that this very issue of *Crisis* was sharply critical of the Administration, yet its pre-election editorial all but endorsed Roosevelt's candidacy. In the light of such amicability between Negroes and the Administration, it might appear that "FDR" merely continued a racially liberal New Deal policy when he ordered an end to discriminatory employment practices by government and defense contractors and established the Fair Employment Practice Committee (FEPC). That Executive Order (8802) was issued only a short time after Roosevelt began his third term. And, if one read only what the *New York Times* carried concerning the executive order, the illusion of continuity and harmony would remain unchanged. There was no consideration of the underlying forces, the organized pressures, which prodded the Administration into several unsatisfactory attempts at placating Negroes and which finally obtained this more acceptable action. This inattention to the influences behind Roosevelt's order was not a journalistic disregard for "academic," non-newsworthy, analyses. The activities in Negro communities throughout the nation which led to the FEPC decree were highly dramatic. But employment discrimination, even in the face of a pressing manpower shortage, was not deemed worthy of report by the major press until quite late in World War II.

Enormous pressure was necessary before the FEPC Executive Order was obtained from President Roosevelt. Indeed, there is no better example of pressure more unanimously and militantly applied against any President in the history of the Negro protest. The paradox is that no public official since Abraham Lincoln had so completely gained the devotion of America's Negroes. It was in these circumstances that a new movement and a new political issue originated. This soon came to the fore as the top-priority item in the civil rights program, the demand for a Fair Employment Practice Committee.

Discrimination in the Arsenal of Democracy

Let us say to the democracies: We Americans are vitally concerned in your defense of freedom. We are putting forth our energies, our resources and our organizing powers to give you the strength to regain and maintain the free world. We shall send you in ever increasing numbers, ships, planes, tanks, guns. That is our purpose and our pledge.

President Franklin D. Roosevelt[3]

While we are in complete sympathy with the Negro, it is against company policy to employ them as aircraft workers or mechanics . . . regardless of their training. . . . There will be some jobs as janitors for Negroes.

President, North American Aviation Co.[4]

In 1941 the American economy was borne upward on an enormous wave of governmental defense spending. Doors previously closed to the unemployed were opened as the wheels of industrial activity began to roll. In the newspapers of the nation, the talk shifted from shortages of jobs to shortages of labor, from the problem of insufficient purchasing power to the depletions that a rapidly booming national income was making on needed materials of war.

In the midst of this economic spurt, which seemed to expunge all thought of the depression years, there were some who expressed alarm as steps were taken to close down the WPA program. This was not the grumbling of a few superannuated workers who could find no place for themselves in a competitive labor market. The complainants were Negro Americans to whom the feverish preparations to "defend democracy" merely highlighted their group's alienation from much that gave substance to the "American way of life."[5]

The nation, faced with severe shortages of skilled workers, established intensive training programs to solve that problem. Yet, non-Caucasian Americans were informed that it would be wasteful to train them as they could not be placed. And an armed service, which strove desperately to fill quotas in its emergency recruitment program, discouraged that same group despite its millions of potentially skilled hands.

Here then were the twin complaints of Negro Americans early

in 1941 as the nation sought to recruit and to supply its military defenses. These were the days when Hitler's armies lay astride all of Europe, when the Soviet Union (prior to June 22) was in uneasy alliance with the Nazis and when the British were only a Channel's breadth from the recent Dunkirk evacuation. Negroes who had been the first fired during the depression were the last to be rehired as defense workers, and then were mainly restricted to "nigger work." Negro soldiers, wearing the uniform of the U.S. Army, were drafted on a discriminatory quota system, trained in segregated camps and assigned to menial types of duty.

During the depression Negroes, undoubtedly, had been the most severely debilitated of all groups. In 1930 they were 9.7 per cent of the total population; about the same time they made up 16.7 per cent of the total relief group. Nationally, almost twice as high a proportion of Negroes as of whites were on public relief rolls; 18 per cent of Negroes received aid by contrast with 9.5 per cent of whites.[6]

Table 1—Comparison of Negro and White Relief Recipients, October 1933, in Cities With Over 50,000 Negroes:[7]

City	Ratio of relief persons to all persons	
	Negroes	Whites
New York, N.Y.	23.9	9.2
Chicago, Ill.	34.4	10.1
Philadelphia, Pa.	34.4	8.2
Baltimore, Md.	28.8	9.3
Washington, D.C.	21.8	2.4
New Orelans, La.	37.9	9.6
Detroit, Mich.	27.6	10.1
Birmingham, Ala.	26.5	10.9
Memphis, Tenn.	11.1	4.8
St. Louis, Mo.	34.3	7.2
Atlanta, Ga.	22.7	9.1
Cleveland, Ohio	43.0	12.4
Houston, Tex.	20.7	8.9
Pittsburgh, Pa.	43.4	15.7
Richmond, Va.	10.7	3.7

Table 1 portrays vividly the dire straits of urban Negroes in the Thirties. In none of the large cities were Negroes found to be as well off as whites, and in most cases the disparity was very substantial. In Pittsburgh and Cleveland 43 per cent of Negroes were on relief. Washington, D.C. exhibited the greatest disproportion between the races with 21.8 per cent of Negroes on relief compared to only 2.4 per cent of whites.

This condition was long-lasting. A census of unemployment in 1937 found 22 per cent of male Negroes unemployed whereas only 15 per cent of male whites were unemployed. The situation concerning females was worse; only 7 per cent of all white women who were looking for work were unemployed compared with 16 per cent of female Negro workers.[8]

War in Europe set in motion the productive forces capable of absorbing America's unemployed, but the process of absorption was an uneven one. In 1940, the Bureau of the Census collected data "in the belief that statistics on potential workers would be useful in the mobilization of the nation's available manpower reserves required to meet military and war production needs."[9] The situation confronting Negroes, it was found, remained severe. White workers received preferential treatment at the hiring gates. This was readily explained by the Census Bureau:

At the time of the census, a very large proportion of the nonwhite workers in Northern cities were unemployed, partly because of their comparative lack of training and experience of the kinds that were in demand, and partly because many employers were unwilling to hire nonwhites if other workers were available. Employment opportunities for nonwhite workers have undoubtedly improved since the time of the census, and will continue to improve in the future as the number of available white workers diminishes, but the reserves of nonwhite labor cannot be fully utilized unless extensive training and retraining is undertaken, and the prejudice against them is reduced or eliminated.[10]

This prediction proved well founded. Placements by state employment services in 1941 increased over placements the preceding year at a somewhat faster rate for nonwhite workers (48 per cent) than for whites (42 per cent). Nonwhite workers, largely Negroes, made up only 11 per cent of the labor force in 1940, yet in 1941 they constituted 21 per cent of all placements by these government employment offices.[11]

This is plainly a substantiation of the "first-fired, last-hired" thesis. Negroes made up a considerably larger portion of the unemployed than did whites during the depression. As the defense effort opened vacancies, Negroes were rehired at a slower rate than were whites. By 1941, the labor reserve was reaching the bottom of the barrel; a bottom made up of a disproportionate share of nonwhite workers.

Only then did the rate of placements for Negroes catch up with that for whites.[12]

But obtaining employment was only part of the problem for Negroes. Employment practices are discriminatory also in the quality of jobs made available to minority workers. When defense jobs were finally opened up to Negroes they tended to be on the lowest rungs of the success ladder. *The Social Security Yearbook* for 1941 reported:

> Nearly 58 per cent of the placements of nonwhite workers in 1941 were in service occupations and more than 31 per cent in unskilled jobs; hence 11 per cent were in all other occupations combined. In contrast, only about 53 per cent of the placements of white workers were in service and unskilled jobs. Only 1.5 per cent of the jobs filled by nonwhite, as compared with nearly 12 per cent of the jobs filled by white workers, were in skilled occupations.[13]

The quality of nonwhite job openings was also revealed as "tending to account for relatively high proportions of the placements in the occupations characterized by low wage levels."

Much the same discriminatory pattern prevailed in the training of Negro workers. Manpower needs were so pressing that a vast program was organized to equip workers with the necessary technical skills. The facilities of this training program were extended to Negroes on considerably less than equal terms.[14]

The manpower shortage facing the nation did not only apply to the production line; the Armed Forces competed with the homefront for manpower. Yet, despite shortages, the Selective Service System operated with discriminatory quotas: the Army segregated its Negro soldiers, the Navy restricted them to messmen and other menial service, and the other branches of the Armed Forces excluded them altogether.[15] In many respects, the discriminatory practices against Negroes which characterized the military programs of the defense and later war periods cut deeper into Negro feelings than did employment discrimination.

Some perfunctory symbolic efforts were made to placate American Negroes. An officer was promoted to brigadier general, a higher rank than any to which a Negro had theretofore risen, and a Negro aviation training program of very limited scope was undertaken at Tuskegee Institute. There were a few other such gains but it is their unimportance rather than their number which precludes their enumeration here. Even these concessions were obtained as a consequence of much pressure and negotiation with the White House.

Negro Morale

Victory demands your cooperation. If the peoples of this country's races do not pull together, Victory is lost. We, therefore, respectfully direct your attention to the laws and customs of the state in regard to segregation. Your cooperation in carrying them out will make the war shorter and Victory sooner. Avoid friction. Be Patriotic. White passengers will be seated from front to rear; colored passengers from rear to front.

(Sign under a large red "V" on a bus in Charleston, S.C.)[16]

The Crisis leaves to its readers the question of whether there is a great deal of difference between the code for Negroes under Hitler and the code for Negroes under the United States of America—the leading democratic nation in the world.[17]

The seriousness of the first-fired, last-hired employment cycle for Negro morale is plain. Though bad enough during the depression years, some consolation could then be drawn from the very pervasiveness of the deprivation. Unemployed Negroes shared hardships which at that time beset the entire nation. And if there were disproportionately more unemployed Negroes than whites, there was substantial equality in the administration of the New Deal relief programs. In addition to the tangible benefits, status-hungry Negroes could feel somewhat cared about as well as cared for.

When, however, the WPA and relief expenditures were cut back and the threat of complete dissolution was made, Negroes had not shared substantively or psychologically in the budding defense boom. Now Negroes met with more patent discrimination at the hiring gates where signs no longer declared, "No Help Wanted," but, "Help Wanted, *White*." This refrain, played to the tune of democratic slogans, was bound to grate on Negro ears.

World War I was heralded as the "War to Save the World for Democracy." World War II propaganda made even greater use of democratic symbols. Much was orated and printed concerning the goodness of the *free* world and the badness of the *totalitarian* world. The doctrine of democracy was urged as the unifying principle by which to weld the populace into a cohesive fighting force. Americans were continually reminded of equalitarian slogans: "The Four Freedoms," "The Atlantic Charter," "The People's War." The enemy was attacked not merely as a foreign foe hostile to national interests but as a totalitarian social and political system destructive of the freedom of its own and of all people.

In a "fireside chat," President Roosevelt assailed the dictatorships as:

an unholy alliance of power and pelf to dominate and enslave the human race. The history of recent years proves that the shootings and the chains and the concentration camps are not simply the transient tools but the very altars of modern dictatorships. They may talk of a new order in the world, but what they have in mind is only a revival of the oldest and worst tyranny. In that there is no liberty, no religion, no hope.[18]

The need to unify the nation in preparation for war resulted in an increasing emphasis on traditional democratic and liberal values. It was a time when the American creed was receiving considerably more than the ceremonial Fourth-of-July type of affirmation.

The history of the Thirties aided, too, in bringing an increased usage of democratic and equalitarian terminology, for it was during that period that radicalism grew in the despair of world-wide depression. The New Deal was, itself, a pragmatic outgrowth of an increasingly radical temper. Consequently, ideological justification and radically oriented rather than purely nationalistic symbols were required to legitimize American involvement in a new European war.

There can be no question but that the Hitler regime itself, in its flagrant assault on democratic values, provided a substantial basis for counterattack in terms emphasizing democratic norms. The Kaiser, in World War I, was successfully depicted as a despot and his regime castigated as autocratic. In World War II, the label of antidemocracy was provided by the enemy himself, who brazenly sought to conquer all in the name of the "master-race" and of the "Fuehrer."

General appeals to the doctrine of equality and freedom would have been sufficient to arouse the Negro's expectations. But countering the Nazi attack on democracy more vitally affected him, for it was directed at a racist philosophy and genocidal practices. While the persecution had been levelled most particularly against Jews, its implications for Negroes were obvious. Allied propaganda reflected this aspect of the Hitlerite threat and challenged it with democratic principles. As *Fortune* declared: "In the consciousness of all peoples in the world, this war is being fought for and against the idea of racial superiority."[19]

Thus, whatever the actual position of the Negro and other minority groups in the defense effort, there can be no doubt concerning their bad psychological condition.[20] The gap between democratic creed and practice widened when depression gave way to war boom, because war, though it brought more employment opportunities even for Negroes, brought a still greater increase in the emphasis on democratic beliefs. These endless appeals to rally to the defense of free men and free institutions seemed but hollow mockery to American blacks. As Roy Wilkins, then editor of *Crisis,* put it:

No agitators were needed to point out to him the discrepancies between what we said we were fighting for, and what we did to him. He did not need the NAACP to show him that it sounds pretty foolish to be *against* park benches marked 'Jude' in Berlin, but to be *for* park benches marked 'Colored' in Tallahasee, Florida.

It is pretty grim . . . to have a black boy in uniform get an orientation lecture in the morning on wiping out Nazi bigotry, and that same evening be told he can buy a soft drink only in the 'Colored' post exchange![21]

This attitude was pervasive; it characterized not only the Negro intelligentsia and professional leaders, nor only the middle to upper classes. The street corner, poolroom, beauty parlor, and general folk talk also expressed it. Stories went the rounds all pointing the same moral: the inconsistency of fighting for democracy abroad in the light of practices at home. One very popular story may serve as an example. A Negro soldier on a Southern bus is said to have resisted the driver's efforts to shift him to the Jim Crow section by taking off his coat and declaring, "Well, I'm fixing to go off and fight for democracy. I might as well start right now."[22] This was a recurrent theme.

In August of 1941, a gun fight broke out on a crowded bus in Fayetteville, North Carolina, between Negro soldiers and white military policemen. Two of the MP's were wounded and a Negro private was shot dead. The editor of the Negro *Pittsburgh Courier* writing of the attitude of the Negro soldiers to the wounder of the white MP's stated flatly, "They were proud of him for it."[23] The same writer went on to report the reaction of "a Negro sergeant, a college graduate and an all-American football star," who declared: "If I've got to die, I might as well die right here fighting for myself as to go abroad and die fighting for somebody else."

Though described by *Fortune* as "a responsible and rather calmly edited Negro journal,"[24] *Crisis* struck the same note:

We shall see what we shall see. Negro Americans might as well discover at the beginning whether they are to fight and die for democracy for the Lithuanians, the Greeks and the Brazilians, or whether they had better fight and die for a little democracy for themselves.[25]

Writing in *Harper's Magazine*, a Negro author bluntly stated: "The Negro today is angry, resentful and utterly apathetic about the war. 'Fight for what?' he is asking. 'This war doesn't mean a thing to me. If we win I lose, so what?' "[26]

Walter White, then executive secretary of the NAACP, told of his horror at hearing from a teacher in a well-known Negro college in the South of the attitude of his students to the war. One of the students, "with infinite bitterness," exclaimed in a discussion of the war, "I hope Hitler wins!" The teacher had then argued that "conditions would be even worse under Hitler." The student had replied:

They can't possibly be any worse than they are for Negroes in the South right now. The Army jim-crows us. The Navy lets us serve only as messmen. The Red Cross refuses our blood. Employers and labor unions shut us out. Lynchings continue. We are disfranchised, jim-crowed, spat upon. What more could Hitler do than that?

But White was to be even more horrified later on, when addressing a Midwestern audience:

I told the story of the Southern student as an illustration of the kind of dangerous, shortsighted thinking which Negro Americans had to guard zealously against. To my surprise and dismay, the audience burst into such applause that it took me some thirty or forty seconds to quiet it. Though I went into as detailed an explanation of the fallacy of such thinking as I could, I left the meeting with a feeling of depression born of the conviction that I had not convinced all of my audience that Hitlerism could and would be worse.[27]

The reaction of this audience to White's story was duplicated by the Negro press in reporting the developments in the national defense picture as it affected Negroes. A comparison of the white and Negro press strikingly illustrates the divergent concerns of the white and Negro communities. Where the one wrote of help needed to make strong the fortress of democracy, the other wrote of the undemocratic evils of second-class citizenship. One wrote of the gallant armed forces of democracy, the other front paged a young Chicago Negro's refusal of induction into service not on the grounds of pacifism or religion but of racial discrimination.[28]

We need not try to decide whether Negro morale was bad because of the Negro press or whether that press merely reflected the concerns of its readers. It was no doubt a reciprocal and cumulative process. The white newspapers might disagree as to how the "free world" could best be defended, but that it was free was axiomatic. Within the Negro press there was disagreement as to strategy and means but the end, to make an unfree world free by ending racial discrimination *during the emergency*, was clear and held in common. These assumptions were probably accurate reflections of the moods of their respective audiences. After attacks on the Negro press in the *Reader's Digest* and the *Atlantic*, an opinion poll was taken by the *Pittsburgh Courier*. This sought to determine Negro reactions to "the crusade which the Negro press is conducting for full integration of the race into the life of America."[29] It drew an almost unanimous affirmative response.

There is bound to be a great deal of difference in the emphases of the Negro and of the white press. The narrower audience and weekly publication of Negro newspapers is likely to affect what is considered newsworthy. But the differences were particularly pronounced during the war years. White newspapers paid scant attention to the discontent Negroes voiced or to the bases of those complaints. The major news story of 1940-41 in the white press concerning Negroes was typically prejudicial reporting of the alleged attack-kidnapping of a "blond and pretty society woman" who "told how she had been pulled from her shower bath by her colored chauffeur, attacked four times and finally thrown into Kensico reservoir. He confessed last night."[30] This story filled many pages in the nation's white tabloids. Fortunately for the chauffeur, despite this conviction by newspaper, an all-white jury acquitted him.

Similarly, white news reporting of a "Harlem crime wave" in 1941 was bitterly resented by Negroes.[31] The irony of these cases is the vast amount of newspaper attention given to them simultaneously with a general disregard for the serious problems confronting Negroes in the defense emergency. This double standard did not escape notice by the Negro community.

On the other hand, Negro editors seized on each incident of Jim Crow in industrial hiring practices or in the Armed Forces and put it forth as vividly as white tabloids treated rape or murder cases. After Pearl Harbor, many writers complained that Negroes were taking unfair advantage of the situation. Criticism came not only from spokesmen for white supremacy; even Mrs. Roosevelt urged greater restraint.[32] The Negro was charged by critics with interfering with the war effort by protesting in an irresponsible manner and at a time when national unity was imperative for survival. The "race" press came in for the heaviest attack. An attempt was made to deny them newsprint and to get the Department of Justice to indict some of the editors for sedition. This did not eventuate, in part, due to NAACP efforts.[33]

The white publishing world was largely as insensitive to the bad state of Negro morale, as was the Government. A few periodicals attempted to state the Negro's case or allowed him to state it in their pages.[34] But these efforts were sporadic and ineffectual. Some efforts were made by the Government to deal directly with the sag in Negro morale. The War Department presented a forty-five minute nation-wide radio broadcast on the Negro soldier. Unfortunately, it was ill-conceived and was resented by Negroes, particularly Undersecretary of War Patterson's defense of continued segregation.[35] A similar reaction followed issuance of an Office of War Information pamphlet, *The Negro and the War*, which was termed "a monumental mistake and disservice to the government and the Negro."[36]

There is only one conclusion possible: Negro morale was desperately low, and Negroes made little effort to hide their dissatisfaction. No statement concerning the war before or after Pearl Harbor by prominent Negro leaders (excepting the Communists) failed to include some reference to its double nature for Negroes—that it was a war for democracy both abroad and at home. But this did not result from a failure of Negroes to support the defense effort. Nor were Negroes, their press and their organizational leaders seditious.

When a Negro sailor, a messman, manned an antiaircraft gun during the Japanese attack on Pearl Harbor, the deed was made much of in all the Negro papers. This heroic act was officially precluded by the Navy policy restricting Negro seamen to menial tasks. It will surprise no one that the Negro press highlighted the irony of the situation. In this and similar incidents, the Negro press and leadership waxed enthusiastic over outstanding deeds by Negroes in support of the war effort.

On the whole, Negroes did not oppose the war or fail to support it either before or after Pearl Harbor. The leader of the most vigorous pressure campaign for Negro rights during the war was A. Philip Randolph, president of the Brotherhood of Sleeping Car Porters, who organized the March on Washington Movement. Yet Randolph left the Socialist party in 1940 because, as he later said, "I felt that the war of the United Nations against the Axis ought to be supported."[37] He became an active member of the Committee to Defend America by Aiding the Allies early in World War II.

The double-sided war aims of Negroes (in this case even prior to Pearl Harbor) is nowhere better illustrated than in one of the "Editor Says" columns of *Opportunity*. The editor of this monthly organ of the National Urban League concerned himself with two items: The first bade farewell to a Negro National Guard regiment called to active duty; the second complained of discriminatory employment practices. Here is how they appeared, one paragraph following immediately on the other:

No one knows now what will be the ultimate disposition of the 369th, but this we do know—that with a fair chance it will be a shining example of the loyalty of the American Negro to his country.

*   *   *

AMERICAN NAZISM. By no other terms can the cruel and deliberate exclusion of Negro citizens from aviation and other industrial plants engaged in filling defense orders, solely because of their color, be described.[38]

Negro dissatisfaction was not with the draft, but with the refusal of Negro enlistees by many branches of the Armed Forces; not with the purposes of defense work mobilization, but with the refusal to hire and train qualified Negro workers. The Negro did not reject democratic doctrine in favor of Nazi ideology; quite the contrary, he insisted on democratic practices in the fight for democracy.

The Negro Protest

And so tonight I am appealing to the heart and to the mind of every man and every woman within our borders who love liberty. I ask you to consider the needs of our nation at this hour and to put aside all personal differences until our victory is won.

There will be no divisions of party or section or race or nationality or religion. There is not one among us who does not have a stake in the outcome of the effort in which we are now engaged.

President F. D. Roosevelt, in a "Fireside Chat"[39]

Negroes are not as naive and tractable as they were in World War I.

Journal of Negro Education, "Editorial Note"[40]

Historically, the militant Negro protest following the Civil War was crushed in the post-Reconstruction Southern resurgence. The removal of federal troops and a series of court decisions gradually established a pattern of two worlds segregated from maternity hospitals to cemeteries. The abolitionist spirit which had sustained a Negro leadership such as that of Frederick Douglass faded away as white reformers turned to other problems.

Left to shift for itself, a new Negro leadership arose to make the best of a very difficult situation. The "accommodationist" policy of Booker T. Washington was "realistic" in that it rejected as utopian any immediate efforts to continue the battle for the principle of full equality. Second class status was accepted as a prerequisite to obtaining any concessions from the dominant whites. A leadership grew up under Washington's tutelage dedicated to ending illiteracy and encouraging an attitude to hard work as the highest virtue. Negroes were to "cast down their buckets where they were," to learn trades and live exemplary lives. According to Washington, "The time will come when the Negro in the South will be accorded all the political rights which his ability, character and material possessions entitle him." In the meantime, "The opportunity to earn a dollar in a factory just now is worth infinitely more than the opportunity to spend a dollar in an opera house."[41]

There was, to be sure, something to be said for the logic of Washington's strategy. But social protest is more than a matter of rational tactics. Many of Washington's public statements deeply offended Negroes who craved a sense of dignity. For example, the way in which Washington greeted Theodore Roosevelt's election in 1904:

The result shows that the great heart of the American people beats true and is in the direction of fair play for all, regardless of race, or color. . . . I shall urge our people to manifest their gratitude by showing a spirit of meekness and added usefulness.[42]

This approach did not go unopposed. The demand for immediate application of the principles of the Thirteenth, Fourteenth and Fifteenth Amendments, for full citizenship, was asserted by the important Niagara Movement. Led by Dr. W. E. B. Du Bois, this 1905 conference of Negro intellectuals reasserted the primacy of political equality. To Du Bois, "manly self-respect is worth more than lands and houses." Furthermore, "A disfranchised working class in a modern industrial civilization is worse than helpless."[43] It was this movement which blended with a revitalization of the white abolitionist spirit to form the NAACP in 1909.

The initiative had come from the white reformers and the NAACP has been an interracial (at the top) organization ever since. Its appeal, though uncompromising and, hence, "radical" by contrast with Booker T. Washington's policy, was mainly upper class and its methods basically conservative. As recently as the early Nineteen-Forties Gunnar Myrdal found:

The branches—and consequently the National Association—have nowhere been able to build up a real mass following among Negroes. The membership is still largely confined to the upper classes.[44]

The characteristic pressure politics of the NAACP has been conditioned by this absence of mass participation in its work. The organization has made its substantial contribution to Negro progress primarily as an intellectual vanguard. Its methods reflect the talents of the "talented tenth,"[45] which are largely legal and public relations in orientation. The success of these activities in such matters as the white-primary cases and, more recently, the famous Supreme Court decision against segregated public schools has lifted the NAACP into the forefront of the organized Negro protest. And by contrast with the period covered by Gunnar Myrdal's appraisal, the Association now appears to have great popularity with the masses of Negroes. But this was not the case prior to World War II.

Of necessity, as an interracial social service agency, the National Urban League and its local affiliates are even more conservative than the NAACP. Founded at roughly the time of the Association's beginning, the Urban League has provided trained social workers in many metropolitan areas devoted to the endless array of difficulties confronting Negroes adjusting to urban conditions. It has always been much concerned with economic conditions and, therefore, was greatly interested in FEPC politics from the origin of the issue of employment equality. Though the National Urban League is a social service agency, its leaders have, throughout its existence, played an important part in the Negro protest by virtue of their prominence, prestige and influence.

Two other strands woven into the movement of Negroes for equality arose to challenge both Booker T. Washington's accommodationism and W. E. B. Du Bois' intellectualism. These were the racial nationalism of Marcus Garvey and the economic radicalism of such socialists as Chandler Owen and A. Philip Randolph.

Marcus Garvey, a post-World War I phenomenon, was less interesting for the ideals he espoused than for the enormous success of his movement.[46] Garvey never won a single concession from whites or got very far with his scheme to found a black "Empire of Africa." However, he achieved a great response from the Negro masses.

Garvey's program was very different from Booker T. Washington's pragmatic compromises or Dr. Du Bois' principled battle for equality in a predominantly white society. The essence of it was a kind of Negro Zionism, a scheme to return and lay claim to Africa which would be resurrected as a world power. He and his followers turned their backs on white society entirely and glorified "racial purity." The mythology included a black empire, a black God, and a black history which proved through past splendors a racial virility that would rise again in future greatness.

Intellectual and upper class Negroes were repelled by Garvey's emotional chauvinism, but never before had anyone rallied so many Negroes in a mass protest movement. Garvey, at his height in the Twenties, declined during the depression; but he left a legacy of black nationalism which survived his deportation from the country.

The post-World War I period produced another group of Negro protestors, the economic radicals. Young Negro socialists rejected Garvey's race nationalism in favor of the international socialist message. Founded in 1917, the monthly *Messenger* preached the doctrine of working class solidarity as a basis for a better world in which all workers regardless of race were brothers. Not very successful as propagators of socialism among the Negro masses, they did have some influence as preachers of mass-action methods. Also, there was a growing popularity among educated Negroes of an economic analysis of the Negro problem. The economic radicals pioneered an agitation for trade-union organization of Negro workers which gradually gained ground. Eventually, the identification of Negro progress with the advance of organized labor became widely accepted in both Negro and labor circles.[47] An important result was the successful organization of the Brotherhood of Sleeping Car Porters under Randolph's leadership which adopted the *Messenger* as its official journal.[48]

With the exception of Garvey's movement there was little organized protest activity successfully involving the rank-and-file Negro prior to World War II. The major Negro organizations were heavily committed to an approach which tended toward conservative methods and leadership. This condition was not changed much by the deprivations of the depression. Negroes shifted with the general white community from a Republican to a Democratic party politics. Very few actually joined the more radical organizations which sought their allegiance, although there was a good deal of Communist influence due to rather widespread naïveté. The National Negro Congress was organized in a vain effort to promote a vigorous protest but its founders could not mobilize the support necessary to prevent its capture by the Communists.[49]

Such were the existing organizations and patterns of Negro protest which might capitalize upon and give form to the bad morale prevalent among Negroes in the early phases of World War II. With discontent becoming more and more severe, the situation was primed for a new upsurge of organized protest.

Negroes in World War II, both before and after formal American entry into the war, insisted on continuing their protest activities rather than suspending them for the duration. The argument was advanced that "just as national morale is stimulated by the catch-phrase, 'the Four Freedoms,' so is minority morale reassured by pressure campaigns for a 'Double Victory' and for 'Victory at Home as well as Abroad.' "[50]

During the first World War, Negroes had also protested race riots, lynchings and discriminations which had grown alarmingly. The NAACP which began the war with 80 branches and 9,282 members greeted the armistice with 310 branches and 91,203 members. Its protest activities were then, too, termed "seditious and enemy inspired." There was even a protest march similar to that used as a threat to obtain FEPC in World War II.[51]

But these protests were unavailing and the similarity to what went on in World War II is largely superficial. The general temper of World War I compared with the later conflict accounts for much of this. Public opinion supported both World Wars, but the character of that support was quite different in the two. To risk oversimplification, in World War II Americans were, as a whole, less naive than their World War I parents. While no one went about publicly singing the depression favorite, "I Didn't Raise My Boy to be a Soldier," no one revived the World War I song, "America, Here's My Boy."

Following the temper of the country in World War I, Negroes had set aside their complaints in the interest of national unity. Dr. Du Bois had, in the *Crisis*, called on Negroes to "Close the Ranks":

We of the colored race have no ordinary interest in the outcome. That which the German power represents spells death to the aspirations of Negroes and all dark races for equality, freedom, and democracy. Let us, while the war lasts, forget our special grievances and close ranks shoulder to shoulder with our white fellow-citizens and the allied nations that are fighting for democracy. We make no ordinary sacrifice, but we make it gladly and willingly with our eyes lifted to the hills.[52]

Here was patriotism of a very high order, for this was not the pen of an "Uncle Tom." Nor was the wartime temper placable for, as Du Bois said later, "With our participation and in anticipation of it came an extraordinary exacerbation of race hate and turmoil."[53]

Compare the *Crisis* editorial following the American declaration of war twenty-three years later:

NOW IS NOT THE TIME TO BE SILENT. We must say all the things that cry aloud to be said—not later, but now. . . . So we must speak even as we fight and die. We must say that the fight against Hitlerism begins in Washington, D.C., the capital of our nation where black Americans have a status only slightly above that of Jews in Berlin.[54]

And Walter White, wearing the mantle of leadership which Du Bois had worn in World War I when the latter had pledged to "forget our special grievances," greeted formal entry into the war with a press release which declared:

Memories of all Negroes except those of the very young are bitter-green regarding the last World War. . . . I urge [Negroes] to remember that the declarations of war do not lessen the obligation to preserve and extend civil liberties here while the fight is being made to restore freedom from dictorship abroad. . . .

Not that White did not support the war; quite the contrary:

We Negroes are faced with a Hobson's choice. But there *is* a choice. If Hitler wins, every single right we now possess and for which we have struggled here in America for three centuries will be instantaneously wiped out by Hitler triumphs. If the Allies win, we shall at least have the right to continue fighting for a share of democracy for ourselves.[55]

But there would be no postponement of the exercise of that right. The galling experiences of World War I had taught that a period of war crisis was precisely the time when Negro demands had greatest impact; when the Negro was needed for his labor and for his fighting strength. It was in this spirit that the great ex-slave abolitionist, Frederick Douglass, had declared after the Civil War:

In spite of legal provisions, the Negro had been a citizen three times in the history of the government, in 1776, 1812, and 1865, and that in time of trouble the Negro was a citizen and in time of peace he was an alien.[56]

The Negro protest in World War II developed swiftly and continued for the duration of the war. From May 1940, when a Committee on Participation of Negroes in the National Defense Program was organized, to the NAACP's "Appeal to the United Nations for Redress"[57] at the war's end, Negro organizations, their leaders, and their press were engaged in a continuous agitation and propaganda.

As early as May 1940, The Committee on National Defense was launched under sponsorship of the *Pittsburgh Courier* and headed by Rayford W. Logan, Howard University professor of history. It was made up of several existing national organizations. Pressure was brought to bear in traditional ways on Congress and the White House as well as before both political party conventions prior to the 1940 campaign. The NAACP, the Urban League and other existing organizations continued their activities in favor of breaking down Jim Crow practices in defense plants and in the Armed Forces.

A few concessions were obtained in this manner but they were insubstantial. A clause was inserted into the Selective Service Act forbidding discrimination in the selection of trainees. However, the Act also provided that "no person should be admitted into the Army or Navy unless he were acceptable to the Army or Navy heads which negated the non-discrimination clause."[58] A bill providing a supplementary appropriation for defense-work training contained a similar clause, with the same ineffectiveness in practice. But these concessions at least paid lipservice to the ideal of racial equality. More desperate days were close at hand.

Despair

THE FIRST NEGRO DELEGATION in the defense period to gain access to topmost governmental levels was received shortly after passage of the Selective Service Act. President Roosevelt, Secretary of the Navy Knox, and Assistant Secretary of War Patterson met with Walter White, of the NAACP; A. Philip Randolph, of the Brotherhood of Sleeping Car Porters; and T. Arnold Hill, of the National Urban League. Coming as it did in the thick of the 1940 election campaign (September 27) the conference took on added potency as a protest activity. The meeting concerned the utilization of Negro manpower by the Armed Forces. A memorandum was presented by the Negro leaders calling for complete and immediate integration of white and Negro servicemen. Unfortunately, there was no public knowledge of this memorandum until after considerable harm was done to relations between the Administration and the Negro spokesmen.

Following the conference, the White House issued a statement that "the policy of the War Department is not to intermingle colored and white enlisted personnel in the same regimental organizations."[59] To make matters worse, the White House press release was badly worded, seeming to imply that the Negro leaders had acquiesced in laying down the discriminatory policy. The United Press reported:

> White House Secretary Early said the segregation policy was approved after Mr. Roosevelt had conferred with Walter White, president of the National Association for the Advancement of Colored People, two other Negroes and Secretary of the Navy Knox and Assistant Secretary of War Patterson.[60]

The Negro leaders joined in an immediate wire of protest to the President expressing shock "that a President of the United States at a time of National peril should surrender so completely to enemies of democracy who would destroy national unity by advocating segregation."[61] But this was not immediate enough to forestall some harsh denunciations among Negroes of the three Negro leaders. Though the Presidential Secretary and, later, the President himself wired back their public regret for the misunderstanding, the affair left very bad feelings and the conference result was decidedly negative. The only gains ascribed to it were a few appointments of Negroes to advisory posts in the defense setup. Though these appointments were applauded, it was widely held that the concessions were motivated by political considerations incidental to the election campaign.

The election issue of *Crisis* provided a graphic example of the frustration Negroes felt when the Administration shifted more and more from the humanitarian concerns of the New Deal to the military needs of national defense. The same issue which lauded the "Roosevelt Record" and carried a full-page picture of the President and his wife as an election appeal (sponsored by the Colored Division of the Democratic National Committee) berated the President for the Armed Forces segregation policy. "The White House Blesses Jim Crow," reported *Crisis*.[62]

The pill was indeed a bitter one to swallow. Almost simultaneously with the fiasco of the conference on military segregation, the U.S. Senate killed the federal anti-lynching bill. These were terribly trying days for Negro morale and unsuccessful ones for the Negro protest. In an unprecedented gesture of despair, *Crisis* devoted the entire front cover of its election issue to this grisly and sardonic rendition of the Pledge of Allegiance to the Flag:

> *"I pledge allegiance to the flag"*—
> They dragged him naked
> Through the muddy streets,
> A feeble-minded black boy!
> And the charge? Supposed assault
> Upon an aged woman!
>
> *"Of the United States of America"*—
> One mile they dragged him
> Like a sack of meal,
> A rope around his neck,
> A bloody ear
> Left dangling by the patriotic hand
> Of Nordic youth! (A boy of seventeen!)
>
> *"And to the Republic for which it stands"*—
> And then they hanged his body to a tree,
> Below the window of the county judge
> Whose pleadings for that battered human flesh
> Were stifled by the brutish, raucous howls
> Of men, and boys, and women with their babes,
> Brought out to see the bloody spectacle
> Of murder in the style of '33!
> (Three thousand strong, they were!)

"One Nation, Indivisible"—
To make the tale complete
They built a fire—
What matters that the stuff they burned
Was flesh—and bone—and hair—
And reeking gasoline!

"With Liberty—and Justice"—
They cut the rope in bits
And passed them out,
For souvenirs, among the men and boys!
The teeth no doubt, on golden chains
Will hang
About the favored necks of sweethearts, wives,
And daughters, mothers, sisters, babies, too!

"For ALL!"[63]

chapter ii

The March to FEPC

> Such a pilgrimage of 10,000 Negroes would wake up
> and shock official Washington as it has never been
> shocked before. Why? The answer is clear. Nobody
> expects 10,000 Negroes to get together and march
> anywhere for anything at any time. . . . In common
> parlance, they are supposed to be just scared and un-
> organizable. Is this true? I contend it is not.
>
> A. PHILIP RANDOLPH[1]

FOLLOWING THE DEBACLE of the September 1940 conference with
the President, Negro leaders intensified their agitation. Walter White
and Philip Randolph had been scorched by the heated cries of "sellout" which arose following the misleading White House press release. One may surmise that this acted as a stimulus to avoid any further appearance of timidity. Meetings and conferences continued to
be held without tangible results, but these were necessary to the
Negro-in-the-street as signs that his leaders were "taking action." The
clamor of protest reporting in the Negro press was intensified and its
bitter tone continued.

How actively Negroes were aroused cannot be told with preci-
sion. Even assuming that, as usual, relatively few persons engage in
any direct and concrete form of protest, the temper of the group as
reflected in its leadership conferences, its press, and its folk talk became increasingly strident. "Bitterness grew at an alarming pace
throughout the country," recalled Walter White, writing about this
frustrating period.[2]

A few weeks after the conference with President Roosevelt on
Armed Forces discrimination, the installation ceremony of a new
president at Hampton Institute, the Negro technical college in Virginia, was extended into a two-day "Conference on the Negro in
National Defense." Its thirteen-point program of recommendations
stated the basic demands of Negroes during the war.[3] But such activi-

ties no longer satisfied as a means of protest. A prominent journalist, George S. Schuyler, scathingly attacked conferences and similar methods declaring: "The masses of Negroes are getting fed up on these frauds." He called for an organization which "would have worked out some technique of fighting other than sending letters and telegrams of protest."[4] The established pattern of conference, negotiation, and reassuring statement by a governmental spokesman, which had characterized much prewar interracial activity, was unsuited to these more critical times.

In keeping with the bitter popular mood when relations between the Government and the Negro leadership had collapsed, the NAACP undertook more dramatic action against employment discrimination. January 26, 1941 was designated "National Defense Day," and protest meetings were held in twenty-three states. Later, the Association called for countrywide picketing of national-defense plants in key cities.

Conservative Endorsement of a Radical Proposal

IN THE MIDST of these thwarted but increasingly sharp protests the March on Washington idea was born and took hold. This proposal for a nationwide mass demonstration for a greater Negro share in the defense effort was put forth in January 1941, by A. Philip Randolph, energetic head of the Brotherhood of Sleeping Car Porters (BSCP).[5] And it was not until the threat of the March grew to major proportions, the date of its scheduled demonstration drawing closer and attracting increasing attention in the "race" press, that Negro leaders were again given personal access to President Roosevelt.

The second meeting between Randolph, White and the President did not come about simply with the announcement of the March. There were months of strategic pressuring by the Negro leadership and counterstrategy by the Administration. Randolph's initial proposal, that 10,000 Negroes "March on Washington" to protest their treatment in the defense setup, met with an unenthusiastic response. Attracting only modest attention in the Negro press, none at all in the white press, the atmosphere in which the project was launched seemed decidedly pessimistic. Commenting favorably but with little hope that the demonstration could actually be realized, the *Chicago Defender* editorialized:

We would like to share Mr. Randolph's optimism that such a mobilization is possible. It is not possible to get Negroes to march in impressive numbers for denunciation of the miscarriage of justice in the case of the Scottsboro boys; it has not been possible to get them to march in protest against lynching, against peonage and poll tax. . . .
It would not be necessary to mobilize 10,000. If we could just get 2,000 black folk to march on the Capitol demanding 'the right to work and fight for our country,' that would be an accomplishment of considerable import. . . . To get 10,000 Negroes assembled in one spot, under one banner with justice, democracy and work as their slogan would be the miracle of the century.[6]

This was not the kind of action which the predominantly conservative Negro leadership was likely to welcome with enthusiasm. The recruitment and organization of Negroes into a disciplined mass movement was unfamiliar even to the more militant northern Negroes. Yet the proposal for the March on Washington was made to a quite conservative group,[7] and it was made by an already prominent figure in the Negro world. In the words of the executive secretary of the National Urban League, Lester Granger: "It was Randolph's immense prestige among all classes of Negroes that made this idea something more than a pretentious notion."[8] It is a measure of the extreme desperation of the Negro leaders that the proposed March was agreed to, however reluctantly. Walter White emphasized this in a letter explaining his endorsement:

On numerous occasions we have pleaded with the President to break his silence and to speak out against this discrimination. . . . But for five months we were given the runaround. Appeal after appeal was made to Washington with little tangible result. Conference after conference was held, and nothing happened. Knudsen [Office of Production Management] refused even to meet or discuss discrimination with any Negro delegation. . . . Discontent and bitterness were growing like wildfire among Negroes all over the country. Communists were trying as usual to capitalize on this. It was only then that Mr. Randolph and several others of us planned the March as a last resort to get some consideration of the plight of the Negro. . . .[9]

The reluctance of the NAACP and Urban League leadership in agreeing to the March was plain. During the entire period that the agitation for the demonstration was taking place (January to July,

1941) it was given no attention in the official journals of these organizations. It was not until the July issue of the Urban League's *Opportunity* that any mention was made of the March, although the coverage in that issue was substantial. However, this came too late to aid the demonstration which was scheduled for July 1. Indeed the FEPC order was already promulgated (June 25) when the issue went to press.

The NAACP's *Crisis* also did nothing to recruit marchers. There was no notice of the March until a very small item appeared in July, which could not have helped had the affair gone off as scheduled. Though the August issue heralded the establishment of the FEPC, it ignored the pressure activity which brought it about. Stranger yet, the NAACP's "Conference on the Negro in National Defense" was set to draw delegates from across the country to Houston, Texas, adjourning only two days prior to the date of the March on Washington! It is true that A. Philip Randolph was to be one of the NAACP conference speakers; but he was announced simply in his union capacity during a period when he was more popularly associated with the March on Washington. It is true, too, that a newspaper columnist reported that the NAACP conference was to "adjourn early in Houston so members can get to Washington in time."[10] However, in its major story on the Texas conference, *Crisis* made no mention of the March and provided no instructions concerning a possible time conflict.[11]

That *Crisis* was thought of as an appropriate instrument for rallying its readers and NAACP members into action is made clear by substantial and repeated solicitations to attend the Houston conference. It is difficult to understand the lack of publicity for the March as other than a deliberate policy.

Despite the fact that the national resources of the NAACP and the Urban League were not given over wholeheartedly to organizing the March on Washington, there was important involvement for this purpose at the local level. In some cities the local March did not have separate officers at first, but organized as a joint-committee of the Urban League and the NAACP.

And while the national NAACP and Urban League did little to organize prospective marchers or use official publications for supporting propaganda campaigns, their support went beyond mere verbal approval. They did contribute financially to the March on Washington Committee; more significantly, White and Granger were important spokesmen and negotiators, and they did not weaken under the considerable pressures of those who opposed the March.[12] The record is one of endorsement and support by these leaders of the two principal Negro defense organizations. It is less a failure of nerve in this particular situation, that they failed to engage in the March on Washington as recruiters and organizers of the Negro masses, than a reflection of the conservative role characteristically assumed by these groups in the historic Negro protest.

To be sure the March idea, as a political pressure technique, did not originate with Randolph's MOWC. "Coxey's Army" and the "Bonus Army" veterans' march on the National Capitol were well-remembered precedents. (President Roosevelt surely recalled the latter.) The Negro leaders, some at least, probably remembered as personal experiences a World War I demonstration in New York to protest discrimination against Negroes. Shortly after America had entered that war, "30,000 Negroes lined Fifth Avenue and gave silent approval of the demonstration" by 8,000 Negroes who marched "to the beat of muffled drums."[13]

However, the parallel between the marches of World War I and World War II is only superficially striking.[14] For one thing, the World War I march was held and was rather successful as a parade, but it garnered no harvest. The World War II demonstration was called off and the hastily substituted victory celebration was sparsely attended, but it exacted what was hailed as the first presidential order concerning Negroes since Lincoln's Emancipation Proclamation.

Calling a national Negro March on Washington was a radical departure from what had previously characterized even the more militant Negro protest activities. The scope of such an undertaking is one important difference. To be successful, a vast amount of organizational work would be required on a grass-roots level. Problems involved in moving several thousand persons, many of them impoverished, to Washington, housing them and otherwise caring for them on their arrival would constitute an enormous task. Also, people who were ordinarily apathetic and apolitical would have to be simultaneously stimulated. None of the existing Negro organizations, conservative or militant, was experienced with such undertakings. Nor was the middle class leadership, or membership, of the primary Negro organizations temperamentally suited to such an enterprise.

Of considerable importance too were the differences between marching down a New York avenue and converging on the District of Columbia. That the latter resembled a Southern city in its race *mores* rather than a Northern one was an obvious deterrent. The treatment Negro demonstrators might receive from Southern-reared white Washingtonians, including the police, weighed heavily in Mrs. Roosevelt's objections to the March.

These difficulties were brushed aside. The primary argument of the accommodationist, so-called realistic, theory of race advancement, held that one must avoid stirring up the whites by pushing reforms too vigorously lest the net result be negative. This argument was rendered ineffective by critical events. Negro conservatives were unable to withstand the militant mood of the frustrated group they sought to lead. However reluctantly, the organizing of masses of Negroes to engage in a national direct-action demonstration came to be widely agreed upon as a necessary action. It was viewed as a last resort, a dramatic gesture to force the white majority to take notice of the dire distress of its Negro brothers.

*"Left-Wing" Coolness and Confusion**

You can't defend Negro rights without fighting against this war.
                                      Daily Worker, May 16, 1941

The Negro people cannot be true to their own best interests without supporting the war.
                                    The Communist, August, 1942

If the "conservative" Negro leadership endorsed the radical proposal for a March on Washington, where were the "radical" Communists? Many cries have been raised by opponents that the FEPC was a Communist-fostered scheme. What part did Communists play in the movement which gave birth to this important civil rights issue? The relationship of the Communist party to the March on Washing-

---

* We have used the term "left-wing"—in quotation marks—to refer to activities which supported the Communist party line but which were engaged in by persons who were not necessarily Communist party members or even favorable to the Communist party *per se*. Thus persons who were left-of-center in the ordinary sense are not necessarily "left-wingers," whereas even conservatives and bona fide anti-Communists who participated in Communist front activities were in that respect "left-wingers."

ton is complex because of the change in Communist war policy precisely at the peak of March activity. To interpret these and subsequent events concerning the March on Washington Movement, it is necessary to trace the complicated twistings and turnings of Communist involvement in the Negro protest.

Given popular stereotypes, the tactic of the March on Washington seems likely to have appealed strongly to the Communists. Such a march would necessarily entail the basic characteristics associated with "militant" movements. For a march, generally, has military connotations and, thus, is a symbol of revolutionary methods, however peacefully conducted. The terminology applicable to such activities is picturesque in conveying a sense of the dramatic and direct involvement of masses outside the regular channels of influence.[15]

However entreating the official words (e.g., in the Bonus March of 1932), a march carries a tone which is the opposite of supplication. One *marches* to Washington, rather than "sends a delegation"; one *demonstrates,* rather than "holds a meeting"; one *demands,* and does not "request" or "resolve"; the participants are not "delegates," "negotiators," or "leading citizens," they are *masses.* The activity is a *movement of direct action,* and not a "conference." The proposals usually are demands in the form of slogans for agitational and propaganda value more than concrete plans for the remedy of a specific problem. Indeed, it is not too much to say that the immediate demands of such movements are not the real purposes of the activity. The demonstration seeks its justification in the strength of its communication as a radical symbol rather than in the attainment of a particular goal. Primarily, a radical demand is not made to be attained but to be fought over, preferably "in the streets."[16]

Such "mass action" strategies have been typical of Communist and other revolutionary radical movements. So-called militant methods were characteristic of radicals who attacked reformist efforts to attain objectives by negotiation at top levels as, at worst, "sellouts" and, at best, "pussyfooting" and "compromise." The basis for this division between right-wing reformers and left-wing radicals on a matter of "tactics" seems plain. It stemmed from a fundamental attitude towards the status quo and thus was more than mere disagreement over means. While reformers might be driven to reluctant acceptance of radical methods (as in the case of the 1941 March), having exhausted "regular," i.e., status quo channels, radicals would utilize reformist objectives as a "strategy" where organizational gains might ensue. The immediate official objectives of such reformist actions are necessarily regarded by the radical as puny by comparison with revolutionary objectives and even dangerous sops to dull the vigor of revolutionary propaganda and class consciousness in the masses. When the reformist adopts radical measures his eye remains on the official goal to which the method is subservient. Direct-action methods are abhorrent to the reformer for many reasons, but when he does resort to them they are instrumental to the goal of reform within the status quo and regular channels, when reopened, are preferred.

This theory seems sound, if not tautological, if radicals are defined as revolutionaries and reformers are regarded as those who seek change within the context of existing constitutional and institutional arrangements. In practice the line between reformers and radicals is not likely to be so obvious, though the distinction in terms of degree of attachment to the status quo retains basic value. Particular circumstances may well make a reformer of yesterday's radical and vice versa.

Such, indeed, is the case with the Communist "radical" who is no longer a revolutionary by virtue of his socialist commitment to basic social change. The strategy and tactics of the worldwide Communist movement are not explainable in the traditional terms which distinguish reformers and radicals. Rather, it is abundantly plain that the touchstone of international Communist activities is to be found in the external situation and policies of the Soviet Union. Whether Communist policy toward war or peace, national defense and military preparedness, is favorable or unfavorable depends entirely on the coalition of forces in which the Soviets are involved. Similarly, whether Socialists and reformers and even reactionary political leaders are to be viewed favorably or unfavorably, for Communists, depends on how such policy affects the strategic position of the Soviet government.[17]

Communists rationalize this as a genuinely radical policy determined always by "scientific" Marxist principles. Thus, the Communist "flip-flop" on the character of the Second World War (opposition before and support after the German invasion of the U.S.S.R.), for the Communists, was not an about-face at all but an entirely consistent policy. The difference in explanation is that Communists regard the defense of the Soviet Union as fundamental to a true revolutionary policy. Declared the *New Masses:*

> . . . the central fact that must be understood is that *the attack of German fascism on the USSR has changed the character of the war.* And one need not apologize for saying that when the character of the war changes, programs, slogans, and tactics must also change.[18]

Thus, the Communist position on the war necessarily affected the attitudes of Communists to the March on Washington. The Nazi attack on Russia was launched on June 22, 1941, three days prior to President Roosevelt's FEPC order and slightly over one week before the scheduled date of the March on Washington. The Communist relationship to the March is, therefore, not deducible from its character as a typical radical-militant strategy. Rather, Communist policy on the American Negro was shaped by the juggling of events imposed first by the Stalin-Hitler pact of 1939 and, then, by the rupture in Nazi-Soviet relations.

American Communists have always pursued a Negro policy more suited to Russian conditions than to American. The early Bolshevik formula for dealing with what were called "minorities groups" was a kind of federalism in which minority nationalities were permitted to continue group existence as constitutent Soviet Republics. Thus, such homogeneous groups as Russians, Georgians, etc., officially maintained local sovereignty in their territorial homelands. The formula, however, was applied more widely than to groups with geographical ties. Cultural and linguistic bonds were cited by Soviet authorities who established a separate "Republic" for Jews in Birobidzhan. This Soviet answer to Zionism was adapted to the American Negro problem in the form of a demand for a "Forty-ninth Negro State" to be carved out of the Southern "black belt."

The policy was much more successful in colonies occupied by European nations than among American Negroes. However, it was a key plank in the Communist position despite its failure to rally Negroes to the Communist party. None of the planks in the Communist pre-Popular Front platform was calculated to win friends at the cost of revolutionary agitation. Rather, Communist policy was based upon the view that the inherent weaknesses of capitalism would produce the crises to which revolutionary demands would become appropriate.

The Communist line calling for "self-determination in the black belt" was a casualty of the shift to the Popular Front strategy of the second half of the Nineteen Thirties. Actually, the policy was never denounced officially; it was simply subordinated to so-called "immediate demands." Thus, in 1938, it was possible for a top Communist to write:

> The program called for . . . the complete right of self-determination for the Negro people in the Black Belt of the South. Such a program prevented the development of a broad movement. The masses did not understand this full program. Furthermore, the LSNR [League of Struggle for Negro Rights] fell into the same sectarian methods of work as the ANLC [American Negro Labor Congress]. It did not base its activity sufficiently on immediate, daily needs of the people.[19]

The strategy of the Popular Front was to stress "immediate demands" which the masses could understand rather than the "full program." This amounted to a concealment of the real aims of the organization.

The desire for a more broadly based movement, however, was not simply a product of the desire to recruit larger numbers to the Communist movement. In back of it lay the new Soviet foreign policy which sought allies for "collective security" against the rising Hitlerite threat. Revolutionary activities by Communists within the United States might or might not advance the proletarian revolution to which Communists officially aspire. The crucial fact was that it could not win American, British and French opinion to the side of Soviet Russia. Symbolically, the *Star Spangled Banner* took its place beside the *International*, and they were jointly sung at Communist public meetings. Everything else followed suit—reformists and social-democrats, previously termed "social-fascists," were now wooed in the name of a common front against Hitler, the main enemy. Negro leaders like A. Philip Randolph, Walter White and others were treated with a solicitude which was incredible by contrast with previous vituperation. Even the Scottsboro case, which the Communists had made their private *cause célèbre*, was reshuffled to provide for joint action between the Communists' International Labor Defense and the NAACP.[20]

Prior to the Popular Front period, Communists viewed politics as consisting of two groupings: revolutionists and counter-revolutionists. In the basic Marxian class dichotomy all political movements, leaders and ideologies are placed into one or the other of these categories. During the Popular Front this classification was altered. The enemies now were the "reactionaries" against whom were allied all "progressives" including, of course, the "vanguard of the democratic peoples," namely the Communists. Reformists and Socialists were now "progressives" too, to be collaborated with in the "Democratic Front," and were no longer referred to as "the chief social supports of imperialist reaction (White, Pickens, Du Bois, etc.)."[21]

The Communists were successful, during the Popular Front period, in infiltrating several liberal organizations many of which they subsequently captured. A primary target was the National Negro Congress (NNC), formed in 1936. Many non-Communists supported the NNC at that time (e.g., Lester Granger, Ralph Bunche and Alain Locke); indeed, A. Philip Randolph was its first president. At the outset Randolph was spoken of most kindly by the Communists; that is, prior to the Hitler-Stalin pact of August 1939.[22]

The treaty between Germany and Russia which marked the invasion of Poland and the start of World War II brought the Popular Front episode to a close. Now, of course, a "revolutionary" strategy was again more suited to the times. Most important, the "Democratic Front" against Hitlerism was strictly *passé*, and the "progressives" of yesterday were again the "misleaders of the masses." The official organ, *The Communist*, declared:

> But particularly misleading and confusing to the masses is the tricky argument used by the reformist and Social-Democratic leaders, directly and indirectly, that the choice for the masses is between a Hitler victory and a Roosevelt-Churchill victory, and that there is no other choice.[23]

Continued relations between Randolph and the Communists became impossible and Randolph left the presidency of the National Negro Congress at its 1940 conference. The Congress became wholly an instrument of Communist party policy from that point on. Shortly after this split, Randolph (literally) "stole a march" on the Communists by making public his dramatic proposal for a March on Washington.

At first the Communist reaction was complete silence. Given the paucity of attention which the Randolph idea initially evoked, this was only to be expected. Surely the Communists would be undesirous of building up anything emanating from A. Philip Randolph. However, when the March began to receive considerable and favorable notice in all the Negro press a "line" was confusedly and hesitatingly fashioned.

The criteria for such a policy were plain, though actually drawing the line was bound to be difficult. The most important item was the utility of such a demonstration in opposing American war preparations. This was balanced off by the fact that the idea for the March emanated from the "right-wingers," Randolph, White and Granger, who were by then restored to the Communist gallery of archvillains —betrayers of the working class and of the Negroes in particular. (The bitter fight for control of the National Negro Congress was only months past.) The situation was further complicated by the two basic demands of the March Committee, both of which were antagonistic to the Communist position prior to June 22, 1941. The MOWC demanded fair employment in defense jobs and equality in the Armed Forces; in short, an equal right to participate in what the Communists regarded as "imperialist war preparations." The problem could have been completely ignored had not two factors made this situation different from other occasions when the "reformist" Negro leadership engaged in some sort of protest activity.

First, the March was not an ordinary reformist protest activity. The product of months of frustration with traditional protest methods, this was a typical militant tactic. Second, the March began to mushroom into what looked like a popular upsurge among the Negro grass roots. Only when that occurred did the Communists take official notice. Had it not caught hold of the Negro-in-the-street as reflected in his press and successful mass meetings, there is every reason to suppose that the Communists would have continued ignoring it in favor of their own activities.

Signs that the Communists were uneasy as to what attitude to take toward the March appeared as early as February 10th, just after Randolph first proposed that a March on Washington be organized. A *Daily Worker* editorial angrily attacked Randolph and White as "Not the Voice of the Negro People."[24] There was no mention, however, of the specific Randolph proposal. When the March, 1941, issue of Randolph's union paper, The *Black Worker*, published a large item calling for Negroes to organize the March on Washington the Communist *Daily Worker* (still not mentioning the MOW as such) carried a blistering attack on Randolph: "A. Philip Randolph Can't Sell This War to Oppressed, Jim-Crowed Negro People."[25]

Though several other items appeared in the Communist press in the interim, from which one may reasonably deduce that the Communists were completely aware of the MOW activities,[26] the March on Washington itself received no formal notice until June 10, four months after Randolph's initial call. "It Can Become the Voice of the Negro People," declared the *Daily Worker*. However, "these Negro leaders support the war, and in doing so are attempting to carry out the policies of the Wall Street labor-haters and Negro-baiters." Hardly a clear-cut call to join the March, the *Daily Worker* did go on to declare:

> We are confident that the Negro people will see in the job march a great opportunity to display their united opposition to the war program and to all of its discriminatory aspects.[27]

As the date for the March on Washington drew closer, the Communists responded to its increasing popularity among Negroes with somewhat firmer support of the idea of marching, but they constantly drew a line between the "job-march" and its "war-mongering leadership." The "Negro March on Capital Can Be a Blow Against War, Jim-Crow," James Ford declared.[28] However, "Randolph's aim is without a doubt to head off any real struggle of the Negro People against this war program." Ford also stated that "there must be complete democracy in these local [MOW] committees of action, without discrimination against anybody on account of their political or other affiliations." This last in response to Randolph's careful measures to keep the Communists out. Randolph, who had lost control of the National Negro Congress despite his presidency of that organization, had no intention of repeating that experience with the March on Washington.[29]

One device utilized by Randolph to keep the MOW free of Communists simply restricted membership to Negroes. This was to preclude Communist packing of conventions with white Communist delegates (as was done in the NNC). While Negro Communists could not be excluded on this basis, the tactic was of some help. The number of Negroes who were disciplined Communist party members was small though the Negro community shared the general liberal-labor vulnerability to Communist influence which characterized the

Nineteen Thirties and Forties.[30] The exclusion of whites brought
forth Communist charges of "black chauvinism":

> Randolph, who finds it convenient to support Roosevelt and the white
> imperialists, among whom are such Negro haters as Carter Glass, Ellender
> and Bilbo, nevertheless states in his article 'Let the Negro Masses Speak,'
> that this is a job 'which the Negroes must do alone, and does not need the
> support of our white brothers. . . .'
> This is but the effort of the bourgeoisie to split the ranks of Negro and
> white workers, to spread a wave of nationalism which can benefit only
> the war makers. Therefore, it is imperative that one of the ringing de-
> mands of the Negro people shall be 'for the unity of Negro and white'
> because this is the only way that problems of the Negro people can be
> solved.[31]

The demand for a forty-ninth Negro state was truly a thing of the
forgotten past!

During the month of June, a great deal of comment in Communist
publications reflected their concern with the enormous and favorable
attention which was at last accorded the March in the Negro press.
The gains (in the form of anti-discrimination memoranda by the
Office of Production Management and the White House), attributed
by the Negro newspapers to the MOWC, added greatly to the momentum of the March on Washington. The Communists, at first,
sought to claim credit for themselves and for their front organizations:

> Leaders of anti-discrimination organizations like the National Negro
> Congress and the Jewish People's Committee last night expressed satisfac-
> tion that their campaign had at last compelled an official recognition of
> the situation but continued to press the fight to make discrimination a
> statutory offense.[32]

Fantastic as it must have appeared to anyone familiar with the
actual situation, the Communists charged that the March was "a
gigantic undertaking . . . the supreme effort of America's big shot
businessmen to win the masses of the Negro people for the war program of the Administration."[33] The next day, the *Daily Worker* declared: "Without a doubt the Roosevelt Administration sanctioned
the proposed 'March to Washington' July 1." This in an item entitled: "Capital Jittery Over Negro March on Washington; Fear
Job Demands Will Defeat F.D.R. Smokescreen."[34](!)

Another effort was made at this time to steal the employment-discrimination issue from the Randolph group. An FEPC bill was introduced by "fellow-travelling" U.S. Congressman Vito Marcantonio.[35] However, the excitement over the March on Washington negotiations with the White House was too much of a morsel to be crowded out of the Negro press headlines. Other such efforts, also to no avail, included a rally protesting discrimination by a New York power company. The *Daily Worker*, in writing this up, revealed the really important Negro protest news item of the period by concluding: "In the interests of both peace and job equality, labor, minority groups, and all fair-minded citizens can throw their full weight behind the Job March to Washington on July 1."[36] The National Negro Congress went so far as to urge prospective demonstrators to register for the March on Washington with them.[37]

One is reduced to pure speculation as to what the Communists would have done had the march gone on as scheduled and the invasion of the U.S.S.R. not taken place. Would the Communists have agitated in the crowd for reckless actions likely to lead to violence between the demonstrators and the police and perhaps a race riot? This was feared both by the Administration and the leaders of the March. Their fears were stimulated by the plain intent of the Communists to assail any negotiated settlement, based on a cancellation of the March, as a betrayal. As soon as negotiations began between the White House and the leaders of the March (prior to the Soviet-Nazi rupture), the Communists warned:

> Backsliding on the part of the initiators of the March is in the making. With bitterness and fear Roosevelt and his agents are getting alarmed. . . . The Negro people must continue their fight against the whole jim-crow set-up. They must not allow any backsliding and turn-coating on the part of the initiators of the March to Washington.[38]

Even after the U.S.S.R. entered the war, the Communists found it difficult to resist attacking the Randolph leadership of the March as "compromisers." Actually, the Communist line was ambivalent in those very confusing days just after the invasion of Russia. The *Daily Worker* front-page story reporting President Roosevelt's FEPC order, while raising some question as to "loopholes," in no way criticized Randolph for calling off the demonstration.[39] The very next day, however, the *Daily Worker* headlined a story: "Flay Randolph for Calling Off Job March to Capital."[40]

Communist floundering about for a line on the "reformists" and "social democrats," after the Nazi attack on the Soviet Union, led to this bit of doubletalk by a leading Communist writing on "The Negro People and the Fight For Jobs":

> Despite its shortcomings, the [FEPC] order constituted without doubt an important victory, not only for the Negro people, but for the whole labor movement and all progressives. The cancelling of the march by the initiators after the issuance of the Presidential Order was strongly and justifiably resented by broad sections of the Masses.[41]

The MOWC leaders had obtained "an important victory" but the March should not have been called off! That this was the condition for obtaining the victory was not noted.

During the balance of the war, which they now supported, the Communists would be most receptive to other such "compromises" in the interest of "Civilian Defense and Morale—A Vital Factor in the Struggle Against Hitlerism."[42] Now, any disruption of production was an obstacle to American aid to the Soviet Union. For example, James W. Ford declared the Nazi menace "left no choice to any people including the Negro people but to resist Hitler and destroy Nazism. The fight against Hitler and Hitlerism is the affair of every loyal and patriotic American."[43]

The Communist attitude to the first FEPC order was already shaped in terms of the new policy supporting the war. However, coming as it did so soon after the change in line there was a brief lag in some aspects of their position. It was difficult to hate Randolph to 1935, love him to 1939, hate him again to 1941 and then, in a day or two, praise him once more as the successful leader of the March on Washington. The MOWC, viewed previously as an instrument of the Administration's effort to seduce Negroes to the imperialist war, now became disruptive of national unity and hence jeopardized the Soviet Union in its struggle against fascism.

A new Negro front organization was formed, but "the Negro Labor Victory Committee was established . . . not for the primary purpose of improving the role of Negroes in the war effort but to offset the March on Washington Movement."[44]

One final problem connected with the relation of the Communist party to the MOWC and the first FEPC order remains to be cleared up. Did the Communists help to build up the March? Were they responsible for its packed mass meetings and were they engaged in the specific organizational preparations without which the projected demonstration could never have taken place?

There is no doubt that the Communists were of no help prior to June when the first item on the March appeared in their press. During June, there was a substantial number of news items in the *Daily Worker* which may have stimulated some readers to plan to march on July 1, despite the negative attitude displayed toward the March leadership. However, the main tenor of these articles was not that of a call to march. One has only to contrast the articles on the MOW with those published during the same period of 1941 preparatory to the "American People's Meeting for Peace." Called for April 5, 1941, the *Daily Worker* systematically issued calls for attendance which, in size and specificity of instructions (including detailed maps), provide an excellent example of efficient mass organization.[45] This was the type of activity at which the Communist party was exceedingly skilled.

Though the Communists tried to take credit for the FEPC, they were neither its initiators nor substantial organizers of potential marchers on Washington. The Communists were hostile to the MOWC, sought to take it over but were foiled by Randolph's precautions, and were caught short in their plans to disrupt the March by the unforseen attack on Soviet Russia and their consequent change in policy with respect to American involvement in World War II.

Organizational Threat or Gambler's Bluff?

BUT IF THE NAACP, the Urban League and the Communists did not organize the Negro grass roots for the March, who did? Even if the March and its success were the result of a gigantic bluff where were the symbols, however false, of a successfully organized mass movement? The *New York Times* and the rest of the white press depicted no threat. The March on Washington was either a real movement which swept up the Negro population of the country in a mammoth grass-roots activity or the Negro press throughout the country joined in putting over a fantastic hoax on the Administration. Walter White was very aware of the poker-game aspect of the situation. At the June, 1941, White House conference, he recalled subsequently:

The President turned to me and asked 'Walter, how many people will *really* march?'

I told him no less than one hundred thousand. The President looked me full in the eye for a long time in an obvious effort to find out if I were bluffing or exaggerating. Eventually he appeared to believe that I meant what I said.

'What do you want me to do?' he asked.

Philip Randolph told the President that we wanted him to issue an unequivocal executive order to effectuate the speediest possible abolition of discrimination in war industries and the armed forces.[46]

Would 100,000 Negroes have marched on Washington the First of July, 1941, had the President not issued his executive order? Would 50,000, which was another often cited figure; or even 10,000, which was Randolph's first figure? There must always be doubt. Surely Walter White was bluffing if he meant to imply that the "mass membership" of the NAACP could provide the "one-hundred thousand" who would march on Washington. Yet, such an implication can readily be drawn from his account of the conversation with President Roosevelt:

We then turned to discussion of the only reason the conference had been called—the threat of a march on Washington. No success attended the President's skillful attempts to dissuade us. The NAACP was the only one of the organizations sponsoring the march which had a large mass membership.[47]

Our examination of *Crisis* has shown that while discontent was aroused to a degree crucial to the building of a militant movement, NAACP members could not have joined the March through reading *Crisis*. The President and his advisors on the Negro problem were not sold on the necessity of taking a step theretofore staunchly resisted merely by appraising the quality of Walter White's unwavering gaze. Nor is it likely that they were unaware of the actual weakness of the NAACP's "mass membership."

Wherein lay the threat of the threatened march? It was a combination of the factors already described. The ill temper of the Negro community during the early days of the war heightened to a fierce pitch by the defeat of the anti-lynching bill, and the rebuff in the midst of an election campaign by the President himself, made it possible to set in motion persons otherwise apathetic and leaders accustomed to less radical courses of action. If the initial reaction of the leaders was pessimistic the subsequent enthuisiasm which caught the imagination of Negroes everywhere galvanized the leadership into action.

The Negro press, which kept hammering away at inequities, provided a powerful communication instrument for the March on Washington agitation. Overwhelmingly, the sentiment of these newspapers favored the March. Even where, as in the case of the *Pittsburgh Courier*, the March was opposed this was not necessarily the reflection of a compromising or "pussy-footing" attitude. Although Randolph lambasted the *Courier* as "the journalistic spokesman of the petty black bourgeoisie" and accused them of wanting "results without risks, achievement without action,"[48] the *Courier* was attacked by a Southern writer as "one of the most radical of the Negro newspapers."[49] During the last months before the March deadline the MOW was easily the major news item in the entire Negro press.

Shortly after Randolph first suggested the March, a Chicago parade to protest discrimination in the defense program was reported: "Following the parade, a meeting was held at which it was agreed that Negroes all over the country should converge on Washington. . . ."[50] Though the marchers "braved zero weather [and] over a thousand persons of both races"[51] joined in the demonstration, there was little evidence of a rapidly organizing mass movement until much later. Even after a stirring call for the March on Washington was published over Randolph's name in the March, 1941, *Black Worker* (organ of the Brotherhood of Sleeping Car Porters, AFL) there was little comment in other sources to signify that here was a substantial movement in the bud. The very next issue of the *Black Worker* (April, 1941) made no mention of the March. It is not surprising that no one from the Administration called Randolph in for consultation or expressed alarm over his idea at that time.

Despite this early quiescence in the activities of the March on Washington Committee, other pressures continued. These were particularly concentrated on the Office of Production Management's co-director, William Knudsen, formerly head of General Motors, who had ignored previous appeals to forbid racial discrimination in defense work. Finally on April 11, Knudsen's OPM co-director, labor leader Sidney Hillman, sent a letter to all defense contractors urging them to eliminate discrimination against Negroes in their hiring practices. This letter only antagonized Negroes further because it was not signed by Knudsen who refused to explain the absence of his signature.[52] Even had both directors of OPM signed the letter it is doubtful that Negroes would, at the time, have been placated. The *Amsterdam News* editorialized:

> Mr. Hillman has spoken boldly, but unless he follows through with something more punitive than a mere plea, his words are going to fall on deaf ears. The policy toward Negro workers in America is well grounded. Nothing short of a major catastrophe will shake it, unless the word to do so comes straight from the top with White House influence behind it. Mr. Roosevelt must be prevailed upon to speak out.[53]

Even though Hillman, soon after his letter, had established the Negro Employment and Training Branch and the Minority Groups Branch in the Labor Division of OPM with Negroes appointed to its staff, this was another "too little, too late" move by the Administration.

Finally, during April, Randolph announced that "plans for an all-out march of 10,000 Negroes on Washington are in the making, and a call will be issued in the next few weeks to keep in their minds night and day the idea that all roads lead to Washington, D.C."[54] The big spurt in organizational and propaganda activity came during May with the issuance of that "Call to Negro America to March on Washington for Jobs and Equal Participation in National Defense on July 1, 1941."[55]

The bold and uncompromising tone of the "Call" was well suited to the mood of the time. Men of color must have been stirred by Randolph's dramatic language and the sheer simplicity of an action which all could understand and in which all could feel a part:

> Dear fellow Negro Americans, be not dismayed in these terrible times. You possess power, great power. Our problem is to hitch it up for action on the broadest, daring and most gigantic scale.
>
> In this period of power politics, nothing counts but pressure, more pressure, and still more pressure, through the tactic and strategy of broad, organized, aggressive mass action behind the vital and important issues of the Negro. To this end we propose that ten thousand Negroes MARCH ON WASHINGTON FOR JOBS IN NATIONAL DEFENSE AND EQUAL INTEGRATION IN THE FIGHTING FORCES OF THE UNITED STATES.
>
> An 'all-out' thundering march on Washington, ending in a monster and huge demonstation at Lincoln's Monument will shake up white America.

It will shake up official Washington. . . .
It will gain respect for the Negro people.
It will create a new sense of self-respect among Negroes.[56]

But emotional satisfactions were not all that the manifesto provided. Not only would Negroes march shoulder to shoulder and by this demonstration of solidarity experience their "mass power." A practical goal rationalized the emotionality; a program simple to grasp by ordinary masses of people and within the official powers of "a great humanitarian and idealist" (as the "Call" termed President Roosevelt). Note this pragmatic emphasis in the Randolph pronouncement:

The Negroes' stake in national defense is big. It consists of jobs, thousands of jobs. It may represent millions, yes, hundreds of millions of dollars in wages. It consists of new industrial opportunities and hope. This is worth fighting for.

Most important and vital to all, Negroes by the mobilization and coordination of their mass power, can cause PRESIDENT ROOSEVELT TO ISSUE AN EXECUTIVE ORDER ABOLISHING DISCRIMINATIONS IN ALL GOVERNMENT DEPARTMENTS, ARMY, NAVY, AIR CORPS AND NATIONAL DEFENSE JOBS.[57]

The announcement of the date, the concreteness of the demands, and the dramatic site selected for the post-march rally, the Lincoln Memorial (its traditional symbolism powerfully enhanced by Marian Anderson's recent protest concert before a throng of people), made this an irresistible attraction to the Negro press. A similar activity involving a like number of whites would undoubtedly have evoked much the same response from the white press (as did the "Bonus Army March" of 1932). During the months of May and June the proposed March on Washington and A. Philip Randolph's activities filled the Negro newspapers.

By May 17 the *Chicago Defender* reported the organization of a Washington branch of the MOWC and the holding of several meetings which "met with enthusiastic response." That same day, the *New York Amsterdam News* gave front page coverage to the MOW. Later, their May 24 issue devoted a great deal of space to the "Organization of [a New York] Local March on Washington Committee . . . Group Making July 1 Plans." By the end of May, the Negro press had come a long way from the pessimistic editorial in the *Chicago Defender* which had worried whether even 2,000 Negroes would march. The *Amsterdam News*, in huge type, blazed forth in its main front-page headline: "100,000 IN MARCH TO CAPITOL."[58] If the editors were bluffing, their editorial and an enthusiastic cartoon betrayed no weakness or flaw in the jubilant façade. And if they were bluffing, so was the rest of the Negro press. Even the *Chicago Defender* spoke of "50,000" preparing for a "March for jobs and justice."[59]

It is plain that the hard core was Randolph's union which put money and organizers into the campaign from BSCP headquarters spread across the country. But there is little evidence which can directly validate the existence of a solid organizational base for the prospective demonstration. The press roared of March on Washington activities and reported packed meetings, but how much of this was sound and fury and how much was concrete manifestation of an organization capable of moving on July 1 is exceedingly difficult to determine. The spontaneity of the movement which Randolph's March had precipitated swept the Negro leadership along in its mounting enthusiasm. This, rather than a highly organized protest, was the main strength of the March. One should be familiar with the restrained tone which generally characterized the Urban League's *Opportunity* to appreciate this comment by its editor:

> Even if the sponsors of the 'March to Washington' . . . had yielded to the advices from high places to cancel the 'March,' it would have been of little avail since the Negro is so thoroughly aroused by the flagrant abuse of his citizenship rights that hundreds, if not thousands, would have descended upon the capital in spite of anything that the responsible leadership might say or do. In that event the Negro would likely have become the prey of other and less responsible leadership than that which guides this orderly and conscientious attempt to arouse America to the injustice which is being accorded its Negro citizenry.[60]

There are a few tangible items beyond the very successful mass meetings making up the documentary record. The National Council of Negro Women was called upon to meet in Washington on the day before and to stay over for the March by its president, the well-beloved educator and leader, Mary Bethune. Another organization, the "AKA has called its members together for a Washington conference in time to participate."[61] J. Finley Wilson, Grand Exalted Ruler of Negro Elks (of which Randolph has been a prominent member) provided a source of strength and was scheduled to address the March rally.[62] Roi Ottley reported:

Buses were hired, special trains chartered. . . . Both the NAACP and the National Negro Congress supported the march actively, and Walter White brought his influence and prestige to the movement. Thousands of dollars were spent. Press and pulpit played decisive roles in whipping up sentiment. And those efficient couriers—the Pullman porters—carried the word to Negro communities throughout the country.[63]

By the end of May, the March Committee had opened two headquarters in New York (in Brooklyn and Harlem). A *Bulletin* announced the formation of committees in eighteen cities and urged: "But *more* must be formed if you feel the necessity of a fight. A fight that must be won. Be the next one to send in the name of your office."[64] These committees were springing up, in many cases spontaneously, though this was not the sole instrument for national organization. It was reported that "Mr. Randolph and his committee are busily engaged making speaking tours throughout the country and interesting all groups in the movement."[65]

In addition to the vast amount of press coverage which now spread the MOW message, Marchers took to the streets for outdoor meetings, poster walks and similar forms of direct contact. Randolph recalls that he and others toured Harlem and other communities "talking up the March by word of mouth . . . in all the beauty parlors and taverns and barber shops, etc."[66]

A financial report published by the New York March on Washington Committee gives indication of substantial activity. Thousands of March on Washington buttons were sold and small donations received.[67] There can be little doubt that this was a thriving movement.

Perhaps the most tangible evidence which could have been provided short of holding the Washington demonstration itself were plans to hold preliminary marches on several city halls on June 27. These too were called off following the President's FEPC order of June 25. But it may be asked whether Randolph would have risked having his hand revealed so close to the date of the national demonstration if he were not fairly certain of the results. True, if the local marches (set for Chicago, New York, Detroit and Los Angeles) were not all failures, the successful ones would receive the major publicity emphasis and help build up the pressures symbolized by the national threat to March on Washington. Whether Randolph and White were bluffing we shall never know, but that they were gambling seems clear. It is doubtful that the Negro leaders or anyone else could have foretold accurately just how successful a March on Washington was in the making in June of 1941.

Victory!

WHEN, IN EARLY JUNE, large front-page headlines in the Negro papers boasted: "MARCH ON WASHINGTON DRIVE DRAWS NATIONWIDE RESPONSE,"[68] the Administration could no longer ignore the MOWC. Mayor La Guardia of New York City, who was handling civil defense problems for the President, arranged a meeting to consider the situation. On June 13, in the Mayor's City Hall office, Philip Randolph and Walter White were urged by Mrs. Roosevelt, Aubrey Williams (of the National Youth Administration) and Mayor La Guardia to call off the scheduled Washington demonstration. Mrs. Roosevelt promised Randolph to "ask the President to discuss the matter thoroughly." But Randolph refused to call off the March declaring, "I'm certain it will do some good. In fact, it has already done some good; for if you were not concerned about it you wouldn't be here now. . . ."[69]

On the same day as the New York City Hall conference Randolph received a wire from Secretary of the Navy Knox requesting him to "come to Washington for a conference on your project."[70] This message from on high aroused the Negro press greatly and raised the prestige and publicity value of the March. Two days later the "project" really got attention. On June 15, President Roosevelt wrote a strong public memorandum to the co-directors of OPM. Though this letter was reported in the white press, the MOW pressures which had brought it about still went unnoticed.[71]

It seems remarkable that the President resisted so strongly the issuing of a formal executive order, but this was what the Negro negotiators had to fight for. There is little reason to doubt that simply a memorandum issued by the President at an earlier date, perhaps at the previous White House conference, would have assuaged most of the Negro leadership. Now they remained adamant despite the strongly worded "memorandum" publicly issued over the President's signature. The issuance of this message, far from leading any of the Negro spokesmen or newspapers to call for abandonment of the July 1 plans, now merely whetted their appetites. Here at last, after months of despair and frustration, was a token of victory. The March on Washington strategy had drawn blood whereas all previous "nice" methods had failed utterly. Little credit was given the Administration for its welcomed action. Rather, Randolph and the March were hailed by the race press as champions of this partial victory. For the first time Randolph and his March on Washington Committee made page one of the previously pessimistic *Chicago Defender*.[72] The buildup of the March went on with increased vigor and with an aura about it of mounting power and of greater triumphs in the offing.

Continued efforts by Mrs. Roosevelt and Mayor La Guardia to get the MOWC to call off their demonstration failed. On June 18 the President personally conferred with the Negro leaders and strongly requested them to cancel the March. He appointed a committee headed by Mayor La Guardia to prepare a "plan of remedy for discrimination against Negroes. It was reported also that leaders of the March made no promise to call off the affair at this conference."[73]

Finally, on June 24 with the scheduled demonstration just one week off, La Guardia met with the March leadership in New York and informed them that the President was prepared to issue an executive order banning discrimination in defense industries. The demand was then advanced that Government employment also be brought within the order and that was done. Executive Order 8802 was issued the next day, June 25, 1941, and the July 1 trek to Washington was called off.

The issuing of the President's order did receive some notice in the white press but little or no attention was accorded the crucial role of the March on Washington Committee.[74] As can readily be imagined, quite the opposite situation prevailed in the Negro press. Despite this publicity, concern was expressed that this may have come too late to forestall the arrival of thousands of Negroes at the capital city. Mr. Randolph, consequently, was requested by the Administration to inform his followers of the "postponement" of the march over a nationwide radio network.[75] For those who had arrived in Washington despite these efforts a "victory celebration" replaced the scheduled protest demonstration. However, "it was not as well attended as had been anticipated."[76] On July 19 the President appointed the nation's first Committee on Fair Employment Practice, and the FEPC became a reality.

chapter iii

Zenith

> The power of the new movement is mysterious. It has
> almost no organization, no big machine for promo-
> tion and publicity. Yet it grips the people's imagi-
> nation and holds their loyalty. Masses of the darker
> common people are looking to Randolph as the Mod-
> ern Messiah.
>
> EDWIN R. EMBREE[1]

THE MARCH ON WASHINGTON COMMITTEE may never have been able
to march, had its "bluff" been called, because of insufficient organization. But it never had to march because of the pervasiveness of Negro
discontent and the success with which the symbols of mass protest
were wielded by the March Committee. FEPC was wrested from a
reluctant President at a time when many whites who cared most for
interracial justice were engaged in a battle to which they gave higher
priority. That is why the state of Negro morale sank so low, and it
was because morale was so low that the Negro community could be
rallied behind the March.

The radical instrument of a mass national demonstration, endorsed
by moderate as well as militant leaders, dramatically symbolized the
cohesiveness of the Negro protest. Its success in obtaining the Presidential order, however, was popularly attributed to the personal
leadership of A. Philip Randolph. He was hailed as "author of the
FEPC,"[2] and "canonized" by a biographer as "Saint Philip of the
Pullman Porters."[3] Even the Communists desisted from personal attacks for a time after their initial effort to discredit him for halting
the plans to march on Washington. Randolph received the most important award in the Negro community when he was designated
Spingarn medalist for 1941. Since first established in 1915, primarily
scientists, scholars and artists had been thus distinguished; this was
a particular honor for a protest leader. Recognition also came from
Howard University, which bestowed an honorary doctorate, and the

Schomburg Collection 1941 Honor Roll. The subject of many laudatory articles in the Negro press, the *Amsterdam News* saluted him:

The rise of A. Philip Randolph to a new and loftier position in the affairs of the race appears to presage the passing of the leadership that has controlled the Negro's destiny for the past 25 years.

Other organizations and other leaders have done some good work, but because their support has not come from the masses, and because they have rushed to get jobs for themselves at every opportunity, their leadership has been weak and ineffectual.

.   .   .   .

A. Philip Randolph, courageous champion of the rights of his people, takes the helm as the nation's No. 1 Negro leader.

. . . already he is being ranked along with the great Frederick Douglass. His name is rapidly becoming a household word.[4]

Unquestionably, "A. Philip Randolph was the outstanding leader of the period."[5]

The March Goes On

IT WAS RANDOLPH who had initiated the "Call to March," and it was his voice which was projected over national radio to announce the victory and call off the demonstration. But, he made clear, only the July 1 date was cancelled; the March as an organization would go on:

It is my aim to broaden and strengthen the Negro March-on-Washington committees all over the United States, to serve as watchdogs on the application of the President's executive order to determine how industries are complying with it.[6]

The over-all reaction was enthusiastic despite an undercurrent of dissatisfaction. Not everyone was convinced that this was quite the "Second Emancipation Proclamation" (as those closest to Randolph labeled it). However, most agreed with Randolph and the other White House conferees who maintained that the "major demands" of the March had been achieved.[7] Like the strike weapon of organized labor, a threatened "mass action" is not an end in itself but a means of pressing demands forcefully at the bargaining table. But " a bargain is a bargain," and the price of the executive order was cancellation of the threatened July 1 March on Washington.

Considerable evidence tends to support this view that the purpose of the action was an executive order. The original "Call to March" had proclaimed this intent. Similarly, the Negro press was specific concerning a Presidential order. When the President sent his "memorandum" to OPM directing them to act toward eliminating discriminatory practices in defense hiring, the *Chicago Defender* editorialized:

President Roosevelt, who has been unflinchingly courageous on so many occasions, should have issued long ago an executive order—not a memorandum—abolishing discrimination and segregation in the defense industries and in the Army, the Navy and the Air Corps as well. Since he has not done so, Negroes must intensify the struggle by militant action against a Raw Deal.[8]

All accounts of the White House conference at which Randolph, White, *et al.*, dickered with the President are in agreement. The President sought to have the March called off for something less than what the Negro leaders asked. *Fortune* emphasized that they held out for an executive order:

At a meeting with the President and ranking members of the Cabinet and the Office of Production Management, the suggestion of an executive order came from the Negro side of the conference table, and was coolly received on the other side. When only a few days were left for preventing an international embarrassment, the Negro leaders were shown a first draft, which committed defense industries but not government itself. The Negroes stood pat. Finally the President agreed to include an order to his administration and the March was cancelled.[9]

Thus, the demand for an executive order ending discrimination in employment by defense contractors and by Government was a major objective of the March, and this was so from the outset. The "horse-trading" did not begin at the White House conference table but at least as early as the President's unsuccessful attempt to placate Negroes with his memorandum to OPM. The *Chicago Defender* emphasized the importance of Executive Order 8802: "Organizations and individuals which had sharply criticized the President's memorandum on the same subject issued to OPM Monday, June 16, were unstinted in praise of his latest action."[10]

Overwhelmingly, the Negro leadership hailed the FEPC order. Roy Wilkins, who has since succeeded Walter White as executive secretary of the NAACP, declared: "The most important item, of course, is that this action was forced on the Administration by the March-on-Washington crusaders. Proving once more that we get more when we yell than we do when we plead."[11] That "more" had been "gotten" Wilkins did not doubt. True, he along with other leaders made it clear that this was only a partial victory, but the President's act was regarded as "a truly momentous one."[12] Wilkins ardently defended Randolph and White from the cries of "sellout" which did arise in certain places.[13]

The factual evidence of such dissatisfaction is sparse. The fear expressed by some that the march might go on from sheer momentum and be taken over by irresponsibles was exploded in the poorly attended victory celebration in Washington. The "aroused masses" were not rushing into the Capitol despite official cancellation of the march. The Communists did, as we have shown, attack Randolph for "betraying" the March in the immediate confusion of that week's change in line caused by the Soviet entry into the war. However, they were not the sole source of attack. The *Defender* reported:

The praise of the President's action and of Randolph's decision to postpone the job march was not shared universally, however. In many sections of the country, leaders while lauding Roosevelt's executive order, pointed out that it provided no penalty for violation of the order.

Similarly Randolph's decision was characterized as a 'sell-out' in some quarters. It might have been an awareness of this reaction which caused him to emphasize that he had 'postponed' and not 'cancelled' the march.[14]

A good case can be made that the White House conferees had not obtained all that the March was originally organized to attain. The "Call to March" had demanded *both* "jobs in national defense *and* equal integration in the fighting forces of the United States."[15] Also, it will be recalled that the previous White House conference (September 1940), following which accusations of "sellout" were raised against Randolph and White, was specifically on the question of Armed Forces discrimination. It is plain that though they got entirely different treatment at the June White House conference than they had at the previous September meeting, the negotiators got less than they demanded.

The NAACP was in session at its Houston, Texas convention when the FEPC order was issued. One can detect echoes of discontent among the delegates. While the body did resolve to "endorse the present MARCH ON WASHINGTON COMMITTEE and its work," it greeted the new executive order with restrained approval as "a step in the right direction."[16] The description, if not emphatic, in the resolution of the limitations of the order suggests that doubts very likely were raised as to whether the march should have been called off. Probably this was agitated by Communist influenced delegates, but the need to so placate them reveals more strength than their regular numerical following could have sustained. "Left-wing" criticism of the MOWM leadership's FEPC victory found enough response to make necessary a compromise resolution which straddled wholehearted endorsement of the March and outright criticism of its "victory."

The enormous enthusiasm which the projected demonstration had aroused was not easily channeled into a victory celebration. At first, many did not understand what an executive order was and how that differed from the platitudinous public statements previously issued from the White House and the OPM. Writing on "Negro Morale" in the *New Republic*, shortly after the 8802 Order, a well known Negro writer, Roi Ottley, failed to appreciate the significance of the new FEPC. He did not even refer to the President's edict as an *executive order* nor indicate that a new Presidential *agency* was established. The gains produced by the March were lightly dismissed as "a public statement [which] broadly condemned racial intolerance and urged the country to drop its bars against the employment of racial minorities."[17]

Ottley wrote that when the March was called off:

The masses of Negroes were bewildered by the sudden turn of events; indeed, many of Randolph's own colleagues were disgruntled by the easy conclusion of the affair. Nothing tangible had been gained, they felt. The recent incidents at the Army camps and the chronic, acute unemployment bear them out. Randolph lost much prestige as a leader. And Negroes now appear to be taking the situation into their own hands and stampeding their leaders, with the result that newer and younger men now are taking the helm.[18]

This was an exaggeration and later Ottley admitted, "As it turned out, Randolph and White displayed considerable statesmanship."[19] This subsequent judgment is undoubtedly more correct, but Ottley did reveal something of the mood of many Negroes just after the March was called off. If a perceptive writer like Ottley could miss the significance of the newborn FEPC, so could many rank-and-file followers of Randolph—and a number did.

The MOWM, like a typical mass enterprise, required the rallying of enthusiasts; and it was a measure of the success of Randolph's movement that it had them. But enthusiasts are of different sorts. Some ardently wave from the sidelines taking vicarious satisfaction in the activities of the participants, so long as these are in the news. Others are more active, participating enthusiasts. Sometimes the activity as such becomes a source of much gratification. This may be exhibited by the devotion of greater energies to dramatic techniques than to substantive goals. It is perhaps not surprising that it was the "Youth Division" of the March which was most enthusiastic about *marching*. And it was the youth group which exhibited the greatest feeling of letdown when "having won" they discovered they would not need to march, at least not just yet.

Meeting in New York on June 28, 1941 the "Youth Division of the Negro March Committee" condemned the decision to call off the march. The resolution forwarded to Randolph suggested:

> In order to take full advantage of the partial gain made, however, and to encourage the Negro people to press forward with vigor to secure their full participation in American life the Youth Division of the Negro March Committee recommends that no momentous decisions be made in the future by the National Executive Committee unless the local committees have been consulted. We further recommend that the National Executive Committee call the Negro masses together to make plans for the postponed March to be held within a period of ninety (90) days after July 1, 1941.[20]

It is necessary to caution that we are dealing with only an undercurrent of discontent; the main stream of public comment hailed the March leadership and Randolph in particular as bearers of a great victory. In this context it should be noted that the vote for the resolution of the youth division was not unanimous (23 for, 14 opposed, 1 abstention). And, while the smallness of the total vote may have been due to the speed with which the group was brought together, the size of the gathering did not indicate an overwhelming mass-passion to march, come what may, within ninety days.

Randolph's reply was lengthy and blunt. It may be characterized as part lecture on the nature and strategy of mass movements and part attack on the motivations of the petitioners. "It is evident," he wrote, "that the youth division missed the main objective of the march, as well as the method and technique of mass action."[21] Randolph's letter warrants extended attention, though, for convenience, we may reduce its bulk to six essentials:

(1) *The specific and main objectives of the march had been won:*
In the first place, the purpose of the march was specific, and not general. It was to secure an Executive Order from the President of the United States abolishing discriminations in national defense . . . [and] in the Federal departments of the Government.

(2) *It is necessary to keep objectives simple to rally the masses:*
These were objectives that the people could understand, visualize, and feel. These objectives were developed in harmony with sound mass psychology; namely that the people cannot struggle for an omnibus program with a multiplicity of aims, but must have one central and vital issue around which to rally. . . .

(3) *The march threat was analogous to labor's strike:*
The strike vote is the positive, tangible expression of the will of the workers to strike if their demands are not complied with. However, the workers know, and so does the union, that all their demands will never be complied with. Therefore, when—as a result of negotiation and conference—the chief aims of the organization of the workers are realized, the proposed strike is called off.
    This does not mean that another strike may not be proposed and scheduled.

(4) *The youth were too enamored of the romantic flavor of the demonstration to appreciate the practical victory:*
The Negro masses who want jobs now would have hurled curses upon the heads of the leaders of the Negro March-on-Washington Movement if they had sacrificed an immediate and practical opportunity to secure employment opportunities for Negro masses in defense industries in order to satisfy a handful of Negro youth who apparently were more interested in the drama and pyrotechnics of the march than in the basic and main issue of putting Negroes to work.

(5) *They were dilettantes and had failed to organize the masses of Negro youth:*
It would seem to me that your first function as a serious group, devoted to the cause of the Negro masses, was to actually mobilize the youth of the country—at least of Harlem. This you never did. You were more articulate about what you hoped to do than what you actually did. It is a grave question in my mind whether the youth division would have actually mobilized 25 youths to go to Washington. There is no tangible evidence to the contrary.

(6) *Some were dupes of the Communists:*

I am really fully aware of the reason for the attitude of the youth division. It is the inevitable outcome of manipulation by an artful and aggressive fraction that religiously follow the Communist Party line as a bible of unerring salvation. It would have suited the Committee [sic] Party perfectly for the march to have gone on with the rejection of the President's Executive Order in satisfaction of the infantile, ridiculous, and tragic technique of dragging the Negro masses lower in the depths of unemployment and impoverishment in order to have a demonstration which might be labeled an expression of the revolutionary ardor of the Negro people.

These were harsh words though a somewhat prickly olive branch was extended. Randolph offered "long, hard, sacrificial effort." This would enable those who "have not themselves gone through the test-fire of sacrifice and suffering" to "morally justify their leadership of the masses of Negro youth." Therefore, though they were not "read out of the party," Randolph later refused to organize a separate youth division.

We shall not deal seriatim with Randolph's letter as many of the points reflecting his views on mass organization will be dealt with in wider contexts. However, it might be observed here that there is something to be said for his youthful protesting zealots. Despite the basic solidity of Randolph's case, one may question whether the executive order could be described as an objective "the people could understand, visualize, and feel." The press and leadership did; and Randolph was a genius at symbolizing the order, not in terms of a legal document, but as analogous to Lincoln's Emancipation Proclamation. The fact remains, however, that the youth were not the only ones (as we have shown in the case of Roi Ottley) to whom the significance of the FEPC order was not clear.

Part of the difficulty lay in the fact that this was a prosaic victory, despite the sense of exhilaration to be derived from the White House's yielding to pressure. The luster of the threatened March shone brighter than that of the order. Randolph would no doubt be right to say that "one can't eat luster." But as a brilliant agitator and propagandist skilled at creating the glitter necessary to attract masses to action programs, Randolph might have been more tolerant of these young romantics, impractical as they no doubt were. When they complained to him, "But to Negro Youth and perhaps millions of other Negroes the March on Washington was received as the hope of a new day," they were reflecting their naïveté. They found it hard to understand why the promised day had not dawned fully developed at the appointed hour. The belief that it can is in political life a powerful myth of which Randolph had zestful experience in his own youth.

Lastly, we may note that Randolph did avoid a frank statement that the executive order had not directed an end to discrimination in the Armed Forces. Perhaps this is the implication intended in the third point of our résumé of his letter where it is maintained that full satisfaction of all demands is not possible in such negotiations.

However, it is one thing to maintain that not all the demands of the March had been met; it is another matter to decide whether Randolph, White, *et al.* had gone into the conference with enough pressure behind them to have held out for more. The President could not be indifferent to the countervailing pressures on him strongly pressed by Southern political leaders. Also, there were definite limits to which the "international embarrassment," which constituted much of the inherent power of the March, could be pushed. Such an embarrassment might well be tolerated if the price of avoidance was too high. The primary Rooseveltian concern of the time was the building up of the Armed Forces and the defense establishment in general. Southerners were not remiss at threatening that disruption and violence would result if civil rights measures were hammered too far, too fast. Serious rioting did occur during the war for which Southerners readily laid blame upon the Negro leadership and press.[22]

Another factor weighing heavily on the Negro negotiators was simply that they had no way of knowing how many would *physically* "march" to Washington. Randolph was fond of saying, "It is time for the leadership to catch up with the followship"; but this, after all, was addressed to the "followship." Even if the Negro leadership was more easily satisfied with the June 25th order than the "aroused Negro masses," what then? Would their "arousement" have sustained an actual march? Therein lay the gamble, therein lay the "magnificent bluff."[23]

The analysis which Randolph's letter to the youth served should not suggest that this was what primarily concerned him right after the FEPC victory. As president of a busy trade-union, he had seen work pile up on his desk during the buildup for the demonstration and the conferences with the Administration's spokesmen. Randolph's lieutenants, too, had been busier with the March than with the Brotherhood of Sleeping Car Porters. And the other leaders of the March had their own organizational fires to tend.

The MOWC, as a committee of leaders of existing groups, officially had no membership of its own and was theoretically but a co-ordinating instrument. The March had been created as a temporary and special activity narrower in programatic focus than any of its components. Its purpose having been achieved the question should be asked, why didn't the Negro March on Washington Committee go out of existence?

Perhaps unusual in organizational experience, the official and the unofficial answers to this question were not very far apart. Officially, the local March Committees would be preserved to ensure their capacity to respond to another march (read "strike") call. Thus, the FEPC and the Administration would be kept on their toes in fulfilling their part of the bargain. Unofficially, the March was nominally "postponed" rather than cancelled in good measure to reassure those who felt let down and to protect the leaders from charges of "sellout."

The usual unofficial reason for continuing a successful organization did not fully apply to this case. None of the leaders who headed the March and represented it in the White House negotiations had to rely entirely upon the March to sustain his leadership. Indeed, to Walter White and Lester Granger the March was more a threat, organizationwise, than a prospective gain. The greater the attention lavished upon the March, the more difficult their respective tasks as organizers of the NAACP and National Urban League. The more adulation heaped upon Randolph, who was getting most of the personal credit, the less easy their own leadership roles would become. This was a sacrifice readily made for a short period and for a specific goal. For them, the desire to continue the March was pretty much as stated, to enforce the executive order.

To a considerable extent the decision concerning the continuance of the March was not up to White and Granger. They could not publicly desert the March or advocate its dissolution without Randolph's consent for two reasons. First, it would be strategically foolish to cut oneself off from the most successful and popular Negro activity of the decade. Second, the "postponement" of the July 1 march had already raised doubts concerning their militancy. No Negro leader would lightly risk the Uncle Tom label; attacks on the

March were only possible, at that time, for insufficient militancy, not for radicalism. Conceivably, the existing organizations could have been charged with enforcement of the executive order—had Randolph agreed.

Randolph's interest in continuing the March was somewhat greater than that of White and Granger. He was, of course, the hero of the March which was synonymous with his name. Also, the character of the NAACP and, to a lesser extent, the Urban League as "protest" organizations was different from the trade-union Brotherhood. Therefore, Randolph had most use for the March, or something comparable, to continue his political protest role. It will be recalled that he had been president of the National Negro Congress which had served as a similar vehicle.

But we should not weigh these factors too heavily as they are somewhat counterbalanced by three others: First, the character of unions in the Negro community tends to be different from their white or mixed counterparts in that all Negro organizations are often called upon to champion the race and, therefore, are part of the Negro protest. Actually, all Negro leaders, whether officially political or not, play something of a protest role. Thus, baseball-player Jackie Robinson, concert-singer Marian Anderson and United Nations diplomat Ralph Bunche have all been cast in that role at one time or another. As Myrdal has said, "Every Negro who rises to national prominence and acclaim is a race hero: he has symbolically fought the Negro struggle and won."[24] Being a trade-union leader was not a handicap to any political-protest aspirations of leadership Randolph may have had. Secondly, the NAACP and the Urban League have much more status today than they had in the Nineteen Thirties and early Forties. Programatic competition from Communist-dominated *causes célèbres* such as the Scottsboro cases, and front organizations like the National Negro Congress, sapped the protest roots of the NAACP and other conservative Negro organizations. The enormous prestige associated with the Supreme Court victories of the NAACP was yet to come. Finally, Randolph was not a formal rival to the NAACP; he was a member of its Board of Directors and might have satisfied programatic or personal desires for protest activity through that organization.

The March continued as an organizational entity essentially for the stated reasons: to insure that the President did not "sell out" the

FEPC and to reassure the Negro public that the March leadership had not "sold out" to the President.

It would be naive to assume that once the FEPC executive order was issued, there was quick compliance with its terms. And this was so not only because of the lag one would ascribe to mechanical and administrative management problems. There is no sharp line dividing the policy-making and the policy-executing processes in government. Indeed it is difficult to see why one should assume there would be unless he held the stereotype of government as an individual organic sovereign. It is far more realistic to recognize that the term "government" (certainly *democratic* government) embraces a complex of power points each of which does not owe its power to the same supporting forces. This is particularly true in the American form of government with its territorial and functional division of powers. If a section of government is ardently in favor of a course of public policy it, and the affected clientele, must still deal with other agencies and their clienteles in the continuous contest for priorities and appropriations. Where a clientele group obtains a declaration of public policy from a reluctant segment of government by dint of great pressure, the struggle is even less likely to end with the victory of a public policy pronouncement. Just as the Emancipation Proclamation by Abraham Lincoln did not bring to a close the struggle for Negro freedom, the "Second Emancipation Proclamation" (FEPC) did not produce a final victory in the Negro's struggle for equality of economic opportunity.

The threat of the postponed national demonstration, set to strike at call, was wielded at once in negotiations concerning the composition of the new FEPC. The capacity of the Committee to achieve its official purposes would be affected greatly by the calibre of those appointed. How many (and which) labor men, Negroes, Southerners, businessmen and Jews should there be? Who would be chairman? These questions had to be answered and would affect the character of operations. The Negro leaders, of course, were consulted on their preferences[25] though they were not given all they asked for, and what they were given was not obtained without a posture of strength.

When two relatively unknown labor men were suggested for the FEPC, Sydney Hillman was telegraphed in politely aggressive language:

IF TWO MEMBERS OUT OF BOARD OF FIVE OR SIX MEM-
BERS ARE TO REPRESENT LABOR THEY SHOULD BE NONE
OTHER THAN THE PRESIDENT OF THE A F OF L AND CIO,
MESSRS. WILLIAM GREEN AND PHILIP MURRAY. WE HAVE
NO OTHER RECOURSE THAN TO MAKE OUR POSITION PUB-
LIC IF LESSER REPRESENTATIVES ARE APPPOINTED BY
PRESIDENT AT YOUR INSISTENCE. WE WOULD REGRET BE-
ING FORCED TO DO THIS BUT WE HAVE A RESPONSIBILITY
TO THOSE WHO HAVE SUPPORTED THE MARCH ON WASH-
INGTON AND GENERAL PUBLIC WHICH HAVE OPPOSED
DISCRIMINATION.

A. PHILIP RANDOLPH AND WALTER WHITE[26]

Green and Murray were appointed though subsequently they
were provided official alternates and never functioned as effective
members of the FEPC. Concerning the chairman, Randolph and
White were unsuccessful in their preference, Mayor LaGuardia.
Mark Ethridge, the racially liberal publisher of the *Louisville Courier
Journal*, from borderstate Kentucky and a Mississippian by birth,
was chosen by the President presumably to reduce Southern hostility.
(Ethridge was later to assuage them to an extent considered ob-
noxious by Negroes.)[27] The Negro leaders were fairly satisfied,
particularly by their success in obtaining the appointment of two
of their race to the FEPC. The NAACP's *Crisis* boasted:

Thanks to the ten-day behind the scenes battle waged by the Association in Washington, D.C. and New York, two Negro members instead
of one were appointed to the Fair Employment Practices Committee over
considerable opposition of Sidney Hillman of OPM.[28]

Randolph, too, was satisfied, for one of the appointees directly
reflected his role in obtaining the order; this was the Brotherhood of
Sleeping Car Porters' vice-president, Milton Webster. The other
Negro appointee reflected the gains made by the Democrats on
Chicago's Negro South Side; he was City Councilman Earl B. Dickerson.[29] Though not an original choice of Randolph and White, he
later proved a most vigorous member of the FEPC. His retention on
the Committee was sought when he was deliberately dropped in the
shuffle of subsequent reorganization.

Finally, David Sarnoff, President of the Radio Corporation of
America and a Jew, completed the "balanced ticket." But the number
of appointments necessary to satisfy these various criteria required

a new executive order to expand the size from that established in the original message.[30]

With the completion of the roster of members of the FEPC a new chapter in the governmental handling of the minorities problem got under way.[31] The Committee, though it began its work slowly and with only a small budget, was hailed with great enthusiasm in the Negro press. The *Amsterdam News* reported, "Defense Firms Hire Negro Workers Right and Left," and named a substantial number. The same paper quoted the director of personnel of Glenn Martin Aircraft Production Company of Baltimore on hiring one hundred workers for skilled and semiskilled jobs:

This employment will not be a mere gesture of calling these people production employees and actually using them as laborers. We plan to see Negroes on production jobs working under white supervision and giving them the same opportunity for training and induction in our services as our white employees.[32]

At last the hiring gates were opening! Small wonder that credit went to Executive Order 8802 and, therefore, to the March. If any missed the connection, it was made for them by the front page of this same issue of the *Amsterdam News* which proclaimed: "FEPC OPENS HEARINGS ON JOB BIAS." *Crisis*, also, reported considerable progress on "The Defense Job Front" with "Two Plants Opened" to Negroes through the efforts of FEPC and an article listing nine "Complaints to FEPC" showing the early functioning of that Committee.[33] Whether FEPC deserved the credit or not, that was where it went; and whether MOWC in turn was responsible for the jobs which were now opening up and FEPC's activity, it was so regarded. Indeed, the connection between the March and FEPC was so close as to lead to some dispute and misunderstanding concerning the nature of that relationship.

When the FEPC staged its first public hearing in Los Angeles on October 20 and 21, 1941, it was inevitably the focus of Negro attention throughout the country. Here was the test of the Committee's power to remedy a long-suffered evil. And, therefore, here was a test of what the Negro leadership had "bought" with the postponed march on Washington. What would and could be the role of the March (to recall Randolph's words) in acting as "watchdogs on the application of the President's executive order to determine how industries are complying with it?"[34]

To the *Amsterdam News*, one of the papers most favorably disposed to Randolph and the March, the results were a disappointment. They editorialized:

> Last week when the FEPC held its first hearing in Los Angeles, the 'Randolph' committee was quite inconscpicuous. We had hoped that whenever the FEPC sat down for a hearing, the M.T.W.C. [March to Washington Committee] would be prepared to place before it information and evidence of discrimination in such concrete form that its work would be simple and direct; that the M.T.W.C. would, in itself, be a sort of investigating body, constantly gathering data and sifting material for the FEPC to study.[35]

This, to be sure, was a gross misunderstanding of the kind of organization which the March was or could be without a drastic shift in character. A mass organization, the March had built its strength upon an apparent capacity to call vast numbers of Negroes to march on Washington. Its ability to command substantial newspaper attention and the belief that it really could "deliver" was the result of dramatic propaganda and agitation. In no sense was it an organization equipped with skilled interviewers to handle complainants; to investigate claims would require professionals familiar with the intricacies of personnel work. As Randolph well knew, and Lester Granger was justly prepared to make known, the National Urban League was precisely such an organization.

Subsequently, Randolph defended the March from the *Amsterdam News'* criticism in much the same terms.[36] However, its editor may have claimed, not entirely without basis, that Randolph was the source of this misconception. When the FEPC first set up its staff and prepared for work, Randolph had urged Negroes to apply for defense jobs in large numbers and to note evidence of discrimination:

> If there is no Negro March-on-Washington Committee in the city and Negro workers who apply for jobs are discriminated against, these workers should make known their complaint to the National Negro Committee to March-on-Washington or to any of the local community agencies. . . ."[37]

In effect, the *Amsterdam News* was asking the March to become a community service agency. This it clearly had not been, and was not then equipped to be. Moreover, Randolph did not intend altering its character in that direction. Even so, the editor of the *Amsterdam News* did reveal the close public identification of the March with the

FEPC. During its first year of existence, the FEPC seemed definitely getting somewhere and the March shared that success. This was the high point in the life of the first FEPC and the zenith of March on Washington popularity.

The March Rallies

SHORTLY AFTER the first FEPC hearing the Japanese bombed Pearl Harbor, and the United States became formally involved in the shooting as well as in the production war. We have already cited statements with which Negroes greeted that event. They can all be brought together in one inspired tongue-lash by Walter White: "Your ancestors came to America on the Mayflower while mine came here on a slave ship. But we're all in the same boat now!"[38]

Only a month after the United States declaration of war a conference of seventeen national organizations called together by the National Urban League resolved "that the Negro was 'not wholeheartedly and unreservedly' behind the government's program."[39] In March, Archibald MacLeish, who headed up the "Office of Facts and Figures," was bluntly informed by fifty Negro organizations' delegates that "the Negro people were cool to the war effort and that there could be no national unity nor high morale among Negroes unless they were given their rights."[40] The "Double V for Victory"[41] campaign, victory against Jim Crow as well as against the Axis, was maintained by virtually the entire Negro leadership throughout the war.

Negroes knew that their manpower was becoming necessary to the war effort entirely apart from consideration of racial justice. But they refused to accept menial and dead-end tasks as their portion. The charge that their patriotism, therefore, had a price tag on it failed to move their determination to push their advantage. (Though, as we shall see, this does not imply that Pearl Harbor had no dampening effect on the type of protest actions which could be strategically employed during an all-out war.)

In the immediate period after Pearl Harbor it was not possible for the Negro leadership to appear to take other than a strongly militant position. The name "Uncle Tom" was detested by Negroes perhaps even more than old "Jim Crow" himself. No Negro could survive that label if his accusers could make it stick. Though Randolph and the March had a little difficulty in persuading everyone at first that the FEPC order was a victory and not further vacillation of the "handkerchief-head" variety, that was a rather mild undercurrent and a temporary phase. The record is plain that the organization with the most militant reputation was the March, and the leader who personified its aggressive tone and bold proposals was Randolph.

As the FEPC hearings got under way the enthusiasm for the March grew and surpassed that of the pre-FEPC period. We might even say that the "followship caught up with the leadership," but that exaggerates the extent to which masses were actively involved at any time. Roy Wilkins wrote, "Everyone and his brother is talking about the Negro in national defense and about employment particularly."[42] Unemployed Negroes did appreciate the jobs which were being made available. The FEPC seemed to work; at least, declared the *Chicago Defender*, "It gave hope to millions of Negro workers whose morale would have been irreparably shattered were it not for their faith in the eventual realization of the Committee's main objective."[43]

The trouble with the FEPC in its first year was not that its enforcement powers were seriously challenged—that would come later. What hampered its work at first was less the political dynamite with which the problem was charged than the sheer administrative difficulty of getting fair employment practices established with a pitifully small staff and a minute budget. Randolph and White sought to use the threat of the postponed march to obtain increased scope for the Committee's operations. The March acted as a watchdog on the continued existence of the FEPC. At the same time, the Committee bore the brunt of considerable pressure urging it to carry out the terms of its establishing order.

One of the principal concerns of the Negro leaders was that the FEPC remain an independent agency responsible only to the President. It was felt that the Executive would be more susceptible to their demands than would the Congress, or administrative officials whose purse strings were tightly held by Congressional committees. Though the FEPC when first established was nominally a part of the Labor Division of OPM, it operated as a separate agency. That is, its budget and continued operations were a matter of White House rather than OPM discretion. This same arrangement continued when OPM was abolished (January 26, 1942) and FEPC moved to the

War Production Board.[44] But here, again, pressure was brought to bear as it was feared that the FEPC would be subordinated to WPB authority.

This time Randolph sought the aid of the President' wife. Shortly after FEPC was established she had written him, "I hope from this first step, we may go on to others."[45] This was (somewhat loosely) interpreted as meaning that she "is in accord with the set policy of the Negro March on Washington Committee that Negroes should not be satisfied with the President's executive order. . . ."[46] Now Randolph wired Mrs. Roosevelt:

UNDERSTAND EXECUTIVE ORDER BEING PLANNED TO CHANGE STATUS OF FEPC AND MAKE IT SUBORDINATE TO ONE OF THE HEADS OF WAR PRODUCTION BOARD. WANT TO REQUEST AND URGE THAT YOU ASK THE PRESIDENT NOT TO PERMIT CHANGE IN STATUS OF FEPC UNTIL COM-MITTEE HAS MET AND DISCUSSED THIS VITAL MATTER IT-SELF WITH A VIEW TO MAKING RECOMMENDATIONS TO THE PRESIDENT ON ITS FUTURE STATUS. NEGROES OF THE NATION DEEPLY CONCERNED ABOUT FUTURE OF COMMIT-TEE BECAUSE OF THE GREAT WORK IT HAS DONE AND IS DOING TO ELIMINATE DISCRIMINATION IN NATIONAL DE-FENSE. IT WOULD BE TRAGIC IF THE WORK OF THE COM-MITTEE IS HANDICAPPED IN ANY MANNER.[47]

Randolph's fear probably was accurately based at the time as was shortly demonstrated by the transference of the FEPC and its subordination to Paul McNutt's jurisdiction in the War Manpower Commission. But that would not come until six months later, and the FEPC hearings went on. The agency remained for the while within WPB but subject to the President alone. Whether this was a result of Randolph's efforts, whether Mrs. Roosevelt had actually interceded with the President, we do not know. But it is clear that Randolph, White, Granger, et al., were not satisfied with the Administration's efforts to incorporate Negroes into the post-Pearl Harbor war effort on an equal basis.

A brief two and one-half weeks after it was publicly announced that he would receive the Spingarn medal for fathering the FEPC, Randolph was cast in the role of outraged parent: "RANDOLPH BLASTS ROOSEVELT'S FEPC," a front-page headline trumpeted, and continued, "Committee is Meaningless, Says Executive. Believes Entire Unit Must Be Overhauled To Be of Service." Randolph complained that he had just returned from a tour of the country and found "that the FEPC has no direct control and supervision over an adequate staff to police and enforce the order." Furthermore, "Most of the men are taken from the old OPM, which is now the WPB, and is under the direct supervision of Sidney Hillman."[48]

In some respects Randolph's language, as reported by the press, was not representative of his actual attitude to the FEPC. It had been in existence for only six months as 1942 began. Even as late as May of that year, Randolph's *Black Worker* front-paged a banner headline, "FEPC IS MAKING PROGRESS AGAINST JOB BIAS." Randolph and his associates were demanding that the FEPC be strengthened. It was purely for this purpose that its weakness was exposed and attacked. The personnel of the President's Committee, at the time, were on good terms with the March leadership and included Randolph's second-in-command of the Sleeping Car Porters, Milton Webster. And, of course, the FEPC was the prize captured by the March—the fruit of victory and the price for calling off the original march. It could not be labeled a failure too quickly if the March was to maintain its status as champion and bearer of victory.

However, the smallness of the staff and the meagerness of funds presented a very serious problem. The hearings which the FEPC was conducting could not publicly and officially prove (however commonly known) the existence of employment discrimination without painstaking investigation and documentation. At the same time, the prestige of the March was extremely high while Negro dissatisfaction continued to be strong.[49] Should another march be threatened? General threats had been kept up in continuous chorus against which the post-FEPC protest went on. Should another national demonstration be scheduled and a new call to march be issued as some were demanding? Or, was there any technique which might offer a somewhat more moderate course with fewer risks but with substantial pressure too?

A physical march on Washington would hardly have been child's play even in the period when its preparation had been undertaken previously. A post-Pearl Harbor march was not something to be contemplated lightly. Notice had been served that the Negro protest would go on, but how vigorously? To the point of sedition? Very few Negroes would go that far on both patriotic and practical grounds. The protest would continue; that is, the Negro leadership would continue to push their demands, but by methods more suited to the times than a mass descent on the wartime Capitol. Could this radical method continue to receive the support of moderates? One of Randolph's staunchest supporters publicly wrote:

> It would not be tactful at this time to organize another march on Washington, for such a move would play directly into the hands of Hitler and other enemies of our country and our cause and the New Negro has no desire or intention to do that.[50]

We can only speculate as to the possibilities of renewing the campaign so that marchers could be organized. We have referred to those who were dissatisfied that the first march had been called off. We may presume that some were quite ready to march again. For example, from Alton, Illinois, a telegram urged:

> DEAR BROTHER RANDOLPH. ARTICLE IN CHICAGO PAPERS APRIL SIXTEENTH STATES WALTER WHITE (NAACP) AND YOURSELF HAVE CONFERRED AGAIN REGARDING THE REESTABLISHMENT OF "MARCH TO WASHINGTON". WE IN ST LOUIS AND ALTON ILLINOIS HAVE BEEN GIVING THIS MATTER MUCH THOUGHT RECENTLY. SOME SEVERAL RECENT CONFERENCES HAVE BEEN HELD WITH THE NAACP PARTICIPATING. WE FEEL VERY CONFIDENT THAT WE CAN ENLIST THE SUPPORT AND ACTIVE PARTICIPATION OF MANY GROUPS AND ORGANIZATIONS IN THIS REGION BESIDES THE LABOR GROUPS WHO CAN BE DEPENDED UPON TO CARRY OUT THIS PROGRAM TO ITS MUCH NEEDED CONCLUSION. WOULD GREATLY APPRECIATE YOUR CLARIFYING THE CAUSES WHICH BROUGHT ABOUT THE CANCELLATION OF THE FIRST PROPOSED MARCH. WE HERE ARE ANXIOUS TO DO EVERYTHING HUMANLY POSSIBLE IN THIS MUCH DESIRED AND LONG OVERDUE ACTION. FRATERNALLY YOURS.
>
> JEROME B. BLACKWELL
> FIELD REPRESENTATIVE DISTRICT
> 50 UMWA [United Mine Workers of America][51]

But whether the march could take place as a physical fact was more than a matter of willing marchers or even of severe travel restrictions made tighter by the requirements of a country now officially and actively at war. More important was the need to nurse along the myth of an actual march for it was realized that the march was more powerful in the threat than in the accomplishment. Even if it would be successful as a march, it was entirely a "one-shot" weapon. How many times can several thousand persons be uplifted from their daily routines and transported considerable distances at a personal sacrifice of money and discomfort? The law of diminishing returns applied. So too would a kind of Gresham's law of political demonstrations, for an unsuccessful march would be bound to reduce seriously the over-all trading value of the Negro protest.

Something was needed to sharpen the threats that a march would take place if action was not taken, something more pointed than a warning but less dangerous than a march. It was thus that Randolph came up with the idea of spectacular rallies, first suggested for Washington, D.C. (the obvious substitute for the march), then extended to major cities with substantial Negro populations: New York, Chicago, St. Louis.

In 1941, the original idea (expressed in the official "Call") had been for "An 'all-out' thundering march on Washington, ending in a monster and huge demonstration at Lincoln's Monument. . . ." One year later, a series of mass rallies was conceived with the most dramatic of them again planned to capitalize on the symbolism of the Lincoln Memorial. This would come very close to constituting the March on Washington Randolph had continued to threaten but had not delivered.

Memories were still vivid of the 75,000 persons who had assembled in dramatic protest to hear Marian Anderson. Though but half of the 1939 throng had been colored,[52] a rally of thirty to forty thousand Negroes would be an overwhelming coup over competitive strategies in the organizational market. Even if not advertised as a "march" on Washington, the net effect might be substantially the same. The idea for such a demonstration in the midst of war was characteristic of Randolph's flair for the sensational.

It is doubtful that the 1941 march, had it not been "postponed," would have been allowed access to the Lincoln monument. In April 1942, Secretary of Interior Ickes, who had introduced Marian Anderson at the 1939 protest concert, refused Randolph's request outright. Randolph replied to Ickes' refusal: "I can understand your position that you feel that this question is too controversial." But, he went on:

Relative to meetings of this sort being inapropos at this time and meeting with the disfavor of the President, may I say that the A F of L and CIO are staging a series of protest meetings from coast to coast fighting against the action of certain Tory senators and congressmen who want to strip Labor of all its rights under the smoke screen of National Defense.

It is my feeling that a meeting of the sort we plan to stage will help immensely in developing a sounder, national unity for the prosecution of this War and the winning of victory over the totalitarian forces. We are just as interested and determined to see America and her Allies triumph in this conflict as the President is and we want to help him, but the moral position of our country is greatly weakened when we profess to be fighting the cause of democracy and deny it to our own citizens because of color.[53]

If another March on Washington was ruled out for the while, and the authorities would not make the Lincoln Memorial available, in what form could the March as a political movement continue? Mere meetings were nothing new. What was needed, Randolph felt, were mammoth rallies so large and so dramatized that they might serve notice of a united community ready to go farther if the Administration did not act. To fill Madison Square Garden entirely with protesting Negroes, and similar meeting places of gargantuan proportions in several other major centers of colored population, might be made a dramatic event capable of symbolizing mass resentment and a determined leadership.

Madison Square Garden is an enormous amphitheater with an official capacity of 14,200. Actually, four to five thousand more places (the floor of the arena is used) must be filled before a political meeting in the Garden overflows into the streets outside. The Chicago Coliseum and the St. Louis Auditorium similarly can accommodate huge audiences. Would the necessary horde of people leave Harlem and other outlying districts of New York to pack the Garden? Could this be done on a similar scale in several cities? Or would row on row of empty seats expose the Negro protest as mere ballyhoo and press sensationalism? Here then was another gigantic gamble, but this time it could be no bluff as substantial sums of money were paid out for rentals and dates were committed for the meeting places.

The transformation of these large meetings into dramatic and forceful protest mobilizations could not take place without a great deal of organizational effort. An enormous output of man-hours was needed in committee planning, fund raising and the administrative supervision that goes with any large-scale enterprise. Whatever doubts may have lingered concerning Randolph's organization for the 1941 march, the 1942 effort left few tactics unexplored.

There is no need to chronicle all the details which constituted the organizational aspects of the rallies. It is important to note, however, that this vast effort was manned almost entirely by highly dedicated persons stimulated by a militant protest movement and a dynamic leader. The scope of what had been undertaken is revealed by the scores of letters Randolph wrote following the meetings thanking those who made up the working volunteers. There were an enormous number of committees such as Finance, Sponsors, Organizations, Literature, Program, Publicity, Coliseum, Ushers, First Aid, Churches, Youth, Speakers, Minute Men and many more. The Negro press, generally, proved even more helpful than in the buildup for the original March on Washington. Indeed a staff reporter of the *Amsterdam News* was specifically assigned to aid the publicity work on the Madison Square Garden venture.[54]

In a plea to the president of the *Pittsburgh Courier* for substantial coverage of the projected rallies, Randolph stressed the large scale on which the activity was being conducted:

The Madison Square Garden will cost about $4500, and the promotion of the meeting itself will be a considerable expense. The committee in Chicago is seeking to get the Stadium, which will accommodate some 25,000 people. This will cost about $5,000 or $6,000 without the promotional expenses. I have no figures on the cost of the Ball Park in Washington.

We are hoping to finance these meetings through contributions from organizations, individuals and the sale of tickets for $.25. Chicago may sell the tickets for $.10 since the object is to get the masses to the meeting.[55]

Raising such large amounts of money is not a light undertaking. It was particularly difficult in view of Randolph's fixed resolve to restrict his appeal for support to Negroes. Following the rallies, Randolph wrote:

In view of charges made that they [the New York, Chicago, and St. Louis mass meetings] were subsidized by Nazi funds, it may not be amiss to point out that of the $8,000 expenses of the Madison Square meeting every dime was contributed by Negroes themselves, except for tickets bought by some liberal white organizations.[56]

Long lists of names were published in the Negro press indicating a wide spread of support from people who contributed small amounts of money to the March.[57] Actually, the meetings were underwritten by the Brotherhood of Sleeping Car Porters. Had the fund-raising efforts collapsed and the collections and the sales of advertising space in the souvenir program failed to cover expenses, it was Randolph's union which was financially liable. This was made plain in a letter to Milton Webster:

The Brotherhood might have to make up any deficit in the funds if they don't collect enough money before the meeting, June 26th, and afterwards the Brotherhood can get back all the money except what it has contributed outright.[58]

Officially, Randolph and the Brotherhood were only a fraction of the wide sponsorship of the rallies. This was purely formal, though it had some substance in the early stages when Randolph sought the backing of all non-Communist Negro organizations. "Fifty Organizations' Delegates Meet and Select Committee Heads . . . in answer to a call sent out by the March on Washington Movement. . . ."[59] was the publicised form of the organization for the rallies in early April. The *New York Times*, a few days before the Madison Square Garden affair reported it was "sponsored by the National Association for the Advancement of Colored People, the National Urban League, the Harlem Branch of the Young Men's and Young Women's Christian Associations and scores of Negro labor and fraternal organizations. . . ."[60]

But the federal structure of the March Committee, in practice, was subordinated to Randolph's continued leading role. It is not simply that he neglected to consult the participating organizations; they were officially represented on the highest policy-making levels of the March Committee. But this separation of policy and administration is, if anything, less realistic in nongovernmental associations than it is in government. The public identification of the March as "Randolph's show" was accurate not only in the sense that he was founder and spokesman; it was Randolph and the people who were loyal only and directly to him who bore the major work load. They looked to him for leadership and directions.

Thus, the special letterhead for the Chicago rally read, "City-Wide Committee for Coliseum Mass Meeting Friday, June 26, 1942, Initiated by March-on-Washington Movement." But except for the phrase "City-Wide Committee" in the title, the stationery identified all the officers and committee members listed as of the MOWM. It should be noted that it was during the buildup for the rallies that the name March on Washington *Movement* came more and more to replace the term *Committee* symbolizing the independent organizational status which was all but formalized by the end of the 1942 mass meetings.

Once again, as in the preparations for the July 1941 march, the official organs of the NAACP and of the Urban League were not used to enlist the support of their members and readers. This contrasted sharply with the use of these journals for their own activities.[61]

True, these and other organizations did co-operate. The chairlady of the Chicago Planning Committee wrote Randolph, "The NAACP is cooperating with us 100%. They have sent three representatives to work with us."[62] But this was not organic unity even within an organization of organizations form. The term "co-operate" was well chosen and the reference to "us" applied to Randolph's coterie of personal followers.

Indeed, the cohesion of this inner group of devoted Randolph followers led to periodic feuding with leaders of the Brotherhood of Sleeping Car Porters whose devotedness to Randolph was scarcely less but whose allegiance was mediated by the organizational structure within the Brotherhood. Inside the Chicago Division of the Brotherhood, there was a stabilized set of relationships, a chain of command, which gave the leadership of the Chicago BSCP authority over its followers. It was they who controlled the Chicago March on Washington Committee. When the Chicago Coliseum rally was established under a separate Planning Committee, its chairlady often availed herself of its quasi-independence of the Chicago MOWC to appeal directly to Randolph for his support. A similar setup in New York was less given to such difficulties thanks to Randolph's ability to intervene more quickly when necessary.

Randolph worked very closely with the committees charged with organizing the rallies, down to the most minute details. For example, he wrote the chairlady of the Chicago Planning Committee concerning necessary tasks even including precisely which songs should be sung at the rally. The flavor of the March and Randolph's leadership is well revealed in this letter:

Dear Neva:
These are some things that should be looked after immediately.
1. Sign across 47th Street and one on the open lot near the YWCA.
2. Perfect the details of the plans for two street parades with fife and drums and banners telling of the Coliseum meeting.

3. Build up plans for a chorus of 1000 voices, and get arrangements for this feature well set.

4. Get plans developed for the decoration of the Coliseum with American flags, especially the stage.

5. Get Clementine McCaggo and her group to plan a skit that will take place from 7:00 to 8:00 P.M.

6. Arrange to have this chorus sing "John Brown's Body," "Hold the Fort," "We Shall Not Be Moved," "A Mighty Fortress Is Our God," and so forth. We don't want any spiritual song that indicates resignation or weakness.

7. I suggested to Burton that a conference of the ministers of Chicago be called for him and Webster to address. A letter to the ministers calling for this conference should be signed by some of the leading ministers such as Reverend Carey, Reverend Evans, Reverend Kingsley, Reverend Turpeau, and a couple of outstanding Baptist ministers.

This conference should be called within the next week because time is growing short. At this conference an appeal should be made for an offering to be collected at each church for the Coliseum meeting.

8. Get some one and put them definitely in charge of organizing some two or three hundred ushers for the Coliseum meeting, and also get adequate baskets or plates to take up collection.

All these details should be well planned and in hand a week before this affair; or otherwise everybody there will be up a tree and helpless.

9. Plan to have sound truck cover the city for about six days before the meeting. The price of this should be looked into immediately.

I hope everybody will buckle down to work and nobody will be crying upon each others shoulders because somebody stubbed his toe. We have got a big job to do and so little time to do it; but it can, must and will be done.

Yours for 50,000 Negroes at the Coliseum meeting.[63]

Shortly thereafter, Randolph followed this up with another letter listing yet another eleven points covering such items as a sticker advertising the rally to be pasted up all over town including "doors, news stands, fences, sides of buildings, etc."[64]

It is clear that Randolph succeeded in directly stimulating scores of persons to devote the many hours of hard work necessary for organizing such activities. But man-hours, however energetically dedicated to the task, could not easily turn empty halls into the mighty and colorful protest which Randolph envisaged. To be sure, the job as undertaken with several months to accomplish it was an easier one than that of moving the same number of people to Washington. Yet the idea of a March on Washington was more dramatic intrinsically than a rally even at Madison Square Garden and even if accompanied within a short time by rallies in other major cities. Engendering the degree of enthusiasm necessary to fill these meeting halls was a stupendous task.

Then too, this was to be an all-Negro affair. Not since Marcus Garvey had rallied millions (it was claimed) of Negroes in his highly nationalistic mass movement, had Madison Square Garden been filled by an all-colored audience.[65] Twenty-two years later, many regarded the March as heir to the Garvey success at arousing mass enthusiasm and even to that ill-fated movement's black nationalism. If white friends were to be excluded, their money and numbers would be missed. But the high pitch of excitement necessary to filling the meeting-halls might be aided precisely by such an emotional "nationalistic" appeal.

Every gift of showmanship for which Randolph was known would be exhausted in the effort to dramatize the meeting. It was necessary that it be felt by all "to be the greatest crusade ever staged since Peter the Hermit struck out for the Holy Land."[66] There was an enormous outpouring of propaganda, in sheer volume even greater than that for the previous year's more grandiose march on Washington activity. Randolph's *Black Worker*, published only monthly and functionally a house-organ of the Brotherhood, devoted practically all of its June issue to the big event. A barrage of leaflets, stickers and posters made it difficult for Harlemites, or residents of any Negro community, to remain oblivious to the March and its forthcoming rally. In Chicago, it was reported:

> This entire colored section is bedecked with flags, placards and street signs reinforced with sound trucks cruising all over announcing tomorrow night's March on Washington Movement's meeting. . . .[67]

Randolph personally, and many of his associates, took to the "soapbox" in a series of enthusiastic outdoor meetings to carry the message deep into the lower-class sections of the colored communities.

The language of the appeal was pitched at the lower-class "mass" Negro not only from the street corner but in all the printed material and advertisements placed in the press. Thus, the slogans ran: "MOBILIZE NOW! MANHOOD, COURAGE, GUTS, DETERMINATION."[68] The street-corner talk was designed to serve a double function: in addition to being attuned to lower-class speech, it was essential that a sense of militancy be communicated to transform what was after all but a meeting into a substitute for the march. Negroes were not asked to attend a *meeting*. The word "meeting" had lost its value in the currency of mass movements as it failed to communicate a sense of strength and action.

Political propagandists face much the same difficulty associated with the stereotyped Hollywood press agent. The superlatives available to dramatize a meeting are limited in number and dissipated by profligate usage. Only a few months before the campaign to fill the Garden, a MOWC victory meeting addressed by Mayor La Guardia was attended by 4,000 persons. Randolph's *Black Worker* had hailed this as "one of the greatest mass meetings Harlem has ever seen."[69] When one speaks of the use of language to arouse 20,000 persons out of the normal state of political apathy to fill Madison Square Garden, the problem should be felt in its full and awesome magnitude.

Insofar as words can communicate a sense of action, the "shock treatment" applied by Randolph's leaflet was trite but effective:

WAKE UP NEGRO AMERICA!
Do you want work? Do you want equal rights? Do you want justice?
Then prepare now to fight for it!
50,000 NEGROES MUST STORM MADISON SQUARE GARDEN
MOBILIZE NOW!

The March was truly digging down to the Negro grass roots, going to the same level as the mass media and popular culture. That is why its appeals for participation read like advertising copy for the latest cinematic press release. In Chicago one multigraphed "flyer" demanded:

JOIN IN THE GREATEST, BIGGEST AND MOST STUPEN-
DOUS AND TREMENDOUS GATHERING OF NEGRO PEOPLE
FOR JUSTICE–DEMOCRACY–FREEDOM AND MANHOOD
RIGHTS IN THE HISTORY OF THE WORLD!
50,000 NEGROES
MARCH
STORM THE COLISEUM!

There was considerably more of the same. These were not halls to be filled but to be "stormed" as if, veritably, the seat of all their troubles, the Bastille itself. Randolph's hopes and energies were directed to a turnout so enormous that an overflow crowd would listen to the speeches over a public address system mounted outside the Garden. Just prior to the meeting, "he predicted 50,000 persons would be in and around Madison Square Garden during Tuesday night's meeting."[70]

To simulate the conditions of a "march" the MOWM sought to convince those whom they addressed that the rallies were being closely watched by the President. The rallies were offered as a demonstration of Negro solidarity which would compel the President to listen. Randolph declared, "The President will move, only when Negroes make him move. He is not going to take action on the Negro's problem unless he is compelled to."[71] The tie-in to the march was made very explicit for the benefit of the press—especially the white press. The *New York Times* reported that the rally:

> may reach a climax in a march on Washington by Negroes from all parts of the country. . . . He [Randolph] expressed the hope that the protest meetings to be held in the next month in New York, Chicago and other centers would prove sufficient in themselves to bring about effective action against 'Jim Crow' employment policies thus making it unnecessary to mobilize Negroes for an actual march on the nation's capital.[72]

This theme was made the major emphasis of the headline with which the *Amsterdam News* reported on the project in its last issue before the New York event took place: "March-on-Washington To Garden on Tuesday, Randolph Reports Roosevelt Concerned Over Rallies to be Held in Key Cities,"[73] With the nation at war, there was good reason to believe this was true. The power of the rally to symbolize the march on Washington and to appear fully militant as a tactic gained all the more thereby.

Very unusual and most impressive of the stunts employed, Randolph adapted the civil defense blackout drill to dramatize and gain support for the big rallies. The main headline of the *Black Worker* in its pre-Madison Square Garden issue demanded: "BLACK OUT HARLEM JUNE 16TH!"[74] The word went forth from the March headquarters: during the rally, "Harlem will be dark, dry and silent."[75] In Chicago, the same scheme was widely advertised by leaflet:

> While the white press ignores most events in Negro life, it will be compelled to take notice of such a Blackout if it is carried out with some disciplined loyalty, unity and sacrifice by Negroes themselves. The following plan of action should be executed:

1. All lights in buildings, homes (with shades drawn), in saloons, taverns, stores, theatres, places of amusement, should be put out during the time of the COLISEUM PROTEST DEMONSTRATION for the Negro's democratic rights, from 7 P.M. to 11 P.M. [This was changed to 9 to 9:15 P.M. on Randolph's advice.]

2. Negroes attending night schools should refrain from attending the night of June 26. The Board of Education should be requested to close the schools on this night. . . .

3. All Negro ministers should be requested to refrain from holding services of any kind and advise and urge their members to go in great masses to the COLISEUM.

Merchants were asked to close and blackout their stores for the specified interval during the night of the demonstration. Signs were placed in store windows announcing the co-operation of the proprietors in the "voluntary blackout." A tremendous amount of pressure was brought to bear to effectuate this tactic, and much is revealed in the language of the appeal for its implementation: the bitter mood of the time, the feeling of many Negroes that, in the past, their race had been less cohesively organized and less militant than other groups, and a sense of power in the spirit of the "New Negro." The leaflet appealing for co-operation in the blackout declared:

NEGRO CIVILIAN M.P.'S. A squad of some 50 or 100 M.P.'s with arm-bands to identify them will be organized to visit both Negro and white business to [tell] them why they should close their doors and extinguish all lights out of respect for and cooperation with the Negro's struggle against a Jim-Crow status and a second-class citizenship in our American democracy. Stores that refuse to cooperate should be black-listed, boycotted and picketted as enemies to the fight for Negro rights.

Our slogan is: THE NEGRO SOUTH AND WEST SIDES. DARK, DRY AND SILENT DURING COLISEUM PROTEST MEETING.

The moral and spiritual power and value of such a stroke in stirring black and white America is incalculable. Jews close down their businesses out of respect and devotion to their religion during their religious holidays. They give up millions of dollars to observe these ancient traditions of conduct and doctrines. Irish never fail to parade in commemoration of St. Patrick's Day, their saint. They drop everything for this symbol of National loyalty.

Of course, had the basic conditions for rallying the community not existed, such stunts merely would have high-lighted the failure. As it turned out, the degree of enthusiasm which the blackouts elicited underscored the almost total involvement of Negroes in the MOWM demonstrations.

All walks of life were represented, some of our most prominent women doctors, lawyers, school teachers, social workers, housewives, and even 'ladies of the evening' having been seen in the Madison Square Garden boxes.

Between 7 P.M. and 1 A.M. Tuesday night, in the area from 110th St. to 126th St., sometimes called 'Harlem's red light district,' these 'ladies' were conspicuous by their absence.[76]

Perhaps the newspaperman who wrote this exaggerated a bit, but it is indicative that he should have so described the degree of cohesion present in Harlem at the time. Just as World War I zealots reputedly pinned yellow feathers on young men not in uniform as a badge of shame, the atmosphere was created that none but a cowardly "Uncle Tom" would fail to participate in the great night of protest in some way. The protest was made a matter of race patriotism; nothing less than universal allegiance was demanded of Negroes.

A similar situation had prevailed in the propaganda for the original march. "Uncle Tom" was again a readymade scapegoat. A Negro columnist wrote:

Interestingly enough, we have received several letters dealing with the March on Washington Movement and cautioning against the forthcoming mass meeting in Madison Square Garden. One such letter expresses the fear that certain people among 'the whites or the Negroes may do rash things that can lead to most deplorable results.'[77]

This was cited by the columnist only to supply a target for ridicule. It can be seen how successfully what was, after all, but a large meeting had become reified as a national mobilization of radical dimensions. The *propaganda* for the rally spilled over into the *description* of the rally: "20,000 Storm Madison Square Garden To Help Bury Race's 'Uncle Toms,'" was a typical caption.[78] The conclusion is inescapable that Randolph succeeded in making the term "meeting" seem utterly inappropriate to what took place in Madison Square Garden the night of June 16, 1942.

Success!

WHEN A. PHILIP RANDOLPH, "escorted through the auditorium by a hundred Pullman Porters in uniform,"[79] strode to the rostrum in New York's Madison Square Garden, he was greeted by a cheering near-capacity audience.[80] His spectacular entrance ("A chef, in white

cap and apron, marched at the head of the procession while fifty
[Pullman Co.] maids formed the rear guard")[81] was a far cry from
the usually sedate middle and upper-class Negro organizational activities.[82]

The meetings organized by the March in 1942 were mass rallies
not only in their size but in their lower class composition and character. In New York, "The prominence of the porters gave the Rally a
decidedly working class atmosphere. . . ."[83] In Chicago:

> The crowd, made up of an overwhelming number of working men and
> women, responded with . . . a deafening ovation to a ringing demand by
> A. Philip Randolph, Walter White and Milton Webster for the right of
> Negroes to participate equally in the defense program.[84]

The programs of the rallies contained much to stimulate the
crowds participating in these demonstrations of racial militancy and
solidarity. In Madison Square Garden there was a musical pageantry
of singers, of a well known band and a choral group singing such
songs as the appropriately titled "We Are Americans Too." But the
most striking example of the function of the rally as a symbol of
militant protest in the midst of a nation at war, was a short play
written especially for the occasion. Roy Wilkins wrote:

> If their reporters were careful workers, the Government men must
> know that the highpoint for the huge crowd of 18,000 persons was the
> little speech of Canada Lee, during the playlet staged by Dick Campbell,
> in a skit at the draft board. Lee, taking the part of a man called up and
> classified 1-A, said something like this: 'I want you to know I ain't afraid.
> I don't mind fighting. I'll fight Hitler, Mussolini and the Japs all at the
> same time, but I'm telling you I'll give those crackers down South the
> same damn medicine!'
> That was the line that 'broke it up.' The crescendo of applause was
> greater than at any time during the meeting. Screams, cheers and hand-
> clapping made the Garden a bedlam. One woman yelled down from the
> balcony: 'Say that again!' The crowd was generous with applause for
> speakers, but that punch line spoken by Canade Lee hit the jackpot so far
> as emotional impact was concerned.[85]

We may thus gauge the temper of an audience which sat for five
hours through a speakers' list which is best characterized as too many,
too long. The introductory remarks (a model of brevity) of the
chairman, Dr. Lawrence M. Ervin, stated that "we have here assembled the national leaders of the Negro people. . . ."[86] This was,
unfortunately, too literally and completely true. *All* the national
leaders were there and were called upon for a "few words" in an

effort to keep the façade of unity which had to that point characterized the March.

The mathematics of the Madison Square Garden program are incredible. There were five musical numbers, an invocation, a benediction, a collection, the usual quota of telegrams (e.g., from Mayor La Guardia), the playlet, plus *fourteen speakers* not counting the fund appeal or the chairman's introduction of each! True, the bulk of the speakers were scheduled to deliver "messages" rather than speeches. But how could that be enforced? We cannot resist conjuring up the image of a frantically fidgeting chairman based on reading one speaker's declaration:

> This is the first time in all of my speaking career—not only from this platform but from most platforms—when I have been limited to but five minutes. Frank Crosswaith is utterly unable to disclose the corners of his soul in five minutes.[87]

Mr. Crosswaith, needless to say, did not cease until he had probed those "corners" at some length. In fairness to him, it should be recorded that his appointment (at Randolph's behest) to the New York Housing Authority had been announced in the introduction to his "message" by the chairman. Also, Mayor La Guardia's wire had named Crosswaith his personal representative to speak for his administration.[88] This, perhaps, makes the length of his speech understandable.

Unfortunately, there were others who found the platform from which they could address the huge crowd an irresistible temptation to "blow their own horn." A newspaperwoman covering the New York rally has since written:

> It was assumed that a common cause had brought the outstanding Negro speakers of the day to Madison Square Garden, but according to the men who 'make book,' everybody tried to get into the act. If the speakers had condensed their remarks, once it had been made clear that the meeting was running behind schedule, the course of events might not have been changed. But with thousands of Negroes listening, there is strong suspicion that the stage of Madison Square Garden became a sounding board for personal ambitions. Speaker after speaker read prepared speeches and in the end their was not time enough for A. Philip Randolph to make the principal address. By contrast, Adam Clayton Powell, Jr., then a New York City Councilman, aroused the responsive audience to cheers when he announced his intention to run for Congress in the approaching elections.[89]

It is plain that the term "messages" was scarcely observed in the orations which piled up in staggering volume. One of the few to adhere to the brevity essential for such an affair, if its drama is not to be drowned in a deluge of words, was Lester Granger, leader of the National Urban League:

The length of the remarks of the previous speakers makes it unnecessary for me to go very deeply in the issues responsible for our being here. Many points have been developed, and even belabored by those preceding me.[90]

And we need not belabor this point. Suffice it to say that Randolph, scheduled to make the only "address," had time to deliver what was barely a "message." Five hours having elapsed since he had made his dramatic entrance with the Porters' band playing "Hold The Fort For I am Coming,"[91] Randolph spent the remaining few minutes introducing Mrs. Annie Waller, mother of a share cropper sentenced to be executed whose cause Randolph had taken up. Randolph had then brought the meeting to a close.

The Madison Square Garden rally was clearly an outstanding success. If it did not provide Randolph with all the rewards his leadership and hard work entitled him to, it was nonetheless a triumph—a *personal* triumph. The *Pittsburgh Courier* reported:

High point in the meeting was the presentation of the genius behind the scenes of the Movement. Hailed as 'the greatest leader since Douglass,' A. Philip Randolph talked briefly, simply. The man who welded the Negro Pullman Car Porters into a mighty organization, received an indication of their respect . . . he rose to approach the speakers' stand amid the extended cheering of an audience which had risen as a man to its feet. . . .[92]

On being introduced, Randolph had received "the greatest spontaneous applause, lasting fully three minutes, only then ceasing at his plea of the lateness of the hour."[93]

The streets outside the meeting places were not overflowing, as Randolph had hoped, but the halls were packed and the "blackout" of the Negro districts was reportedly effective too. This, too, was described in a manner which tended to personalize Randolph's role:

Negroes, who were as willing as other citizens to black out for Mayor La Guardia for an air raid test, were just as willing to black out for A. Philip Randolph for a test of how well democracy could work.[94]

Despite the *faux pas* of the speaker's list and the absurdly long program, the myth of the meeting as Randolph's was too firmly fixed to be shaken by the amount of time particular leaders had to speak to the crowd. A somewhat overenthusiastic account reads:

> At a mass meeting, called in New York in 1942 with almost no advance publicity [sic!], twenty thousand Negroes crowded into Madison Square Garden. They applauded for hours the speeches of Walter White, Clayton Powell, and a dozen others. Although the thousands had been drawn by his magnetism, Randolph did not speak that night at all! [sic] Yet the rally is always spoken of as 'Randolph's Madison Square Meeting.'[95]

There is little doubt that Randolph had managed to put on a tremendous demonstration of Negro protest, greater than anything theretofore produced with the possible exception of the Garvey movement.[96] An all-Negro affair, a preponderantly lower-class audience, a colorful and militant demand for equality, its message struck an impressively uncompromising tone in a nation at war. It was this which was recognized by all Negro commentators on the 1942 rallies and can best be summarized in Randolph's words when he finally gave his "undelivered address":

> Our reply is that not only are we staging this meeting, but one in Chicago and Washington also, and if the President does not issue a war proclamation to abolish Jim Crow in Washington, the District of Columbia and all Government departments and the Armed Forces, Negroes are going to MARCH and we don't give a hang what happens.[97]

A number of factors had combined to produce the ingredients for a highly successful rally. It was during the buildup for the Madison Square Garden meeting that the FEPC hearings were substantially under way—an impressive departure from any previous Federal civil rights activity. This had its fullest impact when plans to "invade" the South were announced. FEPC public hearings were set for Birmingham, Alabama to be held June 18, 19 and 20; only two days following the Madison Square Garden affair and followed almost at once by very successful rallies in Chicago and St. Louis.

These were the weeks when the March movement and the Randolph leadership were at their highest peak. There seemed little doubt that "Uncle Tom" had been buried in Madison Square Garden and that American Negroes were on the "march" behind the militant leadership of A. Philip Randolph.

chapter iv

Decline

Power and pressure do not reside in the few, the intelligentsia, they lie and flow from the masses. Power
does not even rest with the masses as such. Power is
the active principle of only the organized masses, the
masses united for a definite purpose.

A. Philip Randolph[1]

The March on Washington Movement, in the summer of 1942,
was at the very summit of its success. Madison Square Garden was
the setting for a mass rally which was a triumph in almost all respects.
The single flaw was the fiasco of an overly long program which kept
Randolph from delivering his speech. But this looms larger in hind-
sight than it did at the time.

True, had the program gone on as planned, the dramatic skit, the
music, and what were planned as a series of short "messages" from
the major leaders of the Negro community in America, would have
served to highlight the main address. Randolph might have used his
substantial oratorical powers effectively to bind thousands in the
crowd to his movement and leadership. It is tempting to date the
decline of the MOWM from that missed opportunity in the great
rally of June, 1942. One participant, a journalist, tends to such an
interpretation in her memoirs:

The June 16 meeting represented the most unified mass demonstration
I have ever witnessed. The MOWM had reached a peak; from that time
on its strength either seeped away or was funneled in different directions.
Mr. Randolph gave his speech at a later meeting which was held uptown
in the Golden Gate Ballroom, but the shining moment had passed.[2]

Actually, Randolph's identification with the success of the rally
could not be so easily submerged. In retrospect, his failure to speak
was a portent of incipient decline. But, had other factors not devel-

oped to bring Randolph's "shining moment" to an end, this by itself would have been insignificant.

Though Madison Square Garden was packed, most Negroes in New York and in the nation would know of the rally from the press rather than by personal experience. This mediated image centered on Randolph's role almost without exception. An enormous amount of attention was accorded the rally by the Negro press. Similarly, the Catholic *Interracial Review* declared (rather extravagantly): "Surely, the MARCH ON WASHINGTON MOVEMENT marks a turning point in the history of democracy."[3] So enthusiastic were this journal's editors that their entire issue was devoted to the Garden mass meeting.

In rapid order following the New York rally came the equally successful Chicago Coliseum affair. This time the list of speakers was not so formidable though the wide base of organizational unity was symbolized by the participation of Walter White. It was reported that "20,000 CHICAGOANS CHEER A. PHILIP RANDOLPH" who spoke the full hour from 11 P.M. to midnight.[4] A third "monster" meeting took place in the St. Louis Municipal Auditorium on August 14. The Campbell playlet and other dramatic devices were repeated at all the rallies adding greatly to the feeling of militancy which these meetings evoked.

During this period (summer, 1942) the March engaged in a vigorous program of activities. St. Louis staged a "march" on a local defense plant protesting discriminatory hiring practices, and Chicago "marched" on the Merchandise Mart.[5] The most ambitious undertaking, however, was a "Silent Parade" in New York City protesting the execution of Odell Waller.

The March Marches

FOR TWO YEARS the Waller case had been a *cause célèbre* in the Negro community. Waller had been sentenced to die for the murder of his white landlord in a quarrel over crop shares. The Workers Defense League (a socialist-oriented labor defense group to which Randolph was very close), the MOWM and the NAACP were convinced that Waller had acted in self-defense. Efforts were made to commute the death sentence, and the poll tax jury system was attacked as a deprivation of due process.[6] The *New York Times* editorially supported the plea for commutation of the death sentence, declaring: "The faith of colored people in their country is deeply involved in what happens to Odell Waller."[7] Several stays of execution had made a series of appeals possible; indeed, the last postponement had been credited to the MOWM Madison Square Garden rally.[8] However unlikely, it is revealing that the March could be thought powerful enough to influence the Governor of Virginia in this way.

After Waller was executed (July 2, 1942), the funeral became a poignant setting for race protest. The only white man permitted to enter the church where Waller's body lay was Morris Milgram, then executive secretary of the Workers Defense League. A statement Waller had prepared for release after his execution protested his innocence in semi-literate and pathetic language. This was read to the 2,500 persons assembled at the funeral by Miss Layle Lane who represented Randolph and the MOWM. The *Amsterdam News* reported:

> As Miss Lane read the moving statement the crowd gave vent to its grief and outrage. Miss Lane then explained what the March on Washington Movement meant to the Negro and led the crowd in singing "We Negroes are United, We Will Not Be Moved."[9]

In the brief span of two weeks the New York Division of the March undertook the staging of a protest parade. Some effort was made to broaden its appeal by linking other grievances to the Waller case. Considerable bitterness had been evoked when Roland Hayes, "internationally famous tenor, was beaten by three white policemen in Rome, Ga. . . . following a brief argument that his wife had with a shoe store clerk."[10] This had occurred during the buildup for the parade and only one week after the Waller execution.

Advertising the parade, the MOWM circulated a leaflet which proclaimed:

THE MARCH SPECIAL
All Out Everybody!   Be There!
join the
SILENT PARADE
Saturday July 25th
(1) To mourn execution of sharecropper Odell Waller.
(2) To protest

* Brutal lynchings of two Negroes.
* Shameful attack on Roland Hayes.
(3) To abolish the POLL TAX SYSTEM.
Swell the crowd at Union Square, 4:30–6:30 P.M.
Assemble at 56th St. and 8th Ave.–2:30 P.M.
March-On-Washington Movement
2084 Seventh Ave.   MO 2-3350

The organizational efforts in publicising the parade were markedly inferior to the buildup of the recent mass meetings. Time was, of course, terribly short but there were other difficulties under which the organizers labored. There was, at first, considerable friction between the Workers Defense League group and the chairman of the New York MOWM "Division." The latter, Dr. Lawrence M. Ervin, had "objected to the parade on the grounds that no one had consulted him when deciding to have the parade."[11] Miss Pauli Murray, of the WDL staff, attempted to assuage him by stating that "the Workers Defense League would back the parade movement, but felt that the March on Washington should take the lead. She further stated that Mr. Randolph had agreed to the idea."[12]

Eventually the issue was brought to a vote which favored presenting the parade plan to the next regular MOWM meeting. It is clear that most of those present favored the plans but one man who had sided with Dr. Ervin warned "that the March on Washington had a reputation to live up to and must do whatever they do very well. He stated that it probably could be done but it would be a great deal of work."[13] Apparently Dr. Ervin was later satisfied. At a subsequent meeting, he said "that he was hesitant at first about the possible success of this parade because so many of its active members were on their way elsewhere. But wonders have been performed and the parade is a fact."[14]

A good deal of hard work went into the preparations for the parade; Pauli Murray was "loaned" to the March by the WDL, and other organizations were approached for assistance and marchers. Some success was recorded, for example a report that "the ministers have been very fine in supporting this affair and many of them will head up delegations from their churches."[15] There is no record of the NAACP having participated in the demonstration. No doubt there was a deterrent in the insistence of the MOWM that "all organizations have been asked to take part with one stipulation: that they stick to the March on Washington rules and carry March on Washington Posters."[16]

The projected demonstration was given rather sparse attention in the press. What was provided fell far short of the publicity needed to bring out large numbers of marchers and was infinitesimal by contrast with what preceded the Madison Square Garden rally. The planning committee had not relied entirely on the press, however; more direct means of communication were developed such as poster walks and street meetings.[17] This was stressed when fears were voiced that the importance of the Waller affair was not clear to the public. Plans were made to organize a propaganda chain linking each block in the Negro residential districts:

Further comment followed, agreeing that publicity could have been improved. Mrs. Hedgeman felt that word of mouth information is the most effective, and it should be arranged that a publicity person should be assigned to each block to inform the people of that area. One member stated that he believed that the entire March On Washington had been under-advertised. Mrs. Patterson endorsed the block system advanced by Mrs. Hedgeman and all members present seemed willing to assist in this program.[18]

The plans for organizing the neighborhoods on a "block system" were not very successful with less than two weeks available. Three days before the parade, it was reported that, "400 large posters have been distributed and will be on display. 25,000 leaflets have been printed."[19]

It is difficult to estimate the success of this venture. Surely, anything less than several hundred marchers would be a complete failure. But it would take at least a thousand paraders to maintain the public image of the March as a mass organization. On July 25, the March on Washington Movement paraded to New York's Union Square:

Nearly five hundred Negroes in ominous, grim, silence marched to the faint throb of muffled drums with only the beat of their determined feet upon the street, in a non-violent demonstration in answer to violent mob acts of Southerners.[20]

This was considerably less than a sign that the MOWM could, on short notice, rally thousands to "march" under its banners (as had been maintained under the theory that the original march had been "postponed"). True, the "silent" style of the parade did have dramatic impact,[21] and the number of participants was large enough to save face. But, at best, the results were a very minor achievement.

A Negro newspaper did declare, "This was the first demonstration of its kind in New York."[22] However, the reporter was in error. Previous reference has been made to the World War I march of 8,000 Negroes witnessed by 30,000 more persons of their race. In fact, the planners of the Waller parade were explicitly aware of the 1917 demonstration on which their "muffled drums" and "silent marchers" were patterned.[23] Fortunately for the MOWM, no one seems to have appraised the 1942 parade by contrasting the turnout for the 1917 protest.

The relatively poor showing of the Waller demonstration reveals that the March was no longer able to operate the kind of protest which could force a hearing from top governmental officials. Indeed, only twelve days later Randolph's request for an appointment with the President was turned down. How closely related these events were is a matter for speculative analysis. We note that precisely thirteen months prior to the Waller parade the White House conference with Randolph and White had produced the FEPC executive order. Now, Randolph and White were turned down by the President's secretary who pleaded "extreme pressure" on the President's time.[24] It is significant of how dissipated the protest had become that this elicited sparse comment in the Negro press.[25]

The mass rallies of June and July, 1942 had been prompted by the desire to fashion a weapon capable of exacting a strengthened FEPC. By the end of July, outstanding demonstrations in New York and Chicago pointed to successful completion of that blueprint. There were, also, definite indications that the powers of the FEPC would be increased. Yet, on July 30th, President Roosevelt defied the Negro leadership and transferred the agency to the War Manpower Commission, under Paul V. McNutt.

This was one and one-half months after Madison Square Garden, one month after the Chicago rally and five days after the Waller parade. Had five or ten thousand Negroes marched to Union Square on July 25, would President Roosevelt have acted otherwise? Would he, at least, have conferred with the Negro leaders? The definitive answer rests in Hyde Park, New York with the late President. Historical analysis is limited to the countervailing pressures which beset the President and the FEPC in the context of the prevailing situation.

FEPC "Blues"[26]

THE FIRST ANNIVERSARY of the FEPC, June 25, 1942, was greeted with widespread enthusiasm: "FEPC CHALKS UP BRILLIANT RECORD DURING YEAR" was the verdict of the *Pittsburgh Courier*.[27] A series of public hearings had managed to focus attention on the previously neglected problem and tangible gains were registered. When the first hearings were held in Los Angeles, the *Courier* reported: "Cal. Plane Plants Do About Face as FEPC Hearings Open."[28] Similar satisfaction attended the Chicago hearings (January 19–20, 1942), and those held in New York (February 16–17, 1942). But the big test of the FEPC and its ability to stand up under pressure came to a head when the Committee "invaded" the South (Birmingham, Alabama; June 18–20, 1942).

Of course, the FEPC and its staff were aware of the dangers of this undertaking and took pains to soothe Southern feelings. The usual hearing procedure was altered to enable a Southerner on the Committee, Mark Ethridge, to "deliver a statement which was expected to evoke a favorable response from southern industry and labor."[29] Mr. Ethridge presented a "liberal" Southern view in explaining the Committee's work and purposes. He stressed the need for manpower in the war emergency and defended the extending of civil rights and economic opportunity to Negroes. However, he strongly attacked certain Negro leaders "who have adopted the 'all or nothing' attitude, . . . who interpreted 8802 as a second Emancipation Proclamation."[30] This plainly, was an indirect attack on Randolph who responded by demanding Ethridge resign from the FEPC.[31]

The Negro community, generally, was antagonized by the vigor with which Ethridge defended social segregation; said Ethridge: "There is no power in the world—not even in all the mechanized armies of the earth, Allied and Axis—which could now force the Southern white people to the abandonment of the principle of social segregation."[32] However, the reaction in the Negro press was rather less bitter than might have been expected. Of course, no Negro defended Ethridge, or agreed with his views. The *Chicago Defender* seconded Randolph's demand that Ethridge resign and there was a hubbub of deep resentment.[33] But there was also a willingness to let this pass and general satisfaction with the FEPC prevailed.[34] Perhaps this was aided by a strong statement attacking Ethridge by a fellow member of the FEPC, Earl Dickerson.[35] It was felt that Ethridge was not speaking for the FEPC as such.

For a time, the strategy of the Alabama hearings seemed successful —Negro opinion was aroused, but only a comparatively mild and brief flurry resulted. And Southern opinion seemed somewhat placated too —at least the Southern press was divided. Some Alabama papers commented favorably on the hearings, diluting the vitriolic attacks of others.[36]

Thus, the FEPC seemed a potent tool in the effort to eliminate discriminatory hiring practices, even in the South. A regional representative of the FEPC, who had worked in the South, has described the situation at the time of the sudden transfer to McNutt's War Manpower Commission:

> Upon his return from Birmingham, Malcolm S. MacLean, Hampton Institute president who had replaced Mark Ethridge as FEPC chairman, received White House congratulations for a job well done. The FEPC had hit the zenith of its brief glory. With White House sanction, plans were drawn for a broad nationwide offensive to enforce 8802. The prospective budget came to more than $1,000,000 as against the first year's $800,000 pittance. Twelve adequately staffed regional offices were to be established for the prompt investigation of complaints, holding of hearings and routine policing of war industries. Then to the stupefaction and dismay of all FEPC members, none of whom was consulted in advance, came the President's order of July 30 transferring the body from his executive office to the War Manpower Commission, where it would be subject to Mc-Nutt's direct supervision.[37]

It seems clear that the Alabama hearings had aroused "The Jim Crow Bloc"[38] in Congress to bring heavy pressure on the President. The FEPC was the subject of strong attacks by the governors of Alabama and Georgia only a week before the transfer.[39] President Roosevelt's susceptibility to this pressure was a practical indication that "Dr. New Deal" had become "Dr. Win-The-War."

For the Negro community, the FEPC transfer was a much feared calamity. Minority group pressure could influence the President more successfully than it could sway the Congress. This was fully realized by the Negro leadership. Thus, *Crisis* editorialized:

> It is significant that the FEPC which had operated independently on a budget provided out of funds at the disposal of the President, was not transferred to WMC until *after* it had held hearings on discrimination

against Negro workers in the heart of the South—in Birmingham, Ala. The South raged against these hearings and tried to stop them, only to find that Southern Congressmen and Senators were powerless because the committee's funds were not at the mercy of Congress.[40]

The Negro leadership directed an immediate blast at the Presidential office. Randolph and White each sent wires to the President protesting that he had violated his assurances to them (at the White House conference in June, 1941) that the new Committee "would be and would remain responsible to yourself."[41] This theme was picked up in the press reports at the time:

White Charges Roosevelt Acted Contrary to Promise.
Says President Apparently Forgot Statements made to the 'March on Washington' Leaders—Skeptical of McNutt's Supervision.
Stage March on Washington . . . Rescind order transferring Committee on Fair Employment Practice to War Manpower Commission . . . Double Cross . . . These are just a few of the statements heard following the [FEPC transfer]. . . .[42]

But Randolph and White made no effort to reconstitute the postponed "march." Instead, they wielded traditional modes of protest. Their unsuccessful bid for a conference with the President has already been noted. Mainly, the agitation took the form of contacting organizations to shower Washington with protestations.[43] Thus, White wired Randolph a week after the transfer:

HAVE NOT ONLY WIRED PRESIDENT BUT HAVE TELEGRAPHED NAACP BRANCHES IN 34 LARGEST CITIES TO TELEGRAPH HIM AND TO GET OTHER ORGANIZATIONS AND INDIVIDUALS TO DO SO. WILL YOU BE COMING EAST BEFORE ST. LOUIS MEETING ON 14TH? IF SO BE SURE LET ME GIVE YOU SOME OF INSIDE REASONS FOR ABOLISHING INDEPENDENT STATUS OF FEPC.[44]

The St. Louis meeting to which White referred was one of the mass rallies which the MOWM was staging that summer. There is little doubt that the Administration kept a close watch on these activities.[45] The vigorous protestations which his transfer order had aroused led the President, three days after the successful St. Louis rally, to offer a reassuring explanation through Press Secretary Early:

He [the President]regrets that this transfer and the reasons therefor have been so widely misunderstood.
It is the intention to strengthen—not to submerge—the committee, and to reinvigorate—not to repeal—Executive Order 8802.[46]

The White House statement maintained that the work of the Committee would be aided by the transfer because it "will make full use of the various branches and agencies of the Manpower Commission to increase the effectiveness and range of its activities." On the question of independence, the President was reported to have declared that "the committee shall be preserved as an organizational entity" and it "will continue to refer to the President all matters which, in its judgment, require his decision."

But the two major matters were not satisfactorily explained: There was no mention made of the budgetary problems likely to arise if Congressional appropriations were necessitated by the transfer; and the problem of subordination to McNutt was sugar-coated in the phrase, "It will have the friendly supervision of the chairman of the commission." The crucial sentence in the original letter of transfer had read, "In the performance of its duties and functions, the committee shall be subject to the direction and supervision of the chairman of the War Manpower Commission."[47] This proved to be the crux of the matter and the President's "explanation" did not really change things.

That this was the case might have been inferred from a report published only two days prior to the President's explanatory press release: "One immediate effect [of the transfer] was the calling off of public hearings in El Paso, Texas into unfair labor practices, Lawrence Cramer, secretary of the [FEP] committee declared."[48] And the same report stated that Roosevelt "will make no further allotments since Mr. McNutt has been instructed to go through the regular budgetary channels."

But the press release from the White House managed to produce the result intended by the President. Though neither Randolph nor White were taken in by it, its effect was to weaken the solidity and sharpness of the protest they had stimulated. The *Amsterdam News*, which had "buried Uncle Tom" in a cartoon only two months before (in connection with the Madison Square Garden Rally) editorialized:

Meanwhile we shall have to watch the development of future events. Many of us were wrong in condemning President Roosevelt for his appointment of Senator Hugo L. Black to the Supreme Court bench, and we could be wrong [again]. . . . If we keep on the alert we shall soon see whether the transfer has been a help or a hindrance. Until then we withhold any criticism.[49]

The main headline of the *Pittsburgh Courier*, soon after the President's public explanation, declared, "FEPC BACK UNDER ROOSEVELT, July 30th Letter To Be Forgotten, Courier Learns."[50] This unconfirmed and erroneous rumor blazoned forth on page one must have been confusing to the public and helped to take the sting out of the President's action.

Conceivably, had a unanimous Negro press continued to hammer away against the FEPC transfer, a well organized protest may have emerged. But the administrative transferral of an agency within the government is only with difficulty transformed into a "mass issue." And the confused and confusing handling of the matter in the press did little to aid the protest leadership. The issue had been sapped of its organizational potential.

The strange picture was presented of the Republican national committeeman for Mississippi, Perry Howard, calling for the march on Washington to be carried out (this in the context of an attack on "Democratic chicanery").[51] Yet, only two weeks prior, it had been widely reported that "Randolph Abandons D.C. March."[52] Actually, the latter story was not accurate as Randolph took pains to explain.[53] He had said (or meant to say) that a march on Washington was not the sole or immediate weapon available to the MOWM. Whether he had stated it poorly or the reporter had garbled the speech need not concern us, but, typically, the later explanation was less prominently displayed. As we shall see, this confusion over whether the March would ever *march* was an important element in weakening Randolph's mass leadership.

The summer rallies of 1942 were to have been climaxed in a gigantic assemblage in the Washington, D.C. Ball Park. Randolph's *Black Worker* had declared:

> The Washington meeting is most vital and important, because it is the nation's capital and we want official Washington to know of the deep and profound resentment of Negroes to every form of discrimination practiced upon them by the federal government and private industry.
> It is hoped that a meeting mobilizing 25,000 Negroes can be staged.[54]

This, as has been pointed out, was the obvious substitute for the original march on Washington tactic. To have turned out 25,000 Negroes and "blacked out" the Negro section of Washington would have been an achievement capable of pushing the Waller parade fizzle into insignificance. Following soon after the President's transfer of the FEPC, such a rally might revitalize the Negro protest, and also the MOWM.

Randolph attempted to go ahead with this program but it never came off. The plans for the Ball Park rally had been very cautiously considered even before the Waller parade. Randolph realized that this demonstration, more than the others, could not risk failure. Although the great successes of New York and Chicago were still fresh in mind, Randolph proceeded with great care. On June 30, 1942, he wrote to the chairman of the March on Washington Committee in Washington:

My experience with these giant meetings is that we need at least six or more weeks.

We took three months in New York and three months in Chicago. I would suggest that you try to get the date of August 10th or 17th. . . . It is going to take a whole lot of high-powered propaganda and advertising to put 25,000 Negroes in the Ball Park, and if we fail to have a great meeting, it will do the cause of the fight against Jim-Crow more harm than good. It will take a couple of weeks to break the lethargy and inertia of the people of Washington and get them to talk about the meeting. We ought to have a full time man on the job for at least four weeks. Won't you let me know when you are planning to have the next meeting of the Committee so that I may be there?

Five days after the President's startling transferral of the FEPC, Randolph wrote again: "I hope that the Headquarters are open and humming. I plan to come to Washington about a week before the Meeting [now set for September 4] and remain there to help build it."[55] There is little doubt that Randolph viewed this as the major way to "make the President and all officials in Washington know that the Negro's main business now is fighting for his rights."[56]

But the President's public-relations maneuver as received by the Negro community revealed that it was no longer a unanimous feeling that this was the *main* business. The effectiveness of the President's strategy was due less to its inherent cleverness than to what had happened to the position of Negroes since the bitter days of 1940 and '41.

By the first anniversary of Pearl Harbor, the totality of involvement in war was a felt fact. The pace of all war activities quickened as the military draft was stepped up and the casualty lists began to appear with grim regularity. The idea of the homefront as a vital support to the battlefront sank in. Conservative Negroes and "left-wing" Negroes did not see eye to eye on the priorities of the "Double

V" campaign, but the results of their positions amounted to the same thing—a watering down of the vitriolic protest of the defense period. Communists and their fellow-travellers outdid all others in their "patriotic" zeal to subordinate everything to the war effort. Nothing should be permitted to stand in the way of a "second front" to relieve the beleaguered Red Army. For Negro conservatives, the "Double V" was more evenly balanced in terms of the priority of Negro rights, but the traditional, "polite" protest methods were reverted to.

For the mass of lower-class Negroes, who might be expected to be most loyal to Randolph, the war had also produced great changes. An objective recording of opinion would still reveal the circulation of folk tales of discontent and the Harlem riot would reveal continuing frustration, but the temper had cooled in terms of organizational tactics. The hiring gates had been opened sufficiently to quell the urgency of the "bread-and-butter" issue.[57] Partly, they had been squeezed open by the protest which bitter morale made possible. Partly, they had been easier to open thanks to the acuteness of the manpower shortage. Negroes were happy to thank the FEPC and to credit Randolph with much of the achievement, but that was not accompanied by a readiness to continue the increasingly risky and unpleasant business of militant agitation and organized political action.

Perhaps things would have been different had the President launched a frontal attack on the FEPC. But Roosevelt's handling of the pressures which beset him on the issue proved a remarkable example of political finesse.

Randolph's "We Don't Give A Damn" speech (as it came to be called), delivered at the Chicago rally, had been vigorously applauded by the aroused audience. But, on reflection, it was viewed with great apprehension and alienated the conservative Negro leadership and the Communist "fellow-travellers." The Labor Editor of the Associated Negro Press explicitly attacked the speech as likely to weaken the war effort.[58] He also sharply criticised the all-Negro philosophy of the March as likely to intensify racial antagonism. There were no shrieks of "Uncle Tom" outside of Randolph's own group as would certainly have greeted such a statement only the year before. The fighting bite had gone out of the Negro protest.

By the end of August it was clear that a substantial Washington rally was not possible, and Randolph advised his group "to abandon plans for an outdoor meeting for the present and stage a church meeting, looking forward to an outdoor meeting in the early Spring."[59]

Randolph recently summarized the reasons for calling off the Washington rally:

> As I look back on the period, the only reason I can assign was that we were unable to get a place for said rally and to build up a program attractive enough to develop a demonstration comparable to the meetings we had staged in other cities.
>
> Knowing the conservative climate of Washington, among both white and colored people, I was conscious of the need of a program which would touch off a rally of huge proportions and we were unable to get people of the stature we wanted for such a meeting.[60]

Compare the galaxy of speakers at the then recent Madison Square Garden demonstration! But there were already evident in those speeches signs of cleavage in emphasis on the relative priorities of the "Double V." Mary McLeod Bethune had roused the crowd with her fervor: "We have grown tired of turning the other cheek. Both our cheeks are now so blistered they are too blistered for further blows."[61] Yet, she had gone on to say, "Regardless of our trials and tribulations at home, we must not for a moment lose sight of the fact that we must give our all-out, unreserved effort to win the war."

By the time of the Chicago rally Randolph was already experiencing difficulty in obtaining the co-operation of the top leadership. Mrs. Bethune, who was active in promoting war-bond sales, responded to Randolph's invitation with a friendly note of refusal. Without assigning this as the reason for not accepting, she declared, in a magnificent understatement:

> It might be interesting to you to know that there is a contrast being made between the public meetings being held by the Treasury and the public meetings being handled by the March on Washington Committee. I would like to discuss this with you because I do feel that we are all anxious for the winning of this war and seeing democracy in action here and everywhere.[62]

Randolph's response was "that the meetings which we are holding are not in any way intended to hinder the war." The war would be helped if Negroes insisted on "their democratic rights of being permitted to play their part in the Army, Navy, Air and Marine Corps, defense industries, and the government as equals with the white people in this country."[63]

But Walter White was a speaker of stature, and he had shared the Chicago Coliseum platform with Randolph. Was he not available for the crucial Washington rally? He was not, for the NAACP, at last, had severed its alliance with the March. But that story is best understood against the background of the further unfolding of events connected with the FEPC.

Attacks on the President all but disappeared as Mr. McNutt, under whom the FEPC was now installed, offered personal assurances:

> There is no doubt that the work of the Committee will be strengthened. All of the Manpower Commission is behind it. I was amazed at the reaction of some of the Negro press. The Committee will be far better off now.[64]

After a period of jockeying between the FEPC and McNutt, during which its work was at a standstill, agreement was announced and the Committee appeared on the move again.[65] For the balance of the year, the public's view of what went on in FEPC was focused through glowing accounts in the press. Successive front page headlines proclaimed: "FEPC PREPARES TO MOVE AGAINST STREET CAR CO., D.C. CONCERN TOLD TO CHANGE POLICY,"[66] and later, "FEPC Cracks Down on Dixie Shipyard."[67]

This only obscured temporarily (but effectively) the underlying friction between McNutt and the FEPC. Later, a decisive blow would be struck when McNutt, "without prior consultation with the committee"[68] (on January 11, 1943), would summarily "postpone" the FEPC's scheduled hearings on railroad employment discrimination. The Negro press and organizational leaders were to castigate McNutt's action as a cancellation of the hearings and a new betrayal. It would become clear to everyone that, as McNutt then said, "After all, the Fair Employment Practice Committee is under the Manpower Commission."[69] Meanwhile, prior to McNutt's blow at the FEPC railroad hearings, the Negro community was placated.

Randolph Marches Alone

WHEN THE ORIGINAL March On Washington Committee was formed, it was officially an alliance of leaders who brought with them the backing of their several organizations. It was viewed as a temporary stunt, a product of desperation rather than the building of a new mass organization. Why that committee did not go out of existence when its bargaining with the President obtained the FEPC has been explained. But the very success of the March, which made it the outstanding mass protest organization in the Negro community in 1941 and 1942, planted seeds of disunity.

The gradual change in initials from MOWC to MOW*M* symbolized the transformation of the March from a temporary committee to a permanent organization. Separate territorial "Divisions" reaching across the country, separate officers in those "Divisions," and a separate rank-and-file membership attested to the creation of a new entity in competition with its initiating parent organizations. Increasingly, the March Movement acquired a life of its own which revolved entirely around Randolph's leadership.

That astute analyst of the American Negro, Gunnar Myrdal, shortly before bringing the monumental study he directed to a close, wrote:

> The March-on-Washington movement is interesting for several reasons. It is, on the one hand, something of a mass movement with the main backing from Negro workers, but has at the same time the backing of the established Negro organizations. Though a mass movement, it is disciplined and has not used racial emotionalism as an appeal. It demonstrates the strategy and tactics of orderly trade unionism. For the Negro cause it is prepared to use pressure even against the President. But it knows just how far it can go with the support that it has. Randolph, the leader of the movement, has so far (August, 1942) steered its course with admirable force and restraint.[70]

But the equilibrium was tenuous, for the more powerful the March became, the more imbalance there was between its mass movement character and its quasi-federative structure. However, so long as the March could wield mass loyalties with spectacular success, it was organizationally dangerous for the "regular" leadership to leave.

When the NAACP met in national convention, July 14–19, 1942 (shortly before the Waller parade and the FEPC transfer), Randolph's dominant role threatened to submerge the NAACP in the March. It was at this convention that he was formally presented the Spingarn medal as the outstanding Negro of 1941. The published program barely mentions that presentation although, in fact, Randolph excited far more attention than the speeches receiving official top billing.[71] One reporter wrote:

Some 2,500 persons crammed and pushed their way into the church to see and hear the one and only A. Philip Randolph. Nearly that many and more were outside unable to get in. No doubt about it: Randolph is THE MAN OF THE HOUR![72]

The feeling was widespread that the NAACP was impotent, that it was a paper organization led by intellectuals and whites with no substantial following among the Negro grassroots.[73] Another writer declared: "There is no question that Randolph is the man most worshipped by the Negro rank and file now."[74] Indeed, the largest headline across an entire front page of the *Pittsburgh Courier*, the newspaper most hostile to the March, proclaimed: "RANDOLPH STOLE SHOW—CAYTON."[75] If this caption disassociated the *Courier* from writer Cayton's story, the editorial decision to display it so prominently was all the more indicative of Randolph's primacy.

The reaction of the NAACP leadership, whose "show" had been stolen, was not made public.[76] For good reasons they chose not to buck Randolph in the open. Seemingly, they approved the conference resolution which declared:

> We endorse and continue our affiliation with the 'March-on-Washington' movement. We urge our branches to participate actively in the local committees of this movement where they exist, and elsewhere to take the initiative in seeking to organize local 'March-on-Washington' committees.[77]

Horace Cayton sought to explain "the peculiar behavior of an organization" which votes "to assist in the formation of another organization. . . ."[78]

> It is pre-evident the association does not want to endanger its position by taking the active leadership of this new upsurge of Negroes, especially when led by the pretty dangerous A. Philip Randolph. At the same time, the association does not want to lose some measure of control over, and identification with, the Randolph group.
>
> The formula which was worked out at the Convention allows them to do both. For the more respectable elements of the Negro community and the influential whites, the NAACP retains pretty much the same old program.
>
> For the masses of Negroes who have not been given effective leadership, and who are finding Randolph a man's leader, the 'March-on-Washington' committees can be brought forward. Which will be the real organization and which the 'front' organization remains to be seen.[79]

Cayton's view was commonly held, that the March had "a mass following which the NAACP does not have." But the basis of that following was thought to be the outspoken sharpness of Randolph's demands for Negro rights despite the war.[80] This necessarily alienated "Second-Fronters" and frightened the NAACP's dominant conservative group—despite Walter White's continuing official support of Randolph.

The publicised theme of the NAACP convention was the slogan: "Victory is Vital to Minorities." In his message of greeting to the conference, President Roosevelt noted the theme "with satisfaction" and commented: "This theme might well be reversed and given to the Nation as a slogan. For today, as never before in our history, 'Minorities Are Vital to Victory.' "[81] Given the over-all emphases of their primary commitments, the President said what the bulk of Negroes actually believed—and vice versa. But the selection of the theme as officially worded revealed the dampening effect of Pearl Harbor on the Negro protest.

Another factor which became increasingly important in creating a schism between Randolph and Walter White was the exclusion of whites from the MOWM as a matter of policy. Cayton emphasized this in another of his perceptive analyses at the time:

Further, if there are to be two organizations, what relationship will there be between them? The 'March-on-Washington' seems to be a purely Negro organization while the cardinal principle of the NAACP is its inter-racial composition. I suspect that in these times the people who support the NAACP—I mean influential and wealthy white people— would hesitate to go as far as the 'March-on-Washington' movement seems to be going.[82]

Cayton's query as to the relationship of the NAACP and the MOWM was answered swiftly as subsequent events deflated Randolph's prestige. A week after the conference, the Waller protest parade obtained a barely respectable turnout. A few weeks later the President transferred the FEPC and refused to confer with Randolph and White. The March, far from unleashing the postponed march on Washington, failed to organize the planned substitute as efforts to stage the Washington Ball Park rally collapsed. The President's "explanation" of the transfer seemed supported by the agreement between McNutt and the FEPC which apparently continued its successful operations. At this point, with McNutt's "postponement" of the railroad hearings some five months in the future, Randolph called a national conference of the March to convene in Detroit, Michigan, September 26–27, 1942.

Pressures upon Randolph to convene such a conference stemmed from two sources: Within the March, for some time, there was a feeling that the rank and file should have more voice in determining policy. From outside, Randolph was attacked as having no organized program to justify the large following he had attracted.

Because of its original quasi-federative character, officially, the March was not expected to have a membership of its own. This was quickly ignored in the enthusiasm of signing up individuals for the march on Washington. The recruitment of members was made formal at least as early as September, 1941 when Randolph called for a "million Negro-American members" to be "built upon the block basis with a captain of each block."[83]

A membership drive was made an important part of the big rallies of 1942. For example, Randolph wrote his Chicago organizers to "have twenty or twenty-five thousand membership cards for this our greatest opportunity."[84] A few months later, a bulletin reported: "More members were added to the roster of the New York Division of the MARCH ON WASHINGTON MOVEMENT in September than in any other month since the movement came into existence . . . 590 names were enrolled compared with 162 in August."[85] The credit for this successful drive was assigned by the Chairman of the Membership Committee to "his enthusiastic corps of Block Captains." This "block" basis of organization was derived from the view that the MOWM was a mass movement whose *members* were poised to march on short notice.

But the organizational structure placed the formal power in the hands of the initiating committee, which in practice was dominated by Randolph and the leadership of the BSCP. Early signs of dissatisfaction were evident in the complaints of the Youth Division when the 1941 march plans were halted. There was also very serious disruption in the Chicago Division during the period preparatory to the Coliseum meeting and, to a lesser extent, in the New York Division prior to the Waller parade.

In Chicago, a rift developed between Randolph's hand-picked Director and a rank and file group, mainly of young members. The Director was vigorously backed by Milton Webster who headed the

Brotherhood office in Chicago. This bickering threatened the Coliseum meeting preparations but was smoothed over by Randolph. Following that rally, trouble broke out anew. Webster and the Director were accused of "brutal tactics." A letter to Randolph signed by fourteen members claimed that Webster had told them:

Now there's been a lot of talk about what have I got to do with the March-on-Washington, and what am I sticking my nose in for. Well, I'm an officer of the Brotherhood and anything that the Brotherhood has to do with, I have a say so about it. Now there's been some talk about getting rid of Mr. Burton [the Director]. Well I want to say that we have no intentions of getting rid of him. Now I've put it in language that you can understand, so NOW YOU CAN TAKE IT OR LEAVE IT![86]

Webster allegedly prefaced these remarks with the statement: "The March on Washington Movement was conceived by the Brotherhood and is a part of the Brotherhood." Someone, reportedly, "then rose to ask if Mr. Webster meant by his statement that this was not a democratic organization."

The dissidents declared to Randolph:

If it is true that the Brotherhood owns and controls the movement and does not intend to allow *democratic techniques,* then *we have been led up a blind alley,* as we all believed that the time had come when we could sit down together and map out a democratic form of government.

Unquestionably this fracas was instrumental in bringing about the scheduling of a national MOWM conference. Randolph responded with a telegram to the Chicago group to "KEEP STEADFAST IN OUR GREAT CAUSE."[87] A follow-up letter explained why there had been no formal provisions for democratic procedures:

On the question of government of the division, that policy we have discussed before. It was pointed out that the March on Washington Movement grew up as a mass effort, and no attempt was made to subject it to any rigid rules. Such a policy would have been futile and dangerous.

We need plenty of latitude for action. This is why we were able to win the Executive Order 8802 and also the FEPC. I certainly doubt whether we could have done this with a movement hedged in by many rules and regulations.

However, the time has come now for a change in our set up and procedure and we will have a constitution and by-laws. . . .

I hope that as many members as possible attend the policy convention where we will give formal structure to the March on Washington Movement.[88]

Mass movements are perhaps "democratic" in the sense of representing a broad slice of a social grouping, and in lower-class orientation. But the semimilitary strategy of mass action and the messianic
leader-follower relations, which provide the basis for mass cohesion,
are poorly adapted to parliamentary procedures and formal representative processes. It is particularly difficult to delegate authority to
secondary "leaders" who are not themselves supported in their positions by mass adulation. In Chicago, for example, the dissidents were
happy to be persuaded by Randolph personally, but would not take
direction from his appointed representatives. By contrast, an institutionalized bureaucratic setup can functionally distribute authority
because it is not dependent upon mass enthusiasm. To offer a sociological generalization, mass movements achieve discipline through a
charismatic ("personality") leadership process, whereas bureaucratic
organizations provide an authoritative structure of leadership as a
function of formally distributed status.[89]

As the original fervor of Randolph's following subsided, formal
arrangements became necessary if the March was to be continued. In
a sense, when the March was officially a Committee (MOWC) it
possessed the attributes of a successful mass movement. When the
March officially became the Movement (MOW*M*), in actuality, it
was already losing its mass movement character to become simply
one more organization competing for public attention in an increasingly apathetic market.

The external attack which influenced Randolph to seek a more
formal structure was a widespread criticism that the March had no
program justifying its separate existence. Thus, the *Pittsburgh Courier*
editorialized: "All we have so far are ear-splitting generalities and
blowsy platitudes. We do not have a program. Nor does there exist
any machinery for carrying out a program if there were one."[90]

Actually, the March had presented an "Eight Point Program" at
the Madison Square Garden rally.[91] Under the general slogan, "Winning Democracy for the Negro is Winning the War for Democracy,"
the program ranged over the entire civil and political rights fields.
FEPC was far from the only or even major emphasis.[92] Indeed, it
might be urged that the March was better justified in the eyes of the
already existing organizations so long as it restricted itself to the
FEPC issue which it had fathered. The eight-point program, as an
omnibus statement of aims, in effect transformed the March from a

specialized committee of limited purpose into a rival organization. It was *because* it now had a broad program that the March had to justify its competitive existence.

Behind this erroneous claim that Randolph had no program was conservative, middle-class dislike for Randolph as a radical mass leader. Measured by standards of operational efficiency, a mass movement is indeed a chaotic affair. An office staffed by professionals, such as the NAACP's lawyers and trained publicists, is unquestionably better organized than one manned by "lay" enthusiasts. This is particularly true where the laymen are lower class, engaged in largely unskilled "blue collar" occupations. Randolph was widely accused of being incapable of running an efficient organization by those who viewed organizational talents strictly in an administrative sense.[93]

This criticism of Randolph's administrative ability was tied in with the increasing concern for wartime unity. One writer asked, "If Mr. Randolph organizes the discontented among us, just what is he going to do with them?" He expressed the fear that they may "become emotionally engulfed in the fight for themselves to the extent that the value of the service they are giving the nation may be questioned."[94]

Not all the criticisms of Randolph were dominated by conservative or "Second-Front" considerations, however. A widely read Negro journalist, then an independent radical who subsequently moved to the far right, did "not share the Cayton view that the March-on-Washington movement is any threat to the NAACP, more's the pity." But he did regard Randolph as lacking in administrative skill:

The March-on-Washington movement is A. Philip Randolph. Mr. Randolph knows how to appeal to the emotions of the people and to get a great following together, but there his leadership ends because he has nowhere to lead them and would not know how if he had. Every person has his or her limitations, and of course Randolph has his. He has the Messianic complex, considerable oratorical ability and some understanding of the plight of the masses, but the leadership capacity and executive ability required for the business at hand is simply not there. The original March-on-Washington move is now admitted to have been a failure else the current agitation would not be necessary. Moreover there is no organizational set-up or observable administrative ability to keep the MOW movement alive and functioning. Organization is not merely a matter of ballyhoo and oratory, it is a science, and one that is largely a closed book to Mr. Randolph. Mass leadership in times like these also requires a little more guts than any of the Negro leaders possess. I know of none willing, like Nehru and Gandhi, to go to jail.[95]

However interesting this criticism, which was equally scathing in its attack on the "self-perpetuating oligarchy" of the NAACP, it was largely defeatist. No constructive advice was offered as to how the technically skilled apparatus of the NAACP and Randolph's admittedly great mass-leadership capacity could be forged into a working instrument. Whatever hope may have lain in that direction, of an efficiently constituted mass protest organization, devolved upon Randolph alone as the Urban League and NAACP leaders would not participate in the Detroit conference.

There is little doubt that Randolph, who had always stressed the importance of organization for successful mass pressure, was concerned to demonstrate that he could organize the March effectively. But organization, for Randolph, meant building and wielding a cohesive mass membership rather than an efficient public relations apparatus. This was what led to the charges of "empty ballyhoo" from those who regarded organizational programs in traditional terms.

The generality of Randolph's new program overlapped with that of the older organizations. In addition, the major strategy of the March also seemed generalized as it became increasingly dubious that a physical march would or could take place. If general aims and traditional tactics were to be employed, what justification was there for the MOWM? The *Pittsburgh Courier* raised this question following the somewhat misleading report that Randolph was abandoning plans for an "immediate" march on Washington:

In brief, what reason has the March on Washington movement for continued existence if it is to merely duplicate work already being done, to inflame the masses with oratory and then leave them stranded by constantly postponing loudly advertised measures . . . ? how will this differ from the work so efficiently being done by the National Association For the Advancement of Colored People and the [*Pittsburgh Courier* sponsored] 'Double V' Clubs?[96]

It is clear that this problem was crucial and ultimately required resolution. Logically, the alternatives were plain; one should say plain in retrospect: (1) The March could oblige the older organizations and go out of existence. (2) The program could be restricted to the FEPC issue with which the MOWM was closely identified, perhaps changing its name to indicate this specialized purpose. (3) An effort might yet be made to discover a new "mass-action" technique sufficiently militant to distinguish the MOWM from other organizations and capable of refiring popular enthusiasm for the March. (4) The problem of duplication could be brushed aside in the hope that popular support for the MOWM could force co-operation from the older organizations (the NAACP resolution endorsing the March was but two months old).

Naturally, the logic was one of developing events and not simply a matter of rational planning. The first alternative was least appealing. What organization sacrifices itself to eliminate jurisdictional overlap while still commanding substantial support? The March was in a "tailspin," it was reported just prior to the Detroit conference.[97] But if the March was slipping, it had been to the very heights only weeks before and retained considerable strength.

The later course of events would force Randolph into the second alternative, but that was one year in the future. At the time of the Detroit conference, the FEPC issue seemed inadequate to justify a separate organization or positive enough to fire enthusiastic supporters. Despite the transfer of the FEPC, the *rapprochement* with McNutt seemed effective, and the ruckus over the railroad hearings was still half a year off. Randolph's recollection of his reasons for continuing the March after White and Granger broke away tends to jump over the year between the Detroit conference and the establishment of the National Council For a Permanent FEPC (organized September, 1943). He was asked, "Why, as a member of the Board of the NAACP, did you not work through that organization?" His response was that he wanted to "concentrate on FEPC alone whereas the NAACP was a broader organization."[98] That had, indeed, been the basis for continuing the March after the executive order was obtained and later became the basis for the National Council For a Permanent FEPC, but it does not explain the activities of the March at the 1942 Detroit conference and some time thereafter.

It is a combination of what we have stated as the third and fourth alternatives which best accounts for the course of action which ensued. The MOWM, after a brief renewal of its flirtation with the idea of a march on Washington, attempted to fashion a new instrument modeled on the Gandhian civil disobedience tactics. At the same time, it continued to pose as a united front of non-Communist Negro organizations, its original form.

In the light of the then recent NAACP conference resolution binding the two organizations so closely, it is understandable why the March might not regard the rupture as final. One of Randolph's close associates wrote to him the day prior to the MOWM conference:

> Some of us understand that the NAACP is not sending an official delegate to the policy making conference because they believe MOW has gotten away from its original plan of a federation of Negro organizations working jointly on the program of the Negro.
>
> You and I know that they were called in to discuss future program before the plan for this present conference was made. The public does not know this. And it seems to some of us extremely important that MOW have in its statement of policy definite commitment to correlation of program in order that there be no question in the minds of the public as to the intention of MOW to eliminate or nullify in any way the programs of the NAACP and Urban League.[99]

The explanation of the refusal of the NAACP leadership to participate does not lie entirely in the events which transpired between the July NAACP national conference and the September MOWM conference. As we have shown, the FEPC transfer which occurred at that time revealed the weakness of the March. This was particularly plain in the collapse of plans for the Washington, D.C. mass rally. But the other factors which have been described; the increasing impact of the war on both conservative and Communist groups, dislike for the bitter and lower-class style of Randolph's speeches, the increasing apathy of workers gaining entry into defense employment in large numbers in 1942, and concern for the "Garveyite" implications in Randolph's policy of excluding whites from the MOWM provided the situational context.

Astutely, the NAACP leadership chose not to challenge Randolph's popularity at their conference and allowed the resolution strongly endorsing the March to go through. But the structure of the NAACP did not place supreme power in its national conference. Rather, the Board of Directors and the national staff simply neglected to carry out the conference directive. This strategy was applied discreetly and no public proclamation was issued to defend the action. Of course, it could not escape notice entirely, and Horace Cayton sought to explain what was behind the break.

Several factors were considered in Cayton's column: (1) The Association was slow to recognize the competing character of the MOWM; this reflected upon "the insight of the officers" of the NAACP. (2) the NAACP leaders had regarded the MOWM as "a big thing from which they did not want to separate themselves." (3) However, "they were embarrassed by the fact that it was a purely Negro organization in contrast to the interracial character of the Association." (4) The March had become a "hot potato":

> Recently while in Washington every government official questioned me about Randolph and his 'March.' Most of the governmental officials were frankly antagonistic or else scared to death that Randolph was going to throw the country into a bloody series of race riots. A few stated that Randolph's movement was dangerous but was the only thing that got much respect or might be able to gain concessions from the Administration. At least everyone agreed that the 'March' was the hottest thing in the muddled field of race relations.[100]

As Cayton said, "now he [Randolph] is on his own." But it is important to bear in mind that this was not an open break. Indeed, there was little attention paid to the Detroit conference in the Negro press. The NAACP did not attack the March nor did Randolph choose to demand publicly that White honor the recent NAACP conference resolution pledging active affiliation with the MOWM. Both groups avoided a public fracas thus keeping open the possibility of future co-operation. The tone of the rupture in relations between Randolph and the leadership of the Urban League and the NAACP was cordial. Consider Lester Granger's letter to Randolph explaining his withdrawal from the March:

> *Personal*
> I was sorry not to have been able to attend the August 27th meeting of the March on Washington Committee. I should have preferred to say in the meeting what I am setting forth in this letter—namely my inability to carry on further with the Committee. I joined the group in the first place because of the need for a national expression of opinion from the Negro population on discrimination in the defense program. As a permanent organization, however, the March on Washington would demand far more time and responsibility than I would be justified in giving to any movement outside of the National Urban League at this time. There will be important decisions of policy to make requiring close acquaintanceship with developments in local communities, with the personalities of local leaders, and with relationships between local chapters and other organizations in their communities. This is patently impossible for me in view of

the tremendous pressure to which I am already subjected in the Urban League and the increasing duties that have fallen upon our already overworked staff.

These difficulties would stand in my way even if I were completely in accord with the tentative plans for a national policy conference, as set forward in the memorandum addressed to me. As it happens, I strongly oppose certain items in those plans. It seems to me that there is a good deal of refining and definition of objectives, techniques, and principles which must be completed before we are ready to establish a permanent mass movement of the type which the March on Washington now appears to be. The kinds of organizations that should be affiliated, the kinds of statements that can be made in accordance with the movement's principles, the defined responsibilities which must be acknowledged by Negroes as part of their citizenship obligation—none of these can be decided in a large meeting like the Detroit conference without prolonged discussion by planning groups in advance.

I am writing to you frankly, because of my deep personal regard for you and my admiration for the services you have rendered to our race and country. I had hoped before now to have sat down and talked with you to express some of the thoughts that are behind this letter. Perhaps we shall have a chance when you and I both can 'stay put' in New York for a while. Won't you let me know when that appears possible to you?[101]

Randolph replied with equal courtesy indicating he understood that the pressure of other duties might keep Granger off the national committee of MOWM. He agreed that one should not take responsibility for organizational activities unless close contacts were maintained. But, with respect to the character of the forthcoming conference, he wrote:

May I say that the policy conference which we plan to hold in Detroit is not a big delegate conference, but a small body of people who will deal with goals, methods and tactics. . . . The Detroit conference is a planning conference in which intensive discussion of the questions you suggest will be made.[102]

This was indeed the character of the conference which was conceived as a prelude to a full-scale convention. There were only sixty-six delegates, half of whom were from the Detroit area.[103] Two of the items listed for discussion in the thirteen point Call to the Conference concerned the "advisability of calling a large national conference to discuss and adopt constitution and by-laws, goals, policies, tactics, methods and strategy." And the Detroit conference was also "to plan the delegate composition of the national conference and set its date and place."[104]

Thus, the function of the conference was to draft proposals for later action and only tentatively formalize the permanent structure of the March. Randolph's conception of the national convention which the Detroit conference would plan envisioned another spectacular demonstration of the unity of the Negro protest behind the leadership of the MOWM. But Randolph could no longer put off entirely the formalization of the MOWM and the Detroit group would "elect national officers" and "work out broad organizational plans." In particular, they would "plan the setting up of a broader March On Washington Movement National Executive Committee."

Actually, the distinction between the Detroit "conference" and the "convention" which it projected for Chicago at a later date made it possible to retain the highly centralized and personalized leadership of the March with little change. The constitution of the MOWM adopted at the Detroit meeting vested "the power to appoint all Officers of the Organization" in the National Director, namely Randolph, "pending the meeting of the First National Convention."[105]

Thus the March continued much as before, even in formal structure, as the officers would continue to be Randolph's personal choices. The constitutional provisions did specify a geographical distribution of officers which was a limit of sorts on Randolph's selections. Then too, the mere formalization of rules making the national conventions the highest governing body of the organization and requiring such conventions every two years was a step toward internal democracy.[106] However, this very fact meant that the decisions of the Detroit group could not bind the still to come "first convention" which would not be held until three years after the March on Washington Movement actually began.

chapter v

Nadir

A mass movement with a concrete, limited objective
is likely to have a shorter active phase than a movement with a nebulous, indefinite objective.

ERIC HOFFER[1]

THE DETROIT POLICY CONFERENCE of the March on Washington
Movement succeeded in placating the demands from within for
organizational democracy by setting up a tentative constitution. At
the same time, Randolph laid the groundwork for an attempt at re-
vitalizing the March through the projected national convention in
the form of another great "united-front" rally. And, by limiting the
size of the Detroit conference, he was able to avoid for a while
longer the necessity of demonstrating publicly how much (or how
little) strength the MOWM retained.

A Dual Dilemma

BUT THE NEAT formula for assuaging internal discontent while postponing an external test of power could not entirely avoid coming to
grips with major matters affecting the public's attitude to the March.
For the general Negro community, interest in the Detroit conference
was centered on two primary questions: (1) Would the MOWM
attempt a physical march on Washington? (2) Would the movement
continue to restrict its membership to Negroes?

The first question was of obvious import for an organization bearing the name March On Washington Movement. It was increasingly
difficult for Randolph to justify that label without scheduling another
march. He succeeded brilliantly for a time with his giant rallies, but
the collapse of the major Washington rally renewed the problem of
strategy. How could the March maintain a posture of strength with-

out tangible demonstrations of its mass following? At the same time, Randolph was a prisoner of the MOWM name. He and his aides were convinced that the March was too firmly identified with the 1941, FEPC success to risk changing its name to a form less restricted to a particular strategy. Thus, when Randolph sought to make clear that the march tactic was but one form of mass pressure available to the March as an organization he was misunderstood and his influence waned.

The idea of the March as a *physical march* was amazingly popular even late in 1942 when it had become almost a technical impossibility because of wartime housing and travel restrictions.[2] Also, the possibility of a race riot stimulated by a militant display of strength was strongly feared (as Cayton had reported). Yet, when the *Pittsburgh Courier* conducted a straw poll at the time of the Detroit conference on the desirability of a march on Washington, considerable support was registered (see Table 2).

Table 2—Results of Poll Taken by the Pittsburgh Courier*
"Do You Believe That a 'March On Washington,'
with Congress in Session, Would Accomplish Any
Material Good?"

PERCENTAGE ANSWERING YES OR NO

Group	Yes	No
Chicago	58	41
Cincinnati	40	60
Washington, D.C.	28	71
Detroit	60	35
New York City	51	46
Philadelphia	42	54
St. Louis	65	28
Texas	30	68
Tennessee	31	65
S. Carolina	40	57
N. Carolina	27	70
Pittsburgh, Pa.	46	52
Atlanta, Ga.	20	75
Florida	38	60
Louisiana	35	60
Los Angeles	54	44
Ohio	46	51
South	39.4	55.2
North	44.5	51.3
Male	41.3	54.2
Female	44.2	51.7
"Total Vote"	41.8	53.1

* Reported October 17, 1942, p. 4.

The *Courier* strongly opposed the march, and their interpretation of the poll's results in their front page headline was restrained: "VOTE IS CLOSE, BUT COURIER POLL REJECTS 'MARCH ON WASHINGTON.' "[3] Actually, in the major centers of Negro population, outside the South, the march was still powerfully supported. In Chicago, Detroit, New York, St. Louis and Los Angeles, substantial endorsement was registered by more than a majority of those polled. The big blow to Randolph's chances of managing a successful march came from Washington, D.C. where reported sentiment was overwhelmingly hostile. Even so, the MOWM at the time of the Detroit conference continued as a force to be reckoned with. Randolph's problem was to somehow retain his hold on the popular support for the march without risking it in a venture which became increasingly dangerous as the war went on.

The Detroit conference sidestepped the immediate problem of whether to march by recommending to the forthcoming national convention that there be a march on Washington. In effect, the decision was again postponed though the march tactic was nominally retained as justification for the name of the movement. Meanwhile, other types of "mass action" were resolved "including marches on City-halls, City Councils, Defense Plants, Public Utility Works, Picketing, and the sending of mass letters and telegrams. . . ."[4]

In support of this approach the Committee on Organization at the Detroit conference recommended:

a framework around which a membership of sufficient numerical strength could be built so as to characterize the Movement as a mass movement; to fashion an organizational structure of such a model as to provide for the minute-man type of machinery calculated to mobilize into immediate action the entire membership upon short notice.[5]

For this purpose, the "block-plan" of organization was to be implemented, and these basic units would be pyramided into a hierarchy of districts, divisions, states, regions and a full-time national organizer. The ambition was to reinvigorate the now independent MOWM as a mass organization of Negroes theoretically prepared, if necessary, to unleash a march on Washington. But this weapon was not the only one and the "block-plan" would apply the basic myth of the march to less ambitious actions.

Interest was also strong in the second issue, whether the reconsti-

tuted MOWM would be an interracial organization or restricted to
Negroes. It will be remembered that the March was all-Negro from
the outset; one of the original Randolph calls for a march on Washington had proclaimed:

> On to Washington, ten thousand black Americans! . . . We shall not
> call upon our white friends to march with us. There are some things Ne-
> groes must do alone. This is our fight and we must see it through. If it
> costs money to finance a march on Washington, let Negroes pay for it.
> If any sacrifices are to be made for Negro rights in national defense, let
> Negroes make them. . . . Let the Negro masses speak![6]

Critics now viewed the all-Negro policy of the March as a contradiction. How could Negroes seek to break down racial segregation
through a "self-segregated" organization? Furthermore, there was
the recollection of Garveyite "black nationalism" and distaste and
fear for its resurgence. Both the conservative and militant leaders had
viewed the Garvey movement as demagogic and a severe liability on
the Negro protest. The essence of the Negro struggle, they felt, was
integration between white and colored societies in the United States.
Anything which smacked of Garveyite nationalism—which emphasized the separation of the races, even if unaccompanied by a "back-
to-Africa" program—was anathema to the Negro leadership.

But Randolph was determined to build a mass movement of Negroes. He was convinced that there was tremendous untapped power
in the Negro grass roots. But to mobilize that power effectively, the
imagination of the "common Negro-in-the-street" had to be captured
and galvanized into action. None of the Negro organizations, apart
from Garvey's, had ever succeeded in doing this. None, that is, until
the MOWM sprang into being.

Myrdal has warned of the dangers involved in appealing directly
to the Negro masses:

> It should be borne in mind that the easiest means of rallying the Ameri-
> can Negroes into a mass movement are such that they would destroy the
> organization. The Garvey movement demonstrated that the Negro masses
> can best be stirred into unity by an irrational and intensively racial, emo-
> tional appeal. . . .[7]

But, closing his study just prior to the MOWM Detroit Conference, he had regarded Randolph's movement favorably and an exception to his generalization:

NADIR   [129]

When we look over the field of Negro protest and betterment organizations, we find that *only when Negroes have collaborated with whites
have organizations been built up which have any strength and which have
been able to do something practical.* Except for the March-on-Washington movement—which has a temporary and limited purpose and which,
in addition, is backed by the regular organizations—all purely Negro organizations have been disappointments.[8]

Now that the MOWM could no longer be characterized as having
a "temporary and limited purpose," and did not continue to be
"backed by the regular organizations," it was increasingly attacked
for "Garveyism." Randolph, who had directed the "Garvey Must
Go" campaign in Harlem,[9] was sharply reminded that he himself had
then proclaimed: "Only solidarity can save the black and white
workers of America."[10] Randolph thundered back at his detractors:
"The petty black bourgeoisie are always hunting for some white
angel at whose feet they may place the Negroes' problems."[11]

Actually Randolph's belief in an all-Negro movement was not
simply "nationalistic," and he sought to persuade the public that his
policy was not patterned on Garvey's.[12]

Now, the March On Washington Movement is an all Negro movement, but it is not anti-white, anti-American, anti-labor, anti-Catholic or
anti-Semitic. It's simply pro-Negro. It does not rest so much upon race as
upon the social problem of Jim Crow. It does not oppose interracial organizations. It cooperates with such mixed organizations as the National
Association for the Advancement of Colored People and the National
Urban League, and churches, trade unions. Its validity lies in the fact that
no one will fight as hard to remove and relieve pain as he who suffers from
it. Negroes are the only people who must take the initiative and assume the
responsibility to abolish it. Jews must and do lead the fight against anti-
Semitism, Catholics must lead the fight against anti-Catholicism, labor must
battle against anti-labor laws and practices.[13]

This had little in common with Garvey except the principle of an
all-Negro membership. Whereas Garvey had been anti-Semitic,[14]
Randolph had always attacked such chauvinism.[15] Garvey's "back-to-
Africa" policy had no interest in resolving the Negro problem in the
United States; this was Randolph's basic concern. Garvey and the
Klan saw eye to eye in their belief in racial purity—indeed light-
skinned Negroes were barred from the Garvey movement.[16] Randolph supported and would co-operate with interracial organizations.[17] The MOWM was all Negro because "its major weapon is the

non-violent demonstration of Negro mass power."[18] That is, a *Negro membership* is a corollary of a *mass* organization for Negro rights.

This logic for the building of a mass Negro organization was not "a contradiction of Randolph's basic philosophy," as Adam Clayton Powell, Jr. has charged.[19] Randolph had utilized a racial appeal years before in organizing the BSCP.[20] It is significant that when the *Messenger* (Randolph's Negro Socialist journal) became the Porters' house organ, its name was changed to the *Black Worker*. The components of that name are symbolic of a general outlook in the social-politics of the Negro world. "Black" is not a name which rates high in social status. Typical titles of Negro "slick" periodicals are *Tan* and *Sepia*. In the hierarchy of skin colors, a lighter skin is a definite social advantage and marks more upper-class Negroes.[21] Thus, the *Black Worker* designated a lower-class color emphasis.

"Worker" is not a high sounding name in colored or white society. Randolph chose it over laborer, porter, trainman, or any of several more euphemistic titles which might have appealed to a more middle-class and less radical temperament. In this way, Randolph's *Black Worker* reveals his long standing attitude to mass-action politics. He has always been working-class and race-pride conscious.

Even if no all-Negro movement had obtained practical gains until the MOWM wrested the FEPC order from Roosevelt, the appeal to race consciousness was crucial to the building of a mass membership organization. Lower-class Negroes belonged to churches—"store front" more than "stone front"—and to fraternal associations, but protest leadership and organization had been primarily a "talented tenth" activity. It was Myrdal's assumption that appeals to the Negro masses could be made most effectively on a basis of racial emotionalism. If that would be most effective, surely those seeking to organize lower-class Negroes would make use of such appeals.

The decision to build a mass organization as the form of the now officially independent MOWM meant cutting deep into the lower strata of Negroes in the Northern urban ghettos.[22] And, if Negro masses were to be mobilized in huge demonstrations of protest, their wounds had to be uncovered and held up to public anguish and anger. Randolph was a master of this technique. Not that he was merely manipulating such feelings. There is no doubt that he shared deeply the emotions he aroused.[23]

Can anyone profess surprise that Negroes might be responsive to such an appeal? It was a similar cry of bitter despair which W. E. B. Du Bois penned in his *Litany of Atlanta* when a white mob descended on the colored community of Atlanta, Georgia:

> Surely thou too art not white, O Lord,
> A pale, bloodless, heartless thing![24]

The march had successfully channeled those feelings in the Negro community during the dark days of the defense period, and Randolph proposed to build a permanent mass organization on that basis.

There was yet another reason for the MOWM to admit only Negroes to membership. To an important extent, the March was "lily-black" because it was "anti-red." As president of the National Negro Congress, Randolph had been burned badly by the ease with which white Communist representatives of various "front" organizations had taken over. Only a few months before he started the March movement, Randolph wrote an important article explaining "Why I Would Not Stand For Re-Election For President of the National Negro Congress":

> I quit the Congress because it is not truly a Negro Congress. Out of some 1200 or more delegates, over 300 were white, which made the Congress look like a joke. It is unthinkable that the Jewish Congress would have Gentiles in it, or that a Catholic Congress would have Protestants in it, or that the famous All India Congress would have in it as members natives of Africa. Why should a Negro Congress have white people in it?[25]

It was his experience with the Communists in the Negro Congress which led Randolph to view the exclusion of whites as an effective tactic to stymie Communist control. As we have seen, this was not the only reason for the policy, but it was so strongly involved that a newspaper report was devoted entirely to the story that Randolph "says March on Washington Movement bars white members to avoid Communist infiltration."[26] An allied reason given by Randolph was:

> We planned the March to be all Negroes because we wanted the President and the country not to be left in any doubt that this March was the symbol and expression of discontent and resentment of Negroes themselves against discriminations . . . and not some outburst artificially stirred up and manipulated by the artful Communists.[27]

The attitude to Communists since the "Cold War" developed makes it seem odd that Randolph utilized this indirect means for keeping free of Communist influence. Why did he not simply bar all Communists? The truth is that his strategy was somewhat ambivalent.

In the early days of the March, it was reported: "Communists Not Wanted in March to Washington, Declares Randolph."[28] However, while scarcely holding out a welcoming hand, Randolph told the Detroit Conference delegates:

We cannot sup with the Communists, for they rule or ruin any movement. This is their policy. Our policy must be to shun them. This does not mean that Negro Communists may not join the March on Washington Movement.[29]

What probably kept Randolph from a more forthright exclusion of Communists was, first, that the problem would be substantially reduced by the exclusion of whites. Not that there were no Negro Communists, but the primary method of infiltration via the "paper organization" delegates route would be closed off. Another factor making it difficult to directly bar Communists as such was Communist success in labeling direct opposition "red-baiting" and pleading democratic procedures would be violated if they were refused organizational membership. This was very effective generally in liberal-labor circles in the Nineteen-Thirties and Forties.[30] It was particularly so in the Negro community where many agreed with Adam Clayton Powell, Jr. that "there is no group in America including the Christian church that practices racial brotherhood one tenth as much as the Communist Party."[31]

Yet Powell's statement was made at the very time the Communists were soft-pedaling the fight for Negro rights in the interest of wartime unity.[32] For example, the Secretary of the Navy announced (April 7, 1942) that Negro volunteers, previously accepted only for menial types of duty, would be accepted into general service on an "experimental basis." The announcement also specified that "there was to be no mixing of black and white." One scholar has recorded:

Negro organizations reacted to this announcement according to their general orientation to the war and their strategy in the struggle for Negro rights. For example the National Negro Congress [controlled by the Communists] praised the move as 'bold, patriotic action in smashing age-old color restrictions which have prevented the Negro people from full service in the United States Navy.' The National Association For the Advancement of Colored People termed it 'progress toward a more enlightened point of view.' The March on Washington Movement declared that it 'accepts and extends and consolidates the policy of jim crowism in the Navy as well as proclaims it as an accepted, recognized government ideology that the Negro is inferior to the white race.'[33]

It was a condition of the period when the Soviet Union was allied with the United States that there was much confusion over the Communists' purposes and methods. Powell was not the only Negro leader taken in by the Communist demands for "unity" and the "red-baiter" epithet applied against those who saw through the Party line. Thus Randolph pursued a policy not understood by many until years later. This innocence led some to the naive plea that the March and the Communist-front Negro Labor Victory Committee should unite, there being no fundamental difference between them other than one being all-Negro, the other interracial![34]

In view of this situation, it made strategic sense that Randolph emphasized the *positive* values of an all-Negro organization in furthering the wartime protest. It accomplished his basic purpose with respect to both the emotional appeal necessary to attract a mass-membership and the need to keep the March from the fate which befell the National Negro Congress.[35]

"Satyagraha" and "We Are Americans Too!"

AFTER THE DETROIT CONFERENCE, and as 1942 neared its end, the March began to prepare for its first formal national convention. Randolph appointed a full-time national executive secretary to take over some of the organizational tasks, the date of the convention being set initially for May, 1943 (in Chicago).

A period of intensive work ensued in an effort to build the movement. Only modest success was attained, though Randolph stayed in the public print through various activities. As a delegate to the AFL convention (October, 1942), he dramatically challenged the discriminatory policies of several constituent unions. The *Pittsburgh Courier* hailed his "brilliant speech" and declared, "Mr. Randolph's arguments were powerful and his logic unassailable."[36] Though the convention rejected his resolution, his prominence in the Negro community was sustained.

Randolph addressed scores of meetings throughout the country and MOWM branches were established in twenty-four cities. A number of these were "paper" divisions which simply reflected the existence of local BSCP headquarters, but many functioned with considerable activity. There were local "marches" and picketing. In St.

Louis, it was reported that "2,000 Attend Mass Meeting; Discuss 'March To Washington.' "[37] A "prayer meeting" met with less success in New York,[38] but other activities compensated for this. For example, a front-page story in the *Amsterdam News* reported a big "Citizenship Day Celebration" in Brooklyn where "Dr. Lawrence Ervin, chairman of the N.Y. Chapter of the March On Washington Movement, will be the principal speaker."[39] In Chicago, a campaign was launched to break the color line which barred Negroes from employment in public utilities.[40]

But the MOWM could not be built as a mass movement by these quite ordinary activities. The March, at this time, was scarcely more vigorous than many other organizations; there was little to distinguish it in program, in methods, or in expectation of important accomplishment. Randolph still had a following but it was not growing as it had during the period of the summer rallies. Even though the tone continued to be militant it had lost its dramatic impact. By December, the friendly *Amsterdam News* editorialized, "Wanted: A Leader to Lead."[41] While not a direct attack on Randolph, this contrasted sharply with their recent adulation.

Propaganda for a march on Washington was renewed sporadically but it was plain that there was less reality to the threat with each passing day. Twelve days after the first anniversary of Pearl Harbor, it was reported from Cleveland: " 'May March To Save Nation's Soul'—Randolph."[42] A week later a front page item proclaimed, "Randolph Prepares For New 'March' "[43] The MOWM was reported embarking on "a national attempt to mobilize five million Negroes into 'one great mass of pressure for freedom and democracy in America by 1943. . . .' "[44] There was little force to these announcements, however, as the decision of when and whether to march was put off to the forthcoming convention. Indeed, the renewed but vague threats that a march might be called wore thin with unfulfilled repetition. The *Pittsburgh Courier* taunted:

> A. Philip Randolph continues to compound confusion about the frequently threatened 'March on Washington.' To our recollection, this 'march' has been called on and off at least three times, and many Negroes are anxious to know whether there is ever to be a march, and when.
> . . . We are not authorities on organizing marches to Washington or any other point, but it is difficult to see why it should require all this time to get down to the business of marching.[45]

This was, to some extent, a misunderstanding of the nature of the march as a political pressure tactic. But it was clear that the MOWM had about exhausted its FEPC glory and its limited-purpose name was increasingly a handicap.

Unless a Washington, D.C. rally could be staged, a repetition of the big meetings, even if possible, would not really help. A feeble effort was made to do something on that order as a Washington press release announced: "MARCH ON WASHINGTON MOVE-MENT WILL HOLD A MONSTER MASS MEETING in the Vernon Avenue Baptist Church at 3 p.m."[46] But it would take more than the word "monster" to make this serve as a national symbol of a rejuvenated March. A new and dynamic substitute for the march became increasingly urgent if the MOWM was to survive.

It was to the Gandhian movement in India that Randolph turned for his inspiration. The Indian struggle for independence from Britain had been of interest to Negroes for a long time. This was more than anti-colonialist sympathy, for Gandhi's preaching against the caste system was bound to have implications for Negroes in America. Indeed, the very weapon of *satyagraha*, variously translated as passive resistance or civil disobedience, had originated in South Africa where Indians and Negroes were lumped together as "blacks." Gandhi had not objected to this as such or sought to raise the status of Indians above Negroes. Rather, in his first imprisonment in Johannesburg, "Gandhi set an example by putting on clothes assigned to Negro convicts."[47] Thenceforth, his activities were followed very closely by the American Negro press.

The power of *satyagraha* derived from Gandhi's religious belief in the capacity of truth and love to triumph over even violent oppression.[48] To be successful, the *satyagrahas* had to discipline themselves to respond to violence with genuine love for the aggressor. Whatever the punishment which they would suffer for their "non-cooperation" with unjust laws, it must be accepted as necessary to redeem the sins of the world. It was Gandhi's capacity to organize such a movement effectively which made him the outstanding religious and political leader of the twentieth century. Thousands of his followers submitted to beatings and imprisonment and somehow emerged emotionally strengthened. As Gandhi taught: "When the fear of jail disappears, repression puts heart into the people."[49]

Temperamentally, Randolph is far from a Gandhian pacifist. Not that he feared jail or never risked personal danger.[50] But he has been a radical political and labor leader rather than a religious saint. He had long represented the spirit of the Negro revolutionary poem:

> This must not be!
> The time is past when black men
> Laggard Sons of Ham,
> Shall tamely bow and weakly cringe
> In servile manner full of shame.
>
> Demand, come not mock suppliant!
> Demand, and if not given—take!
> Take what is rightfully yours;
> An eye for an eye;
> A soul for soul;
> Strike, black man, strike!
> This shall not be![51]

It was his capacity to communicate this sense of emotional outrage and militant protest which constituted his charisma. Could the Gandhian techniques be successfully adapted to American Negro purposes under Randolph's leadership? Probably not in the full Gandhian sense. But "non-violent, goodwill, direct action" methods (as Randolph termed them) might be used as a political technique independent of its religious justification. There are those who believe that without the religious component *satyagrahas* could not steel themselves against provocations and resist only passively. But, as Eric Hoffer has observed, "The True Believer" is a product of political as well as of theistic religious fervor.

Furthermore, Randolph did not intend to plunge his followers into civil disobedience activities without preparation and training in self-discipline. Thus the announcement read, "MARCH ON WASHINGTON MAY CONFERENCE WILL PONDER PROGRAM OF CIVIL DISOBEDIENCE."[52] The new campaign seemed ideally suited to the situation then confronting the MOWM. As Randolph came to realize that the prospects for a wartime march on Washington were fleeting it was essential that the May convention come up with something befitting the spirit of the March.

It was at least successful in keeping the movement before the public eye.[53] The reaction from the Negro press was generally negative but attentive. The *Pittsburgh Courier* editorialized:

A. Philip Randolph is guilty of the most dangerous demagoguery on record.

The 'March on Washington' plan was bad enough, but alongside a call to civil disobedience, it seems quite sane.

For a stated period Mr. Randolph is suggesting that colored citizens disobey all Jim-Crow laws as a demonstration of their dissatisfaction with them (and presumably he is prepared to lead the way) but there is to be no violence![54]

The editorial then declared that Southerners would surely greet such a campaign with violence, that American conditions were different from the situation in India where a colored population greatly outnumbered the whites, and that it had not worked in India either but, instead, produced "bloodshed and imprisonment." The *Chicago Defender* was sufficiently sympathetic to carry the rebuttal: "RANDOLPH REFUTES CRY OF 'CALAMITY HOWLERS.' "[55] Randolph explained that the civil disobedience campaign was not levelled against the war and would not be directed against defense plants or the Armed Forces. It would be concentrated against Jim Crow accommodations in public places, including the South, but above all it would be non-violent.

The campaign was to take place during a one-week period, but there was some ambiguity as to when that week would be set aside. The May convention would first decide "when, as and if the program of civil disobedience and non-cooperation is initiated. . . .[56] But Randolph, at the same time, planned to make the convention into more than a "conference" by calling upon Negroes, during the convention, to observe " 'I AM AN AMERICAN TOO' WEEK WITH SLOGAN 'DEFEAT HITLER, MUSSOLINI AND HIROHITO BY ENFORCING THE CONSTITUTION AND ABOLISHING JIM CROW.' "[57] During this week there were to be " 'I AM AN AMERICAN, TOO' Marches on the city halls . . . from coast to coast. . . ."[58] Thus the convention week would not be the occasion for carrying out civil disobedience activities as such, but the anti-Jim Crow marches were easily confused with the passive-resistance agitation.

Just as the rallies of the previous summer had been transformed by Randolph into something far more dramatic and unifying than mere meetings, he now sought to make the convention into a national symbol of wartime protest by the entire Negro community. The meeting was referred to as an "all-out National Negro Conference."[59] This bid for unity was also plain in "Mr. Randolph's suggestion that the Negro organizations throughout the country plan and execute 'I AM AN AMERICAN TOO' WEEK. . . ."[60] An effort was made to issue the formal call to the conference over the names of prominent Negro organizational leaders. Thus, Walter White was again approached—but he passed the decision to the NAACP Board of Directors:

> The Secretary [Mr. White] reported that he had informed Mr. Randolph that in the light of the Board's decision at its September 1942 meeting to the effect that 'it would not further our common objective to divert any considerable part of the energies of the Association to the establishment of the proposed new, permanent organization (the March on Washington Movement),' this would require Board approval.
> The Secretary requested that a small committee of the Board be appointed to discuss the matter with Mr. Randolph.[61]

These efforts were unsuccessful and the list of sponsors was generally restricted to a hard core of Randolph's immediate circle of friends and associates. Not many months earlier, Randolph was swamped with prominent speakers on the Madison Square Garden platform! Despite its Detroit Conference resolution that "the March on Washington Movement is not and is not intended to be a rival Organization to any established agency already functioning to advance the interests of the Negro,"[62] it was so regarded. Worse, it was no longer felt to be too strong to ignore; at least the wartime risks involved now outweighed whatever mass support was still available through Randolph's leadership.

Failure to support the militant March movement was no longer an automatic sign of vacillation in the struggle for equality as it had tended to be during the 1941–1942 period. The formerly general cry of "Uncle Tom" at signs of conciliatory compromise was dulled and infrequent. Indeed, events now intervened which led Randolph himself into activities increasingly removed from the mass-action program of the MOWM and, before long, to concentrate his attention on the establishment of an entirely new and different organization.

Demise

THE MYTHICAL INDEPENDENCE of the FEPC, now an "organizational entity" within the War Manpower Commission, was exploded sharply on January 11, 1943. Paul McNutt exerted his "supervisory" authority and "indefinitely postponed" the FEPC's scheduled hearings into discriminatory employment policies by the railroads.

Surely this was the moment to unleash the march on Washington if it retained any reality as a pressure weapon. One of Randolph's top associates in the MOWM wired him:

MCNUTT'S ACTION REGARDING RAILROAD HEARING AND FEPC REQUIRES DRASTIC ACTION. MOBILIZE NAACP, URBAN LEAGUE, CHURCH GROUPS, TRADE UNIONS, FRATERNAL ORGANIZATIONS TO MARCH.[63]

There is no record of Randolph's reply, but the public record speaks for itself; there was no call to march. Instead, representatives of many interested organizations made the trek to Washington for futile conferences with McNutt. "So many delegations swarmed about his office, that, on January 19, he refused to receive any more."[64]

Shortly thereafter, the chairman of the FEPC and two other members resigned. The FEPC staff, which had prepared the railroad cases in readiness for the hearings, also resigned. But though the *Chicago Defender* suggested they do so,[65] the colored members of the Committee held on. It is interesting that at this very time the Negro adviser to the Secretary of War, Judge William H. Hastie, was hailed as a race hero for his resignation blast at military discrimination. For that, he received the Spingarn medal the very year after Randolph's award.[66]

Of course the situations were different. The FEPC posts carried no salaries and it was not necessary to resign to speak out. As adviser to the War Department, Hastie had been ignored more than he could bear, but his voice was stilled by his official position. Milton Webster and Earl Dickerson sought to reconstitute the FEPC which had wielded tangible power through its embarrassing public hearings and Presidential citations. Also important in explaining why Webster did not resign was the close connection between the stymied railroad hearings and the Brotherhood of Sleeping Car Porters.[67]

It must be remembered that Randolph's Brotherhood is a railroad

union. As such he has had definite ambitions for expanding its jurisdiction to take in categories of workers other than Pullman porters.
Dining-car employees, maids, yard workers, redcaps, and now Negro
firemen were involved with the BSCP, sometimes leading to jurisdictional conflicts with competing unions. For example, there was
considerable rivalry between Randolph's group and the redcaps'
United Transport Service Employees of America, CIO (UTSEA),
led by Willard Townsend.[68] This jurisdictional rivalry inevitably
spilled over into the arena of political leadership contests.[69]

Precisely at the time Randolph was preparing to launch the 1941
March on Washington drive, the Brotherhood called a Negro Firemen's Conference in Washington (March 28–29, 1941). This resulted
in the Provisional Committee to Organize Colored Locomotive Firemen. The basic problem underlying this activity stemmed from tech-
nological changes in the duties of railroad locomotive firemen. The
shift from coal-burning steam engines to Diesels made the firemens'
jobs more attractive and Negroes were being rapidly displaced.
Furthermore, contracts between the operating railroads and the "lily-
white" Brotherhood of Locomotive Firemen and Enginemen, in
effect, deprived colored firemen of seniority rights and barred pro-
motion to higher grades.[70]

When the FEPC was created, Randolph moved at once to utilize
this agency for advancing the organization of Negro railroad
workers. In September, 1941, the BSCP announced the formation of
a National Citizen's Committee To Save the Jobs of Colored Locomotive Firemen, nominally headed by Mrs. Roosevelt and Mayor
LaGuardia.[71] Their previous role in negotiating the halt in plans to
march on Washington will be recalled. One year later, Milton Webster was named chairman of a subcommittee of the FEPC "to investigate and hold hearings on problems of the colored locomotive firemen who are being displaced by younger white firemen when Diesel
engines are put on."[72] When these hearings were scheduled, pressure
was exerted on McNutt who then intervened.[73]

It is important to realize that it was not only Randolph who held
"the key to saving the Fair Employment Practice Committee is to
save the Railroad hearings."[74] The entire Negro community—that is,
its press and leadership—rallied behind the issue. It was felt that,
"Swinging wildly at Randolph, the administration hit the Negro."[75]
But the top leadership—Walter White, Lester Granger, Dr. Bethune—

would have nothing more to do with the March as the protest vehicle.

Randolph persisted with the MOWM as a separate organization, but it became increasingly clear that he could not "go it alone" if he wished to influence the President with respect to FEPC and the crucial railroad hearings. When the FEPC seemed completely moribund and "post-mortems" were published bemoaning its death,[76] Randolph called a "Save FEPC Conference" to convene in Washington, D.C. (February 15, 1943).[77] Official sponsor of the conference was the BSCP's Provisional Committee for the Organization of Colored Locomotive Firemen, but the press release went out under the March On Washington Movement name. It was this conference which eventually led to the formation (in September, 1943) of the National Council for a Permanent FEPC.

The crucial aspect of the Save FEPC Conference was its effort at unifying a broadly based organized protest behind the FEPC. For this, organization outside the MOWM had become essential. It was necessary if Randolph was to preserve his close identity with the FEPC issue, for other leaders and organizations had adopted it for their programs and activities.[78] And it was strongly indicated as a device for rallying support behind Randolph's efforts to organize colored locomotive firemen.

These factors of "self-interest," or at least narrower organizational strategy, should not be stated as if they were the *real* motives rather than a *principled* concern for FEPC. Randolph's basic sincerity on the issue is not questioned—the factors of ideological principle and organizational leadership were intertwined and not in substantial conflict. What changed was the *strategy* by which Randolph could pressure the Administration into sustaining a vigorous FEPC.

It is true that the communication of the strategy of mass action required the romanticising of mass movements as such, and the militant language employed often seemed an end in itself. Many of Randolph's followers did respond to the style of the March as if it were the goal. The exchange between Randolph and his youthful adherents when the original march was called off exemplified this. There were many times when Randolph, too, seemed swept up in radical symbolism beyond the call of oratory. Mass appeals are most suited to his temperament and talents, yet his organizational leadership has been adaptive to new conditions. In the main he exhibited, at each decisive point, a readiness to alter tactics to meet changing situations. At the same time Randolph's reputation is remarkably free of charges of opportunism. While strong criticisms often have been levelled against Randolph, these have seldom questioned his integrity and devotion to principle.[79]

The change in organizational emphasis, though gradual, is unmistakable. For a time, the FEPC issue had been greatly deemphasized by the MOWM. From the Detroit Conference to the period of McNutt's intervention in the FEPC's railroad hearings, the March was more involved in such matters as the Senate's filibuster over anti-poll tax legislation.[80] Even greater attention was given to the problem of discrimination in the military services—particularly to the case of Winfred W. Lynn who refused induction claiming violation of the 1940 draft act prohibition of racial discrimination.[81] The only substantial educational pamphlet ever issued by the March was entitled, *The War's Greatest Scandal! The Story of Jim Crow in Uniform*.[82] And, as we have seen, the new civil disobedience tactic was directed to Jim Crow in public facilities rather than to employment discrimination or the FEPC.

Following McNutt's action, the FEPC issue moved back into the forefront of MOWM activities. Several thousand stamps were printed and distributed bearing the legend, "Make FEPC Permanent For Jobs and Justice, March On Washington Movement." This reflected the idea gradually gaining currency that the FEPC should be established by statute as a permanent agency of government. But that development took place over a period of almost an entire year. At first, the MOWM continued to claim the issue and there were no plans to turn the broad but temporary "Save FEPC Conference" into a permanent group. Instead the March renewed the preparations for its now renamed "We Are Americans Too" convention, and the date was advanced from May to the July Fourth holiday to provide more time for organization.

The future of the March depended on the impressiveness of its Chicago convention. If the "We Are Americans Too" activity could be staged as a rally on a par with the summer, 1942 successes it would publicly symbolize a thriving movement. Simultaneously, it might provide a much needed spurt to MOWM morale which was slipping badly. In March, Pauli Murray wrote Randolph:

Somewhere between the mass meetings of last summer and today, the March on Washington Movement has lost ground rather than gained it. . . . I get the impression from reading the press that you are a leader without a movement.

. . . My inquiries about the various branches of the MOW in places outside of Washington all bring the same answers—internal dissension, lack of direction, defeatism, inability to carry forward with a sense of crusading for freedom.[83]

The test was made even more crucial by the comparisons inevitably involved in the scheduling of major gatherings by other organizations shortly before the MOWM affair. Now it was a Communist controlled group, the Negro Labor Victory Committee, which filled Madison Square Garden with an estimated 25,000 persons.[84] That it was not an all-Negro gathering is too esoteric a point to have mattered much; more important was the question of what the March could do to outshine its rivals.

Similarly, the NAACP held an Emergency War Conference, June 3–6, in Detroit clearly competing with the "We Are Americans Too" activity. The NAACP conference even boasted a "monster mass meeting held in the [Detroit] Olympia stadium, June 6."[85] Now Cayton wrote in sharp contrast to his appraisal of the previous year:

Walter White and the NAACP have got the ball. They're in the lead again. . . . A year ago it was different. Phil Randolph stole the show—but completely. He dominated every meeting with the possible exception of the Willkie meeting, and there he received a tremendous ovation. This year I don't think the name A. Philip Randolph was mentioned at the convention. . . . there was never a person so completely ignored as was Randolph at the NAACP convention.

I'm anxious to see what's going to happen in Chicago where the March on Washington has its national convention. Unless they've got some tricks up their sleeves—unless they come up with some plan of action which can be implemented by rank and file organizations in local communities, I'm afraid they won't have much chance.[86]

The most crushing feature of Cayton's analysis was the assertion: "In spite of its middle-class orientation . . . it seems that the NAACP is making more headway in working with labor than is the more nationalistic and sectarian March on Washington." Cayton did grant that "it may be that Randolph's appeal is greater in the working class and lower middle-class than is that of the NAACP. Randolph may still have a following that the Association has not tapped."[87]

But the March was unable to hold on to its earlier primacy. The status of the FEPC had fallen to the vanishing point and dragged the March down with it. Randolph participated with, rather than assuming command of, the Negro protest which descended on McNutt and the Roosevelt Administration. When Roosevelt was forced to give in to this pressure—the 1944 election was but one year away—it was Earl Dickerson rather than Milton Webster who forced his hand.[88] Roosevelt issued another executive order and appointed a new FEPC.[89] Webster was retained and Dickerson dropped, but whatever glory attended this successful exertion of pressure did not go to Webster, Randolph and the March—a far cry from the first FEPC establishment.

Then, only ten days before the MOWM convention where it was to play a vital role, the civil disobedience campaign received a fatal blow. On June 20, 1943, "the worst race riot of the year broke out in Detroit, Michigan, in which 34 were killed, 25 of whom were Negroes."[90] John Rankin of Mississippi told the House of Representatives it was due to the "crazy policies of the President's Committee on Fair Employment Practice in attempting to mix the races in all kinds of employment."[91] The report of the "lily-white" Michigan Governor's committee investigating the riot blamed "the positive exhortation by many so-called responsible Negro leaders to be 'militant' in the struggle for racial equality."[92] This was precisely what the conservative Negro leadership had feared might be the outcome of Randolph's activities. On top of the already diminishing ardor of the Negro community for "direct-action" protest methods, these riots marked the finish for whatever enthusiasm may have remained.

Meeting so soon thereafter, the MOWM had to go through with its scheduled discussion by a panel on "non-violent, good will, direct action—what it is and how it can be applied to abolishing Jim Crow."[93] But the *satyagraha* technique was doomed for the duration of the war and could no longer hope to provide a substitute for the march as the weapon of a militant mass movement.[94] Indeed, the great wartime upsurge of Negro mass action had run its course.[95]

The *New York Times*, at last, gave the "We Are Americans Too" convention as much, and in some instances, more, coverage than did the Negro press. They reported: "Conscious of deep feeling running among Negroes following the recent riots in Detroit . . . officials and civic leaders of both races had been watching 'the March on Washington' with apprehension." And the story was headed:

DECIDES AGAINST MARCH ON CAPITAL, CHICAGO CONVENTION DEFERS PROPOSED MASS APPEAL FOR REDRESS OF NEGRO GRIEVANCES, RACE TENSION RELIEVED, MOVEMENT HAD EXCITED FEARS OF OUTBREAK CLIMAXING FEELING FOLLOWING DETROIT RIOTS.[96]

The decision whether to march on Washington was delegated by the convention to its national officers with no recommendation or time limit set. The civil disobedience campaign received formal endorsement but the resolution was to prove nothing more than a gesture. No marches on city halls accompanied the convention as originally planned, and the convention contented itself with "an open air mass interdenominational and interracial prayer meeting . . . at the Negro soldiers' monument."[97]

Randolph and some of his followers sought to convince each other that the conference had been a great success. One of the vice-presidents of the BSCP wrote him:

You are quite right about the conference at Chicago, it was the greatest action conference ever held for Negroes in America and there is one thing of which I am proud, it proved to the second story pigeons of the stuffed shirt group that you could go just as fast and as far without them as you could with them.[98]

This appraisal had little substance. The discussions at the convention were organized around important topics and conducted by able men both in and out of the MOWM.[99] But this was scarcely different from what other organizations did, and measured in terms of attendance (barely more than a hundred delegates) it must have been a gross disappointment.[100] Judged by the more ambitious standards of maintaining and building a huge mass movement—which had clearly been Randolph's earlier view of the March—the "First Convention" formally established the March On Washington Movement but really marked its end as a mass movement.[101]

The activities of the March following the Chicago meetings, increasingly, were directed into channels complementary to the activities of the National Council for a Permanent FEPC which Randolph formed three months later. An effort was made to form a "national non-partisan Negro political bloc, with branches in the various local communities in the country."[102] This was clearly derived from the

new emphasis on obtaining FEPC legislation and the lobbying operations to which Randolph now turned. On June 25 and 26, 1944, a
National Non-Partisan Political Conference was called to meet in
Chicago. Efforts at involving other organizations in this activity again
were without success and only ninety delegates attended.[103] However, the newly launched National Council for a Permanent FEPC
provided the mechanism for a united front behind the FEPC issue and
Randolph turned his leadership activities into that organization.

The March really died at that point though it lingered on officially
as late as 1947.[104] Its last national conference was held October 19,
1946 in Chicago where Randolph's opening address all but called for
dissolution:

> As to the continuance of MOWM, I cannot see justification for it un-
> less a well defined and developed program of action for the elimination
> of discrimination in employment, which is different from any program
> now carried on by any existing organization, is initiated.
> As I see it, the fight for FEPC is the most effective approach to this
> problem and the National Council For a Permanent FEPC is better quali-
> fied in composition and mass appeal to do this job than MOWM or any
> other organization I know.[105]

The door was held ajar for those who wished to continue the
MOWM by "fighting for civil and economic rights through the non-
violent, direct action strategy." But, in any event, "the changing times
and public psychology require the discarding of the name March on
Washington Movement." Thus Randolph gave formal utterance to
what had been plain for some time: "While Marching on Washington
is still in order, no movement will command the respect and mass
allegiance of the Negroes whose name indicates that which it is not
doing."

Despite Randolph's gloomy prognosis, the delegates voted to
continue the organization. It was necessary that Randolph obtain
an official burial for the March on Washington name for fear that
the movement, however small its last-ditch following, would become an irresponsible vehicle for black-chauvinism. The remnants
of Garveyism found the MOWM's all-Negro policy congenial to
their "nationalistic" views, and they sought in Randolph a replace-
ment for their fallen idol, Marcus Garvey. One such neo-Garveyite
wrote Randolph:

Mr. Randolph I have asked you in vain to take leave from the Brotherhood and come on and give us the kind of leadership that only you can give at this time and the kind that Black America is thirsty for. *You alone* must make the decision. It means get ready to die. But you'll have many like me who will stand up with you through thick and thin. Announce to the world that you accept the leadership of Black America, and that you are ready to join hands with our mother country, and black people everywhere. Not in hate of other people but in love for your own people. Yes you Mr. Randolph can do today what Mr. Garvey wished he could have done.[106]

This group, which called itself "Black Nationals," had been submerged in the March during its earlier, more successful days. Now, Randolph found it difficult to obtain their consent to disband. Consequently, the fiction of organizational life was continued though Randolph's activities were directed elsewhere. One of the last items in the files of the March is a letter to "all officers of the MOWM" calling for "an immediate campaign to participate in the present plans of the National Council [for a Permanent FEPC]."[107]

All that remained of the March on Washington Movement was transformed into a bookstore to pay the rent of the national headquarters as long as there was official breath in the organizational body. That store, bearing the name March Community Bookshop, still exists as a pallid monument to what was one of the most remarkable mass movements in American political history.

chapter vi

FEPC After the March

There were Jews and many Negroes in this agency.
Let's face it. That fact was the subject not only of
whispering campaigns but of derisive shouts on the
floor of Congress. Until Congress itself comes to believe citizenship is not a class prerogative, there is
little hope of settling the problem at the grass roots.

MALCOLM ROSS[1]
Chairman, FEPC

A. PHILIP RANDOLPH had a large stake in the success of the FEPC. As
the agitational leader who pressured its establishment he was chief
beneficiary of its glory. As head of the Brotherhood of Sleeping Car
Porters the FEPC provided a governmental weapon in his efforts to
expand the union's jurisdiction over new categories of railroad workers. Thus McNutt's peremptory "postponement" of the FEPC's
railroad hearings was a double blow at Randolph's prestige and organizational leadership. Indeed Randolph never fully recovered the
enormous stature he had attained in 1941 and 1942.

Randolph lost face not only because the FEPC seemed dead. His
failure to wield the kind of protest which had boosted him to the pin-
nacle of leadership, however legitimate the reasons, spelled the end
of the March on Washington as a mass movement and reduced Randolph to the level of other major Negro leaders.

Were he purely a radical agitator he might have gone ahead with
the bold program of the MOWM. Had he done so, it is quite probable
that serious punitive action would have been taken against him. And
such martyrdom would have popularized the label, "American
Gandhi," which many had pinned on him. From what we have observed of Randolph it seems likely that he was indeed tempted, but
he is the old radical turned practical through his very success as an
agitator-organizer. His radical style remained, its mode of speech and

action came naturally and sincerely into his continuing activities, but it was controlled and compromised by "the art of the possible."

Thus, it was not through the March that Randolph turned loose the pressure which would force the President to supersede Paul McNutt. Milton Webster did not resign in protest from the FEPC or risk his position as did Earl Dickerson in publicly violating McNutt's authority. Rather, the protest that was unleashed took channels which brought Randolph back into formal alliance with the established organizational leadership—Negro and white.

Randolph's "Baby"

THE IMMEDIATE FORM of renewed co-operation consisted of pressures (delegations and negotiations) brought to bear on the Administration to revitalize the FEPC. Success was apparent in the issuance of a new executive order and the rescheduling of the railroad hearings.[2] The second FEPC was removed from McNutt's control and made an independent agency within the Office of Production Management. Although the language of the new order was somewhat stronger than the original, the weakness of the new FEPC was soon revealed. At the conclusion of the hearings, the operating railroads and unions blatantly refused a directive to cease their discriminatory employment practices. The cases were then certified to President Roosevelt who appointed a special mediating committee, but this functioned as a mere "pigeon hole" and no action resulted. The experience made clear the need of a statutory basis for the enforcement of FEPC decisions.

This was not the only factor leading to a growing conviction that legislative support for FEPC was crucial. A congressional committee's investigation into the authority of executive agencies subjected the FEPC to considerable harassment.[3] At the same time, the funds of the reconstituted FEPC were brought under congressional control by a measure forbidding the use of appropriations for agencies created by executive order after one year unless specifically authorized by statute.[4] Thus the hope that Congress could be by-passed, with appropriations drawn from the President's general emergency funds, was shattered. Even if there were no ambitions to establish the FEPC on a permanent basis, the retention of the wartime President's Committee would require a pressure-group strategy appropriate to influencing the Congress.

Finally, though the Normandy ("D-Day") landings were almost a year away, there was increasing apprehension that postwar problems were not far off, that wartime "boom" would collapse in peacetime "bust." Minority groups were especially vulnerable because they lacked job seniority, and the realization grew that the FEPC was only a temporary, emergency agency. Understandably, this led to a conflict of concerns between the pressures necessary to support the wartime FEPC and the desire to establish a permanent agency. But as long as the wartime FEPC fought for congressional appropriations, the National Council for a Permanent FEPC had to subordinate its efforts for legislation to lobbying for continuance of the temporary presidential agency.

It should not be assumed that Randolph was now without a following or without stature as a leader. Only by contrast with his previous rise did his decline appear so steep. He now shared the leadership but his place as a top spokesman for American Negroes was retained. Moreover, his shift from the glamorous mass action of the March to the more prosaic strategy of the National Council for a Permanent FEPC was astutely timed to save his hold on the issue.

The National Council represented a broadening of the alliance behind the drive for a permanent FEPC. However, the new organization as first constructed enabled Randolph to maintain a tight grip upon it. The Council's Washington office, opened early in 1944, was manned by people of his choosing accustomed to regarding him as "the Chief" (an informal title of respectful adulation by which Randolph is known in the BSCP). Mrs. Anna Arnold Hedgeman, who headed the staff, came directly out of the MOWM.

The official policy-making arrangements in the National Council were also conducive to maintaining Randolph's control. A wide representation of organizations drawn from minority, religious, labor and liberal groups provided a broad facade of unity and shared leadership. Nominally, even the chairmanship of the Council was shared by Randolph with a co-chairman, the Rev. Allen Knight Chalmers. But the device of limiting the size of the Executive Committee facilitated manipulation of the leadership. Though all co-operating organizations had representation on the Executive *Council* the smaller

Executive *Committee* made the practical decisions. To be sure, even the Executive Committee was considerably broader than the MOWM top levels had ever been. As an interracial organization this naturally followed, but the particular groups represented were narrowly drawn and it was not until 1946 that the NAACP, AFL, and CIO national bodies were provided membership on the Executive Committee.[5]

The pattern of organization was a distinct carryover from the MOWM. (It should be remembered that the March was still in existence, an affiliate of the National Council, and in process of hopefully preparing its National Non-Partisan Political Conference to be held in Chicago, June, 1944, on the third anniversary of the 8802 Order.) Randolph proceeded to establish local affiliates of the National Council which provided the basis for individual membership. In this way he brought with him the personal following built up over years of national touring. In many communities the MOWM simply transformed its operations into National Council activities. The core, as with the March, was the nation-wide network of BSCP Divisions, and their possessive attitude to the Council was the same as it had been to the MOWM. Randolph continued his trips through the country but, whereas previously he had organized March on Washington units, now he set up local councils for national FEPC legislation.

The organizational activity behind FEPC was now interracial—at least officially. But in the early period of the National Council's work, this was more apparent than real. There were, to be sure, many white groups affiliated with the Council, and Randolph received support and funds from white, socialist, labor leaders like David Dubinsky of the International Ladies Garment Workers Union. But the fear of Communist infiltration, and the priority white liberals assigned to maintaining wartime unity, led Randolph to emphasize work in the Negro group.

Subsequent organizational developments would find the Negro community playing a definitely subordinate role in many campaigns for state FEPC laws. Paradoxically, Randolph's National Council was attacked for overemphasis on the Negro interest in FEPC. Thus, Louis Kesselman has written:

> Especially vigorous were the charges that the Negro viewpoint was being represented to the exclusion of nearly all other minority groups and that the committee was dominated by individuals hand-picked by Randolph and loyal to his point of view. Part of the criticism came from the

Communists who were bitterly opposed to Randolph's leadership, but much of it came from non-Communist groups and individuals who were concerned lest the movement fail for lack of appeal to all minority groups.[6]

Actually, there was little pressure from non-Negroes for involvement in the National Council until the war drew to a close. The largest white minority group with a substantial interest in FEPC was the Jewish community,[7] but the forces at work in Jewish organizational programing during the war placed other issues in the forefront of their activities. Priority was naturally given to Jewish support of the fight against Hitler—a name which firmly unified Jewish interests behind the "arsenal of democracy" idea.[8]

This concern predated the war when American Jews had developed substantial programs to counteract anti-Semitic activities in the United States and abroad.[9] Huge sums were raised to succor the horde of refugees escaping the Hitler terror, and horror grew as these brought news of what they had fled.[10] The magnitude of the persecution overwhelmed the apathy of even the most disinterested American Jews. Many reacted like Max Lerner: "Before I could get educated as to the relation between myself and Jews elsewhere in the world, six million of my brothers and sisters had to die."[11] The stench from the gas chambers and human furnaces at Dachau seeped into every corner of American Jewish life.

Consequently, employment discrimination against Jews, which certainly existed,[12] did not assume paramount importance in Jewish organizational work until after Hitler was defeated. Though there were definite steps taken to cope with the problem, its relative role was far less than that assigned fair employment by Negroes.[13]

Kesselman maintains that Jews were slow to act against employment discrimination even prior to the war, ascribing this to the "sha-sha" ("hush-hush") tactics pursued by the more conservative agencies.[14] The American Jewish Committee and the Anti-Defamation League of the B'nai B'rith are generally assigned to the "quiet" category whereas the American Jewish Congress has a history of "mass activities, such as protests against the present [Nazi] German government, a boycott against German-made goods, and mass meetings."[15] The latter organization early established a Commission on Economic Discrimination (in 1930).

However, these differences, with respect to FEPC, can be overdrawn. The American Jewish Congress was a part of the Chicago Bureau on Jewish Employment Problems which explicitly restricted itself to "non-militant methods."[16] This Bureau, founded December, 1937 by the Congress and the B'nai B'rith, was later joined by the American Jewish Committee and the Jewish Labor Committee. All of these played important roles in postwar campaigns for national and state FEPC bills.

Further evidence of a conservative Jewish approach to the employment discrimination problem is found in a memorandum on FEPC issued during the war. The Coordinating Committee of Jewish Organizations Dealing With Employment Discrimination in War Industries (established in 1941) criticised the FEPC for its primary reliance on the public hearing technique.[17] It attacked "extremist sentiment" and the "forces which clamor loudly for Utopia to arrive tomorrow." Emphasis was placed upon methods "without fanfare and without publicity," reserving public hearings for situations where less aggressive tactics fail. The approach of the FEPC, it was claimed, "all too often serves to divide our citizenry—whatever the reasons therefore—rather than unite them in a common cause." Plainly the war effort was uppermost in Jewish concern at the time, and to a greater extent than in the comparable Negro organizations.

Thus, the Jewish groups were aware of the FEPC from the start (note that the establishment of the Coordinating Committee of Jewish Organizations coincided with the creation of the FEPC). A number of Jews served on the FEPC staff and Jewish organizations supplied it with cases of discrimination. But the secondary role which FEPC was assigned by Jews during the war was resented by Negroes. The *Pittsburgh Courier* caustically attacked the Jewish leadership for seeking to benefit from the FEPC without paying the price of a hard-fought pressure campaign:

The Fair Employment Practice Committee was set up to combat job discrimination against minority groups including JEWS and Negroes. Jews did not help to force the creation of this agency. And, as a matter of fact, they stood off on the sidelines to see how it was going before they began to avail themselves of its power and authority. They didn't want to go off on the deep end.

When they perceived that the FEPC might be of service to them, they swung into line. They not only asked the Committee to add impetus to its fight against discrimination of which Jews were the victims, but they insisted on bigger and better representation on the staff of the Committee. They began to demand jobs which the Committee had and some it did not have.

That is all right. They deserve the jobs. But what did they do when the Committee was recently knocked on its heels by the President's letter of July 30? [transferring FEPC under McNutt.] Did they make any move to keep the Committee in power and authority? Did they, as Negroes did, rally to the aid of the Committee?

Maybe they did, but there is not much record of it.

There are some foxy Jews. We believe that they should not be so foxy, that they should FIGHT with us if they hope to share the benefits of our fighting.[18]

The emotional pitch of this editorial, captioned "Some Jews Are Like Foxes," had marked anti-Semitic overtones. But, despite repetition of the stereotype "foxy Jews," the *Courier* disclaimed any such intent: "Intelligent, thoughtful Negro leadership deplores any evidence of anti-Semitism among the Negro masses." Moreover, they called for united effort and deplored the fact that "some Jews, as some Negroes, do not realize that we should work together for the common interest."[19] This hoped for co-operation would come about, but not until after the war.

The last official action of the wartime FEPC recommended to President Truman "that you continue to urge upon the Congress the passage of [permanent FEPC] legislation. . . ."[20] When it became clear that the wartime agency was dead, a hard-fought lobbying campaign was launched by the National Council in the Seventy-ninth Congress (1945–1946).

In the House of Representatives, the bills were "bottled-up" in the Rules Committee despite favorable action by the House Labor Committee. To get a bill to the floor for a vote, in the absence of a rule from the Rules Committee, is a most difficult task. Efforts at both a discharge petition and the Calendar Wednesday methods for by-passing the Rules Committee failed.[21]

When the Seventy-ninth Congress reconvened in January, 1946, the Randolph forces succeeded in bringing the Senate bill to the floor. This "Senate-first" strategy was assailed by "left-wing" groups who accused Randolph of inept parliamentary management for not awaiting House action.[22] But the Negro leadership, including Randolph's trade-union rival Willard Townsend, came to his defense, and the National Council kept control of the issue.[23]

Whatever the merits of the competing strategies, and competing organizational efforts to seize command of the issue, the Senate smothered the FEPC bill. Despite the fact that President Truman was on record as favoring FEPC, as was the 1944 national platform of the Republican party, it proved impossible to close debate, and the bill succumbed to a Southern filibuster (January 18–February 7, 1946).[24]

The National Council moved swiftly in a desperate effort to save the day. Technically, there was still time in the session to pass the bill in the House and to obtain cloture in the Senate. A strategy conference met in Washington (February 22–23) and plans were laid to threaten reprisals at the polls in the oncoming 1946 congressional elections.

In rapid order, Save FEPC Rallies were held in New York (Madison Square Garden) and Chicago, echoing the days of the March On Washington Movement.[25] Indeed, Randolph attempted to organize a new march under the aegis of the National Council. Nor was this mere bluster for the February 22 strategy conference:

... REPRESENTING 43 NATIONAL ORGANIZATIONS AND 28 LOCAL COUNCILS RECOMMENDED AS A MAJOR SUGGESTION SINCE POLITICAL STALEMATE SEEMS TO BE AT TOP THAT WE HAVE A MARCH ON WASHINGTON.[26]

Now that the war was over and there were definite signs of recession and fear of unemployment,[27] it would seem that conditions were favorable for renewed militancy. But the situation was quite different from the defense-emergency period. The liberal-labor and other minority groups were now active once again in the civil rights area, and FEPC was an attractive issue to feature in organizational programing. Even Randolph was not willing to conceive of a new march as an all-Negro activity.[28]

Furthermore, the "left wingers" were pressing hard to capture the issue at a time when they were no longer concerned with preserving national unity. They were vigorous in attacks on the National Council leadership, and would soon fill Madison Square Garden in a threat to march on Washington themselves. The language they now employed in their agitation is revealing of the changed situation in which the "left wing" threatened to take over the militant civil rights fight:

WHERE WERE OUR LEADERS?

. . . Were they on the firing line? No . . . respectable people don't fight. They adopt resolutions. They gabble, they fulminate, they deplore. Every time the Negro masses get a collective notion that they want to fight fire with fire . . . meet mob violence with violence. String up a white man every time a black man is sacrificed on the altar of white supremacy. Our social respectable folks have a collective conniption fit. Well, there is nothing respectable about a rope around your throat. . . .

WE WILL MARCH ON WASHINGTON[29]

Ultimately this threat failed, but the renewal of militancy by the "left wing" made it exceedingly difficult for non-Communist reform groups to adopt radical tactics for fear of losing organizational control. The Communists had two major advantages when such methods were used: (1) They were highly disciplined and would prolong meetings until their hard core remained after the less dedicated "masses" departed. (2) The emotional, agitational level necessary for enthusiastic mass support is not easily regulated. All negotiated agreements, however satisfactory as reform accomplishments, are vulnerable to charges of "cowardice" or "unprincipled compromise." Thus, mass-action organizational efforts during the Thirties and Forties were feared by reformers even when they may have provided effective instruments for the attainment of their goals.

When the original March on Washington was endorsed, the same danger had existed—up to the entry of the Soviet Union into the war. However, the desperate state of Negro morale then prodded the leadership into what was recognized as a risky course. Now, the morale situation was not nearly so pressing, nor were Negroes without white allies. These allies, however, (particularly the CIO) finally rejected the march strategy, and the plans were dropped in favor of electoral reprisals against anti-FEPC congressmen.[30]

Despite a successful Democratic party primary fight against Missouri Congressman Roger C. Slaughter, who had cast a crucial vote in the Rules Committee blocking floor action on FEPC,[31] the results of the 1946 elections were very disappointing. Randolph regarded the composition of the new Eightieth Congress (1947–1948) as proof that a period of reaction had set in and as a typical characteristic of postwar times. His activities now reflected a loss of confidence in the feasibility of legislative-lobbying methods for achieving substantial civil rights gains.

In 1944, Randolph had resisted great pressure from friends and politicians who sought him as candidate for the new Congressional district which would give Harlem its first Negro congressman.[32] Similarly, he had then refused to endorse any presidential candidate "on account of the fact that I am connected with a movement which is sponsoring Bills in the House and Senate for a Permanent Committee on Fair Employment Practice which has bi-partisan support. . . ."[33]

Now, in 1946, Randolph accepted the chairmanship of the National Educational Committee for a New Party formed by many ex-socialists, socialists and other non-Communist liberals (e.g., Walter Reuther, Norman Thomas, John Dewey and David Dubinsky).[34] This was linked, too, with the pre-"Fair Deal" Truman who, it seemed, had yielded to the prevailing "spirit of reaction." The *New York Times* reported, Randolph "denounces Truman emergency labor legislation proposals; urges formation of new political party."[35] In 1948, Randolph publicly endorsed Norman Thomas for president.[36]

Actually, Truman had successfully placated the general Negro community with a strong speech to the NAACP and the Committee on Civil Rights' forthright report of 1947.[37] He achieved even greater popularity among Negroes as a result of the 1948 Democratic party national convention fight over civil rights which resulted in the Dixiecrat exodus.[38] But Randolph, like many others, was convinced Truman could not possibly win the election; liberals might just as well go down to defeat with principled minor parties.

Plainly, 1948 was a confusing year for reform politics, and for a time it seemed that the traditional confines of the two-party system were breached. Truman, of course, succeeded in a classic upset against seemingly insurmountable odds, which included the opposition of Henry Wallace running on the Progressive party ticket and with the support of the Communists. The Wallace movement helped make the election year an important turning point in liberal-labor politics; a widespread campaign against Communist organizational infiltration was spurred in reaction to this highwater mark of "left-wing" influence.

The NAACP, Urban League, American Jewish Congress, CIO, and many other groups "cleaned house" with increased vigor as the "Spirit of Teheran" froze in the "Cold War."[39]

Sharing the Top

MEANWHILE, following the 1946 filibuster and the general malaise which engulfed liberals after the congressional elections of that year, the National Council for a Permanent FEPC appeared bankrupt. This condition was more than a figure of speech as the organization was heavily in debt to individuals who had loaned money for the unsuccessful campaign, to staff for back-pay, and to printers with unpaid bills for propaganda materials.

Matters were made even worse by a rift which developed between Mrs. Hedgeman (the Executive Secretary) and Randolph. Mrs. Hedgeman resigned in a public statement attacking the National Council leadership when almost the entire staff was discharged as an economy move.[40] Recriminatory exchanges produced a minor scandal, and it seemed to mark the end of the National Council. Such was the situation described by Mrs. Hedgeman's successor, Elmer Henderson:

> After the bitter filibuster and defeat of the bill in the 79th Congress interest in the measure took a sharp decline and disillusionment and discouragement overcame our supporters. A great amount of confusion was created in the mind of the general public after the sudden resignation of the former executive secretary and the recriminations which followed. This confusion has never been cleared up and both Mr. Manly and I have been confronted with it constantly. For nearly a year there was no activity and no contact at all between our Washington office and the field. During that period many people believed the issue dead and the National Council disbanded.[41]

This was addressed to Roy Wilkins not in his NAACP capacity but as chairman (since 1946) of the Executive Committee of the National Council. Shortly before Mrs. Hedgeman's resignation, the National Council had ceased to be entirely Randolph's "baby." He continued as co-chairman, with the Rev. Allen Knight Chalmers, as before; but the Council's organizational base was now greatly broadened by sharing the top.

Previously, the NAACP (and the Urban League) had a rather nominal affiliation with the Council. Walter White could not move against Randolph in an open maneuver because he personified the issue in the Negro community; also, the "left-wing" problem forced a measure of unity among the staunchly anti-Communist leaders.

They defended Randolph on the Senate-first strategy and rejected a united front with Congressman Marcantonio's followers. But, beneath the surface, there was friction.[42]

A complex of factors were involved: the rupture over the March, lingering resentments from the 1942 NAACP convention where Randolph "stole the show," disagreement over priorities for issues—the NAACP was closely identified with competing issues such as anti-poll tax and anti-lynching bills—and general organizational rivalry for funds and the loyalty of followers.

After the war, the FEPC issue (despite Walter White's reluctance) was given top priority by organizations in the civil rights field.[43] This decision grew out of the need to concentrate pressures in the Congress on one bill. Although Jewish organizations now worked closely with Negro groups,[44] the Jewish defense agencies could collaborate best on programs directly connected with Jewish problems. FEPC as an issue was important to a number of groups: it satisfied the Negro militants' emphasis on the laboring masses and their neo-Marxian economic interpretation of politics; it satisfied the Negro conservatives operating in the puritanical Booker T. Washington tradition which glorified hard work and learning a trade as the path to racial advancement; and it satisfied the programatic needs of the Jewish defense agencies because the importance of employment discrimination against Jews was increased by the relative diminution of anti-Semitic activities of the Coughlin variety in the postwar period.[45]

The Jewish agencies, after the war, made substantial financial contributions to the National Council, testified at legislative hearings, provided propaganda materials and loaned the time of competent personnel. Following the post-filibuster reorganization of the Council, Arnold Aronson, representing the National Community Relations Advisory Council (NCRAC), became secretary of the executive committee.[46] He played a leading role along with Roy Wilkins from that time on. Randolph remained a key figure, to be sure, but Wilkins and Aronson assumed much of the active administrative direction of the Council and, thereby, influenced policy and strategy greatly. Under the skilled guidance of these experienced staff-men, a very efficient operation was made possible.

Wilkins and Aronson seem quite different from the "up-through-the-ranks" leadership of the BSCP and the similar "idealists" attracted

to Randolph's various movements, such as the March.[47] The accession
of these professionals reflected a change in the kind of organizational
leadership which was taking over the fair employment issue.

Agitational types, dominant in the March, had continued with
Randolph to control the National Council thus keeping possession of
the FEPC "ball." Their failure in the Seventy-ninth Congress, though
suffered in collaboration with the staffs of other organizations, could
eventuate in either outright seizure of the issue by others or co-
optation of competing leaders into commanding roles. Though the
NAACP did toy with the former strategy, it was not a real possibility.[48] No single organization could monopolize the issue at that stage,
a federative effort was inescapable. Given Randolph's pessimism over
what he regarded as the historically ordained postwar reaction, and
the deep financial indebtedness of the Council, the latter course was
readily accepted by all sides.

FEPC could not become the prime symbol of the civil rights fight
(prior to the Supreme Court's school desegregation decrees) without
attracting those organizations with long-established interests at stake.
Nor could Randolph succeed in a national lobbying operation without
engineering clear signs of broad and intense public support. In the
absence of direct and spontaneous grass-roots pressures—as in the
hey-day of the March movement—the wielding of organizational en-
dorsements and activity must symbolize the community of interests
involved. These organizations in turn needed the issue for the programs (and annual reports) which justify their existence; and Randolph needed them for the influence they represented, the talented
professionals they possessed and the funds they could supply.

The National Council, following the post-filibuster (1946) reorganization, was widely representative of all non-Communist groups
interested in FEPC, at the policy-making top as well as in affiliations
and supporting activities. Liberal, labor, church and minority groups
rallied to support FEPC bills introduced into Congress over the next
several years. Despite a succession of vigorous efforts, however, they
were without major political success.

The financial deficit with which the reorganized Council began
was never entirely overcome. Elmer Henderson, the Council's re-
placement for Mrs. Hedgeman, had to go on a *per diem* basis after
little more than a year and later, reluctantly, resigned for a better
position. But the political situation was a greater factor in this failure

than the shortage of funds which it helped produce. As Henderson wrote, "With the election of a Republican Congress in 1946 and its record in the First Session, many formerly active workers have expressed the belief that there is absolutely no chance for passage."[49] This was regarded as confirmed during the subsequent session of the Eightieth Congress. "Although committed to FEPC by their platform of 1944, Republican leaders evinced little interest in the issue and made no effort to bring it out of committee and before Congress."[50]

The National Council was utterly unsuccessful during the Eightieth Congress; but Randolph, through another bold activity reminiscent of the March, helped pressure two important new executive orders from the President.[51] A *New York Times* front-page headline announced: "TRUMAN ORDERS END OF BIAS IN FORCES AND FEDERAL JOBS."[52] This climaxed the organization by Randolph and Grant Reynolds of a civil disobedience campaign directed primarily at segregation in the military services.[53]

Randolph had informed a Congressional committee, "I personally pledge myself to openly counsel, aid and abet youth, both white and Negro . . . in an organized refusal to register and be drafted."[54] Senator Wayne Morse cautioned him, "It may well lead to indictments for treason and very serious repercussions."[55] Randolph persisted—shortly thereafter he mounted a "soapbox" outside the March Community Bookstore, former headquarters of the MOWM, to specifically urge draft-eligible men in his audience not to register with their draft boards and to refuse induction. "He announced he was prepared to 'oppose a Jim Crow Army until I rot in jail.' "[56]

Efforts to isolate Randolph from the rest of the Negro leadership were largely unsuccessful. Though the NAACP could not officially endorse his activity and declared themselves "dubious about this method," they avoided outright condemnation.[57] Indeed the effort was greatly aided when the NAACP announced the results of its poll of draft-eligible Negro students which "found . . . that 71 percent were sympathetic with the A. Philip Randolph-Grant Reynolds civil disobedience campaign. . . ."[58]

The Urban League executive, Lester Granger, played a similar role. He was spokesman for a group of prominent Negroes who met with the Secretary of Defense, James V. Forrestal, and representatives of the military branches. The Granger statement announced, "The group agreed that no one wanted to continue in an advisory capacity on the basis of continued segregation in the armed services."[59] This point of view—of indirect support of Randolph's campaign—predominated over outright disassociation such as that offered the investigating Senate committee by a Negro member of the Massachusetts FEPC. Even this was hedged by a reference to Negro loyalty "in another war. . . ."[60] No one asked the witness, Mr. Elwood S. Mc-Kenney, concerning Negro behavior in peacetime.

President Truman was now in a position much like that of his predecessor when he too confronted Randolph in the White House. The difference was that Truman was in the midst of a difficult presidential election campaign and that civil rights was an important part of his bid to northern urban voters.

As chairman of the newly created League for Non-Violent Civil Disobedience Against Military Segregation, Randolph threatened organized non-compliance with the military draft "unless President Truman issues an executive order against segregation."[61] But FEPC was closely connected with this effort for Randolph argued that military service is a species of Federal employment. He asked a Senate committee at a public hearing:

. . . how could any permanent Fair Employment Practices Commission dare to criticise job discrimination in private industry if the Federal Government itself were simultaneously discriminating against Negro youth in military installations all over the world?[62]

Thus, the two executive orders reflected the dual demands uppermost in Negro protest activities ever since the defense emergency of pre-World War II days. Randolph was again able to demonstrate the power of dramatic mass-action methods, when directed against a President. The Congress, however, was less vulnerable to such strategies. Reformers seeking legislation are necessarily ensnared in lobbying operations, parliamentary log-rollings and procedural mazes which make it difficult to pinpoint responsibility and vitiate threats of electoral reprisal.[63]

Mobilization and Frustration

THE SURPRISING RESULTS of the 1948 election brought Harry Truman back to the White House and a Democratic majority back to Capitol Hill. With them came the high hopes of the National Council leaders (including Randolph) who regarded the situation as now ripe for enactment of FEPC. But delaying tactics in both Houses kept the bills from floor action and the 1949 session passed without significant progress. This stalemate was intolerable to the proponents who viewed the election as a mandate for civil rights.

. A vigorous show of strength was called for by the NAACP which took the initiative in forming a "National Emergency Civil Rights Mobilization." Organizational delegations from all over the country were called upon to descend on Washington (January 15–17, 1950) to greet the reconvening Congress. This *ad hoc* organization was headed by Roy Wilkins, NAACP, as chairman; Arnold Aronson, NCRAC, secretary; and Herbert M. Levy, American Civil Liberties Union (ACLU), assistant secretary. The effort, theoretically, was broader than FEPC and, thus, broader than the National Council. Actually, all other items were subordinated to the FEPC issue.

The directors of the Council and of the Mobilization overlapped, but the public leadership of Wilkins made the NAACP's role more recognizable and they deservedly received credit for the mobilization's success. It seems plain that the separate effort was also welcomed by the NAACP as a means to move Randolph from his monopolization of the FEPC limelight.

Randolph's reaction to all this was what might be expected; reserved in public and, we may conjecture, rather less reservedly negative in private. The *Black Worker* reported:

The National Council for a Permanent FEPC is to receive the cooperation, in the present session of Congress, of the Civil Rights Mobilization Committee. The Mobilization's steering committee is functioning principally as a lobbying group among the various senators and representatives.

Although, Pres. Randolph, as Co-Chairman of the National Council for a Permanent FEPC, sees no need for another co-ordinating organization working principally for a Federal FEPC, he is nevertheless willing to give his wholehearted cooperation to the Mobilization groups if such an effort will hasten the federal anti-discrimination law.[64]

As a mobilization, the effort was a great success. There were 4,218 "regularly accredited delegates . . . from 33 states."[65] The organizers claimed, "All observers, including veteran newspaper correspondents, agreed that the Mobilization was the greatest mass lobby in point of numbers and geographical dispersion that had ever come to Washington on behalf of any legislation."[66] Delegations swarmed over the Capitol buttonholing congressmen, and the leaders were promised, at a White House conference with the President, "the FEP would be brought to a vote 'if it takes all summer.' "[67]

But if FEPC was to be put across, the crucial test of the Mobilization would be its ability to break the conservative Republican-Dixiecrat alliance.[68] This required constant pressure on the bloc of liberal Republicans and northern Democrats, many of whom were more ardent before their urban, minority-group constituents than in behind-the-scenes maneuvers. A sign of the failure to crack this coalition appeared in the open hostility of the Republican leadership to the Mobilization.

When delegations visited Congressman Joe Martin . . . Massachusetts (Minority Leader) and Congressman Leslie Arends . . . Illinois (Minority Whip), and sought their aid for FEPC, each of them replied: *'What are you coming to us for? Why don't you go to your friends? You elected the Democrats. Why are you asking us for help?'*[69]

At first, it appeared that this was just bluster and that the huge civil rights lobby of 1950 had succeeded in pressuring enough congressmen to have its way. On January 20, an effort by Congressman Eugene E. Cox (D.-Ga.), to restore the power of the Rules Committee to "bottle up" legislation indefinitely, was defeated. (In 1949, a "twenty-one day rule" had been enacted limiting the period of time the Rules Committee could keep a bill from the floor.) This seemed a crucial test and the civil rights proponents were jubilant.[70]

However, Speaker Sam Rayburn (D.-Tex.) refused to grant the floor to the chairman of the committee ready to report favorably on FEPC, so the same situation prevailed. Discharge petitions failed again, but this time the "Calendar Wednesday" technique succeeded in bringing the measure to a vote (February 22, 1950).

The "House-First" strategy was, at last, given a chance, but whatever feelings lingered that Randolph had erred in 1946 for not following a similar course were soon dispelled. The opposition now carried the day with a flanking assault on the heart of the fair employment bill. A substitute amendment was proposed by Congressman Samuel McConnell (R.-Pa.) stripping the measure of all enforcement powers and was carried by a vote of 222 to 178. This was the crucial test, with opponents voting for the amendment and proponents against.

Though the "amended" bill was now passed, the proponents termed it "a far cry from H.R. 4453 as originally introduced and . . . *unsatisfactory* to all supporters of effective FEPC legislation."[71] They had voted for the weak bill on final passage, however, hoping that it would enable them to keep the issue alive and "force" the Senate to act. But the situation again illustrated the complexity of electoral mandates, as opponents in somewhat vulnerable situations could point to their record vote "for" FEPC. The proponents, of course, sought to make clear that "the friends of FEPC are the 178 Congressmen who opposed adoption of the McConnell amendment."[72]

Shortly thereafter, on March 8, 1950, the independent existence of the NAACP-led Mobilization was ended in a merger with the National Council. A final report explained:

> Since the Mobilization was not conceived as a permanent organization, conferences were held with the executive committee of the National Council for a Permanent FEPC, the pioneer organization behind this legislation. It was agreed that the National Mobilization would cooperate with it in a united effort to secure enactment of FEPC in this Congress. This involves practically no change, since the organizations sponsoring the Mobilization have been the mainstays of the National Council. A new letterhead has been issued: 'National Council for a Permanent FEPC in cooperation with the National Emergency Civil Rights Mobilization'. . . .[73]

There was no explanation of why the separation had been maintained for two and one-half months following the Washington mobilization. The question arises whether the Mobilization leadership would have returned to the National Council had it been credited with passage of an effective FEPC bill in the House. It is likely that a successful new organization would have found little reason to reunite with the unsuccessful "pioneer organization" if it sought to retain full public credit for its victory.

The Wilkins-Aronson leadership put on a better lobbying show than had the Randolph-Hedgeman group. At the same time, whatever organizational differences there were had far less to do with success or failure than the obstinate political hurdles institutionalized in the American legislative system. The pathway between electoral mandates and public policy is a labyrinth of obfuscating procedures blocked by scattered and dimly identified wielders of great power. To be sure, these can be made to yield eventually to a clear and actively organized majority. But few matters are ever the subject of widespread concern, and organizational efforts usually take place in an arena of general apathy. The problem of how to pressure important civil rights legislation through the American Congress continues to plague its advocates.

Of course there was no difficulty in knowing who the *staunchest* opponents in the Senate were, when the joint National Council-Civil Rights Mobilization lobbyists turned to the upper chamber. The big problem there would be how to close off debate after free speech degenerated into all-out filibuster. But the parliamentary situation still provided a murky screen behind which covert opposition to FEPC could operate effectively. "Leaders of the Democratic party, boasting a majority in the Senate, were bold and vigorous in their public affirmations of support for FEPC, but singularly weak, hesitant, and inactive on the Senate floor."[74]

In charge was Senator Scott Lucas (D.-Ill.), the majority leader, nominally a firm advocate of FEPC. At the end of the first session (October 19, 1949), he had promised that it would reach the action stage immediately after Congress reconvened. During the second session, he issued periodic promises that it would be taken up at a succession of later points. At last he declared it would be wise to wait for House action first; but when the House acted, he and the President put it off so that the expected filibuster would not wreck the appropriations for the European Recovery Program.

Lucas assured the proponent lobbyists that the bill would soon be acted on and declared:

It is not a question of just when F.E.P.C. will be taken to a test, but of the enthusiasm and determination with which a filibuster will be fought when it goes to the floor. A determined fight will be waged—and I mean 'determined.'[75]

But the "filibuster" which followed was a sham. The bill was moved on May 8, put to one side for two days while another matter was debated, then was returned to for a leisurely consideration of the technical motion that the bill should be the next order of business before the Senate. The *New York Times* reported:

When Senator Scott W. Lucas of Illinois, Majority Leader, moved ten days ago that the bill be called up, Washington expected one of the toughest, most gruelling fillibusters in history to be started by the Southerners.

Developments have not borne this prediction out. Instead of all-night sessions with hoarse and weary Southern Senators drawing crowded galleries, the Senate has quit before dinner time.[76]

Two separate efforts were made to invoke cloture but each fell short of the constitutional two-thirds (sixty-four favorable votes) required by Senate rules.[77] Actually, cloture would have failed even if only two-thirds of those present and voting were the rule for ending a filibuster.

Table 3—Two Senate Votes on Cloture, Eighty-First Congress*

| | | May 19, 1950 | | | July 12, 1950 | |
	Total	Yea	Nay	Not Voting	Yea	Nay	Not Voting
Total	96	52	32	12	55	33	8
Republicans	42	33	6	3	33	6	3
All Democrats	54	19	26	9	22	27	5
"Northern"† Dem's.	32	19	6	7	22	6	4
"Southern"‡ Dem's.	22	..	20	2	..	21	1

* Source: roll calls in *Congressional Record*, Vol. 96, Part 6, 7299–7300; and Vol. 96, Part 8, 9981–9982.

† "Northern" includes all non-southern senators.

‡ "The South" includes Alabama, Arkansas, Florida, Georgia, Louisiana, Mississippi, North Carolina, South Carolina, Tennessee, Texas, and Virginia.

"Who killed Cock Robin?" Could either of the major political parties be saddled with the responsibility?

After the first cloture vote (May 19, 1950), *Crisis* declared flatly: "DEMOCRATS FAIL FEPC." And indeed, in the 1950 Senate, Republicans had a better record, from the FEPC proponents' viewpoint, than had the Democrats[79] (see Table 3).

It was understood that another cloture effort would be made later in that session, and the *Crisis* editorial was plainly directed at urging the Democratic leadership on to stronger effort.[80] They were particularly perturbed over the number of absentees (non-voting under the circumstances was equivalent to a negative vote), several being from outside the South. The statistical assessment of blame by *Crisis* was more evenly bipartisan, but with twelve votes providing the margin of defeat, the Democrats showed up poorly:

So neither the Republicans nor the Northern Democrats can blame the Dixiecrats. Cloture on FEPC was blocked by northern and western senators of both parties, nine Republicans and twelve [actually thirteen] Democrats.[81]

Crisis did not editorialize on the second cloture vote (July 12) but their earlier pressure did stimulate the Democrats to a somewhat better effort (Table 3). The net Republican vote for cloture remained the same (despite individual changes) while the Democrats accounted for the three additional votes. If we paraphrase the *Crisis* editorial assessing the first cloture vote, there were now sufficient Democratic votes outside the Solid South for cloture to have succeeded had all Republicans joined in the effort. But this is an involved and esoteric argument offering little solace to ardent Democrats seeking the political support of the Negro and other minority-groups. Though there were now twenty-two Democrats for cloture, the simple story told by *Crisis* assigning party responsibility for the first cloture vote still applied:

> The Republicans produced 33 votes for cloture on the FEPC bill. They should have—and could have—done better, but they did put the Democrats in the shade. The man on the street cares little about the elaborate excuses that will be offered. As far as he is concerned, the vote on the FEPC proposition was 33 Republicans as against 19 [22 on the second attempt] Democrats. In his book the Republicans are far ahead in proving their friendship for FEPC.[82]

From the minority-group viewpoint, as a party the Republicans showed up better than the Democrats—in the Senate.[83] What of the House? Here the crucial test was the vote on the amendment introduced by Congressman McConnell substituting a "voluntary" FEPC for the original bill introduced by Congressman Powell. Apart from the fact that McConnell was a leading Republican and that the Republican House Minority Leader supported the amendment, the voting record (Table 4) reveals what was commonly

Table 4—House Vote, February 22, 1950, on McConnell Substitute Amendment, Eighty-First Congress*

	Total	Yea	Nay	Not Voting
Total	431†	222	178	31
Republicans	170	104	49	17
All Democrats	260	118	128	14
"Northern"‡ Dem's.	159	23	128	8
"Southern" Dem's.	101	95	...	6
American Labor	1	...	1	..

* Source: roll call in *Congressional Record*, Vol. 96, part 2, 2253–2254.
† Vacancies account for this discrepancy from the full membership of the House.
‡ "Northern" includes all non-Southern Democrats.

understood; most Republicans opposed FEPC with enforcement powers and maintained that their proposed "FEPC" satisfied the party's platform pledging enactment of FEPC legislation.[84] This the minority-group leaders would not accept, and they advised their followers to vote against all congressmen supporting the McConnell substitute.[85]

On the other hand, the Democratic Speaker of the House had hindered the FEPC effort,[86] and the Democrats constituted a majority of the House. Even so, only 49 Republicans voted against the McConnell amendment compared with 128 Democrats. The 118 Democrats voting for the substitute included 23 from outside the South who joined 104 Republicans to emasculate the proponents' bill.

Where was party responsibility to be placed? President Truman, publicly most ardent for FEPC, had included it in his State of the Union Message convening the second session, and had been elected despite the 1948 crack in the Solid South over the civil rights fight. There were questions raised concerning the vigor of his efforts behind the scenes, but that situation was too obscure to be utilized for effective campaign propaganda.

Arthur Krock has written:

Very seldom do informed observers agree with Representative Marcantonio, yet a good many did when he remarked . . . 'It is obvious to everyone . . . that everybody wants civil rights as an issue but not as a law, and that goes for Harry Truman, the Democratic party, and the Republican party.'[87]

The charge that our political system makes it extremely difficult to assess party responsibility was amply borne out in the divisions over FEPC in the Eighty-first Congress.[88]

Following the second and final defeat in the Senate, Aronson appraised the situation with respect to National Council hopes for electoral reprisals and a renewed campaign in the next Congress:

In analysing the cloture vote, he [Aronson] pointed out that six Republicans . . . and six non-Southern Democrats . . . had voted against cloture on both tests. Only four of these men . . . are up for reelection this year and all come from the states which are removed from centers of minority group population and pressure. Even assuming that every other member of the Senate could be prevailed upon to be present and to vote favorably, he said, the thirty-three recorded negative votes supplemented by the vote of Senator-elect Smathers, would be more than sufficient to prevent cloture. Accordingly, Mr. Aronson concluded, prospects for civil rights legislation in the 82nd Congress appeared dim under the existing cloture rule.[89]

The logical deduction from this was that the Senate rules had to be changed, and a campaign was developed around that issue. In 1952, the National Council was again bypassed for a "Leadership Conference On Civil Rights" with the major slogan, "ABOLISH RULE 22 IN '52."[90] This campaign was without success—indeed the anti-civil rights attack on the "twenty-one day rule" in the House, which had been beaten down in the Eighty-first Congress, was now triumphant and the power of the Rules Committee was restored.[91]

Though the issue of FEPC nominally has been kept alive in the Congress, the only bill to leave committee in either House, from the 1950 defeat through 1958, was on July 3, 1952, reported out with no possibility for action, only three days before adjournment. Perhaps the most significant thing about this Senate bill was the deliberate change in its title to avoid the initials "FEPC."[92] By now, other civil rights issues dominated the activities of minority-group leaders; housing and educational discrimination problems had moved to the forefront.[93]

FEPC was not a dead issue but it was superseded by other concerns in a time of full employment and congressional stalemate. Discrimination was (and remains) substantial with respect to the *quality* of jobs open to minority workers. But, to the "man-in-the-street," job discrimination has meant simply a total refusal to hire any minority persons.[94] It was the fear of a postwar depression and mass unemployment of minority workers which had raised the issue to the apex of the civil rights battle. Thus, though Negroes and other minority groups were still victims of job discrimination, the "bread-and-butter" urgency of the issue was greatly diluted.

State FEPC and Professional Leadership

THOUGH THE National Council for a Permanent FEPC and the National Emergency Civil Rights Mobilization have faded from existence, the issue continues high on the list of favored civil rights demands.

Efforts to enact FEPC legislation have continued on the state level where proponents have scored a series of successes ever since New York led the way in 1945. There are now (January, 1958) thirteen states with enforceable FEPC statutes.[95] Half of these victories were obtained during the period of greatest agitation for a permanent Federal FEPC (1945-1950). By 1949, seven of the states had enacted FEPC with "teeth."

When the National Council effort collapsed in the 1946 filibuster, and the congressional elections which followed made the situation seem hopeless, the proponents registered their strength locally where it still counted. But this belief that the national fight was doomed acted as a kind of "self-confirming hypothesis," and the local activities drained energies away from the national organization. Victorious state groups, by their very successes, found the issue less urgent. Defeated groups became all the more pessimistic. Other local programs crowded the organizational budgets and the man-hours available to the national campaigns.

Thus, Elmer Henderson (National Council Executive Secretary) informed Roy Wilkins in 1948:

In a number of states in the North and West, our local supporters turned their attention to state bills. In states where they were successful, they tended to feel their objectives achieved. In states where they lost they became further disillusioned and discouraged. . . . One significant but in a way important development for us has been the creation of so-called permanent organizations as an outgrowth of the FEPC fights in many areas. These organizations have paid professional leadership and their own budgets and fund-raising problems.[96]

Of course, the 1950 Mobilization could not have been so successful in the number of delegations which descended on Washington had the state groups not returned, for a time, to the national issue. But the consequence of that failure repeated the experience of 1946.

Even during the height of the Mobilization, the state organizations were scarcely appendages of the National Council Mobilization leadership. The character of the local FEPC organizations had changed considerably from the initial period of National Council control. They now co-operated as entirely independent groups rather than as mere branches of the Council.

Randolph, as the pioneer FEPC agitator, dominated the national issue through most of 1946 and shared, rather than lost complete control thereafter. The necessarily centralized handling of a lobbying campaign at the Washington level made it difficult for rival leaders to capture the issue. As noted, this would have required the public establishment of an obviously competing organization.

But on the local level the bulk of Randolph's grass-roots following evaporated with the demise of the March. At first (1944-1945) many of the state affiliates of the National Council were dominated by the BSCP and remaining MOWM activists, but whatever strength they retained was restricted to the Negro community. Indeed, the heritage of the March was such that they were distrustful of whites and wary of Communist infiltration. The consequent charge that Randolph over emphasized the Negro interest in FEPC will be recalled.[97] When he turned his attention to other matters during the Eightieth Congress, Randolph's local contacts were broken and other groups carried the issue into the State legislatures.

Generalizing about a large number of differently situated and only loosely connected organizations while retaining fidelity to the facts is a difficult business. State FEPC proponent groups varied from place to place over the country. There were important differences in the demographic features of their locales; for example: the importance of a Spanish-speaking population in Colorado and New Mexico contrasted with the Midwest. NAACP branches were more vigorous in Detroit than in Chicago where the Negro community has been extremely difficult to organize effectively. The Jewish population and, therefore, its organizations are not uniformly distributed. These organizations also vary in local strength, so that in Massachusetts the American Jewish Congress was more important than in Illinois, where the Anti-Defamation League and the other Jewish agencies predominated. Furthermore, some of these factors differed at particular periods during the decade of local FEPC activity.[98]

Despite these and other important differences, as a whole the state organizations around the 1946 period took on an increasingly professional character in their operations. That is, the active leadership of many of the state campaigns was increasingly placed in the hands of men who practiced human relations work as a career. This had been noted by Elmer Henderson in his 1948 analysis. The significance of this is not simply that a more efficient management of the state campaigns ensued, though that occurred. This efficiency also took place on the national level with the bringing of professional personnel like

Wilkins, Aronson and Maslow into top National Council posts after 1946.

In the states the pre-existent organizations which took over the FEPC issue had operated for years with large professional staffs. To be sure, these men were "under orders" as employees of the "lay" boards of directors of their organizations. Many of these "lay" leaders were also personally active in the state FEPC campaigns on decision-making levels. Nor is it possible for the professionals to operate contrary to the explicit wishes of their boards. But the day-to-day operations of these campaigns were performed by the professionals who, unavoidably, made much of the actual determination of policy and strategy.[99]

The increasing role of the professionals is not introduced here to criticize the later leadership behind the FEPC issue with labels of "bureaucracy" or undemocratic procedures. On the contrary, they have devoted themselves with great energy to the task of educating and activating the members of their organizations and the general community. Their work is a positive contribution to the future of practical democracy if American ideals are to be more than mere shibboleths. Randolph's leadership of the March on Washington Movement was certainly not more democratic; as has been indicated previously, it was less formalized and, therefore, more unrestricted. But its mass movement orientation was substantially different, and professionalization is an important item in that difference.

Community intergroup-relations programs have followed the history of social welfare and charity work in this respect. The professional today is an accepted and crucial leader in the operations of institutionalized "social work." But this was not always the case; "Social casework . . . has had a long general but a short professional history."[100] It was inevitable that as communities and groups faced up to the problems of intergroup relations—race riots, slum ghettos and unequal economic opportunity—that trained men would be called on to do a full-time job. The FEPC issue picked up some of these men early in its development when "Metropolitan Councils on Fair Employment Practice" were created in a number of cities. These paralleled the work, locally, of the President's national FEPC which also hired such professionals. In 1946, the National Association of Intergroup Relations Officials (NAIRO) was formed in explicit recognition of this trend. And, as noted, many of the major groups

behind the state FEPC campaigns were organizations which operated on a large-scale professional basis long before the FEPC issue.

These organized groups are among the institutionalized channels
through which community action on minority-group problems ordinarily flows. They are generally limited in their political activities
because of their dependence on funds from sources which demand de-
ductibility under the internal revenue laws. This tax-exemption problem is a serious obstacle to the organization of effective electoral
reprisals. The problem has increased with time and complicates the
political efforts of civil rights advocates on a number of issues. It
shapes the kinds of activities through which the affected organizations
may pursue their objectives, tending to make it safer to conduct
"educational" rather than forceful political campaigns.[101]

As the established organizations whose lay boards are composed
of prominent community leaders they are necessarily conservative in
their methods. Their dominant concern is practicality. A test of
strategy and goals ordinarily leads to an emphasis upon maintaining
rapport with established wielders of power, i.e., "the people who
count." But within the margins of activity which such conditions
allow, they carry considerable influence and often can be more effective than the more militant leadership.

Consequently, they do not tend to originate new issues through
such bold ventures as the March which led to the FEPC, or the later
Truman orders following Randolph's civil disobedience campaign of
1948. The FEPC issue was created when Negro morale was in a
critical situation. The established Negro leadership followed Randolph with reluctance and with concern for the channels of influence
which they had so carefully constructed over the years, i.e., relations
with the White House and other high governmental and non-govern-
mental officials and leaders. After President Roosevelt established the
first FEPC, the issue gradually passed through the "gateway"[102] of
popular acceptance (among the public sympathetic to civil rights
goals) and became an increasingly important part of the programing
of human relations organizations. Indeed it was a sign that the issue
had "arrived" when the "professionals" took over. That leadership
continues the campaigns for FEPC in the states yet to be won and
spurs existing fair employment practice commissions on to more
effective enforcement.

Again the White House

CAMPAIGNS FOR CONGRESSIONAL enactment of FEPC became dormant because of what was described as late as 1956 to be "an informal coalition of Southern Democrats and conservative Republicans [which has] continued to be the principal roadblock to any civil rights legislation."[103] However, the national issue continued on the presidential level where it first arose.

The political processes through which the President is selected make him more vulnerable to civil rights balance-of-power pressures than the Congress. The latter body contains representatives of varied constituencies many of which are beyond the reach of FEPC advocates. To win New York or Illinois without the support of organized minority groups is difficult enough to make presidential candidates very sensitive to those interests. This is repeated in a number of northern and western states. Of course, the Senators from those states face similar pressures, but their influence is diluted by Senators otherwise situated—most obviously, but not all, from the South. This dilution is further watered down by the apportionment of constituencies in both Houses in a manner favorable to the less populated states.[104]

State FEPC campaigns suffer a similar handicap. A state legislator from Chicago's Negro Southside is obviously vulnerable to FEPC pressures—even if that community is but little organized on the issue. An Illinois governor is less vulnerable, but regardless of party he can be counted upon for at least public support of Negro demands. He can win only with great difficulty if opposed by the bulk of urban voters. With minor exceptions, it is the southern "downstate" districts which counterbalance the strength of the Cook County representatives in the Illinois state legislature. The disproportionate representation provided these non-metropolitan areas is the problem yet to be overcome in Illinois and several other states with substantial, but concentrated, minority-group populations. [105]

The possibility that the Negro vote might return to the Republican party played a tempting part in the campaign to re-elect President Eisenhower. Similarly, the record of Adlai Stevenson as Governor of Illinois during two state FEPC campaigns was important in his appeals to minority voters.[106] The weight assigned to civil rights by presidential hopefuls is a continuing and increasing process.

But no President ever had more reason to appreciate the power of minority voters than did Harry S. Truman.[107] His executive order establishing a Fair Employment Board in the Civil Service Commission in 1948 reflected the pressure of A. Philip Randolph's civil disobedience campaign. It was issued on July 2, and was more than remotely connected with the 1948 election campaign. The order affected only government employment which was, technically, already covered by a provision of the Ramspeck Act of 1940.[108] But the Truman Board provided something of an enforcement mechanism while the Ramspeck Act amounted to nothing more than a verbal declaration.

The outbreak of the Korean war in 1950 raised the issue of a more far reaching executive order once again. The proponents sought to convince the President that the new emergency paralleled that of 1941 during which Roosevelt had established the first FEPC. Arnold Aronson reported:

> On July 16, 1950, the National Council for a Permanent FEPC, through its co-chairman, A. Philip Randolph, wired the president urging that he 'issue an Executive Order similar to President Roosevelt's 8802 . . . as an integral factor in mobilization of manpower against North Korean Communist aggression.'[109]

On February 2, 1951, Truman issued Executive Order 10210 authorizing the Secretaries of the Defense and Commerce departments to require and enforce nondiscrimination clauses in government contracts. But the proponents were dissatisfied and continued their pressure. Opponents in Congress argued that specific legislative authorization was necessary to set up any new machinery requiring additional expenditures. The proponents argued that there was sufficient existing authority based on various statutes and that the Russell amendment (which had led to the death of the original FEPC) would not require congressional sanction for at least a year.

A vigorous campaign was carried on to coincide with the simultaneous tenth anniversary of the first FEPC order and the first anniversary of the invasion of South Korea. The governors of seven states proclaimed the date "Fair Employment Practice Day" and similar proclamations were issued by the mayors of eight major cities. A feature of the campaign was a commemorative ceremony at Roosevelt's grave in Hyde Park with Mrs. Roosevelt participating.

Finally, Truman announced a new executive order (No. 10308,

December 3, 1951) creating the President's Committee on Government Contract Compliance. The Committee was composed of eleven members, five drawn from several government agencies and six representing the public. The function was an advisory one with the responsibility for enforcement resting with the heads of contracting agencies. A report was issued by this body which:

found the nondiscrimination clause, required by Executive Orders 8802 (1941) and 9346 (1943) to be in every contract entered into by an agency or department of the Federal Government for materials, supplies, or services, 'almost forgotten, dead and buried under thousands of words of standard legal and technical language in Government procurement contracts.'[110]

The contract compliance agency was reconstituted by President Eisenhower's Executive Order 10479, on August 13, 1953, and placed under the chairmanship of Vice-President Nixon. Finally, on January 18, 1955, Eisenhower issued another order (10590) establishing the President's Committee on Government Employment Policy to replace Truman's Fair Employment Board. The two orders carry on the earlier efforts in the fields of government employment and hiring practices by private contractors to the government.

None of these presidential agencies has duplicated the Roosevelt FEPC in size of staff or scope of operations, nor has the public hearing technique been restored to favor. They have, however, registered definite gains via negotiations with top management. Though the Vice-President was a staunch foe of FEPC when in the Congress, his handling of the Committee on Government Contracts evoked favorable comment from FEPC proponents.[111]

The large problem of employment discrimination remains for a fully empowered and budgeted agency. The approach through the contract clauses cannot reach far enough, and the small staff can scarcely hope to cover the job even within its limited jurisdiction.

There is little likelihood, however, that the Negro will come rapping at the White House door as sharply as he did in 1941 over the issue of fair employment practices. FEPC as a prime symbol of civil rights has given way in the public mind to other issues. But it stands in readiness should the fear of large-scale unemployment and depression reactivate its dramatic significance. Meanwhile, a steady increase in minority-group economic opportunities continues to reflect substantial gains from the years of campaigning for FEPC.

Epilogue

> And it is a significant mark of his [the Negro's] progress that he won most of these rights for himself on the field of legal battle; in earlier campaigns for simple justice he relied upon the leadership of sympathetic Southern whites, but in the series of historic actions in which he regained the franchise and saw the limits of legal segregation progressively narrowed, he fought under his own banner and in his own right.
>
> HARRY ASHMORE
> *An Epitaph for Dixie*

FOLLOWING THE WAR and the frustrating campaigns for a national FEPC law, it seemed that Negro militancy had been exhausted and that the spirit which once sustained the March was completely gone. The NAACP continued its lawyers' work in preparing the endless cases, running down citations, obtaining witnesses and filing briefs with little immediate contact with the mass of Negroes. The liberal white leaders found scanty support for measures vitally affecting Negro interests on the community level, and it was an unexpressed belief in these circles that the bulk of Negroes simply could not be organized effectively. The mood dropped back to the level of apathy which Myrdal had explained as characteristic of lower classes generally and, therefore, of the Negro community more than of the white.

A remarkable change has occurred over the past few years. Negro self-reliance is increasingly a fact in American political life, North and South. There have been times when the Negro's protest may have been fiercer, but never before has he voiced his demands with greater confidence in his own power. What has produced this energetic tone, and where does it lead in the difficult trials to come? What are the consequences for the leadership which must steer the organized Negro protest?

[178]

The long-run factors are those which have uplifted the Negro from conditions of rural bondage and pulled him along in the general urban transformation. These are the forces reshaping the nation's economic structure and, inevitably, its socio-political patterns. Sectional uniqueness, the Old South with its rigid stratification of caste and class, is mortally wounded—despite the violent thrashing about and the shrieks of defiance. And the surest sign of the nearing demise of old-style white supremacy is the flouting of traditional caste roles by southern Negroes. As the Rev. Dr. Martin Luther King, Jr. put it to the 1956 NAACP convention in San Francisco: "You can never understand the bus protest in Montgomery without understanding that there is a brand-new Negro in the South, with a new sense of dignity and destiny."

Among the short-run factors which have produced this renewal of Negro militancy, echoing sharply the days of the March on Washington Movement, the clearest catalyst has been the decision of the Supreme Court finding that segregation *per se* was a denial of rights guaranteed by the American Constitution (*Brown* v. *Board of Education*, 1954). Technically this was a ruling purely on legally required *school* segregation, but that was indeed a technicality to the general populace (and this popular view—that *all* government-imposed segregation is unconstitutional—is fast becoming legally correct). For the Negro community it was a tremendous stimulant to political organization and cohesiveness. Blamed or praised, the NAACP was properly identified by whites and Negroes as the primary organization behind the litigation. Those who praised hailed the NAACP for its leadership of the Negro to a new plateau in the struggle for human equality. Those who condemned have managed to circulate the widespread misconception that the NAACP is a radical organization headed by irresponsible leaders.

The paradox is that it was *because* the NAACP has been a basically conservative body in its methods that the Supreme Court became the battle ground on which the NAACP has so often fought. For years, the NAACP was attacked by Negro militants for its "legalistic" approach to Negro rights. It is ironical that the most conservative strategy available, directed at what is historically our most conservative political institution, should have brought the NAACP to the forefront of the militant Negro protest today.

In the Forties, during the height of the March on Washington

Movement, the "talented-tenth" methods of lobbying and litigation were repudiated. Militants attacked the traditional leadership as too concerned with politeness and respectability. It was this repudiation which led to the rise of a new organization and the birth of the FEPC issue. At the present time, the success of that epitome of moderate strategy, litigation, has precipitated a situation in which moderates are perceived as radicals. Such are the unanticipated consequences of social tactics that the "conservatives" cannot shake the radical label, at least not short of dropping all efforts to implement the decision in the school cases. But that they surely will not do, for among other reasons it is their organizational victory.

Furthermore, so bitter has the pro-segregationist camp become that even the most moderate actions are immediately castigated as if they were revolutionary in nature. (E.g., the Autherine Lucy case, which was simply an effort to enroll one Negro girl as a graduate student in the University of Alabama. This was not even dependent on the 1954 Supreme Court decision.) This has relieved the moderate Negro leaders of the necessity of defending their "middle way" from the attacks of Negro radicals. The legal principle having been established, any move for implementation in the Deep South has been greeted with such resistance that potential rivals have no choice but to support the present leadership.

Extremist southern reaction to the Supreme Court decision, and particularly to the intervention with federal troops in Little Rock, Arkansas, has made it virtually impossible for moderate whites to speak out in Deep South communities. Thus it is true that the communication bridges between whites and Negroes have been destroyed resulting in a short-run loss for interracial harmony, as traditionally conceived in the Deep South. This may be a heavy price to pay for the gains obtained elsewhere, particularly for the groups immediately involved who must operate in an oppressive atmosphere intimidated by extremist groups. But it is a necessary price if the goals of moderate Southern action are ever to advance from the level of platitude to the concrete objectives capable of marking off specific increments of progress.

One benefit is already registered—a moderate achievement as a result of the breakdown of moderation in the Deep South. The modest gains represented by the substance of the civil rights bill of 1957 are less important than the symbolic significance attached to the failure of the Southern senators to filibuster. The moderation which could not be expressed publicly in deepest Dixie (with some heroic exceptions) was strategically successful in the southern caucus of the U.S. Senate. To say that it was merely politically astute to allow the first civil rights bill in over eighty years to pass the Senate is to ignore the real question—why was it politically astute? The answer is to be found in the new political power of the Negro which has resulted from the solidification of his organized protest.

For if it is true that the White Citizen's Council has the NAACP to thank for its growth in numbers, as is pointed out by those who bemoan the resurgence of Negro militancy, it is equally true that the NAACP has benefited organizationally from the immoderate attacks upon it by white supremacist forces. The southern states have helped produce Negro cohesion with their efforts to harass the NAACP under barratry and other statutory interferences with the freedom of organized political action. And this, in turn, has had dynamic consequences for minority group politics.

It is true that a middle way between "now" and "never" has to be found if ideals are to become reality without the price of transition becoming too large. Even highly sympathetic friends of the Negro may balk at paying the social costs should these involve the creation of new and equally dire problems. But is it really fair to ask or reasonable to expect the Negro to take on this responsibility as his primary concern? The finding of the middle way is the task pre-dominantly of the white community, and it is right that the white leadership be "unreasonably" goaded into action by the Negro organizations. Apart from this fitting the proper roles of victims and culprits (the general white community has at a minimum been cul-pably negligent), the Negro cannot maintain his reborn solidarity, cannot conduct the political education of his people through the calculated rationalism of the more-comfortably situated groups. The big problem for the Negro leadership today is how to resist the easy path of relying once again on white philanthropy for their primary organizational sustenance.

This was the fundamental insight which A. Philip Randolph had provided in his leadership. In a way it is the lesson taught by Booker T. Washington too. The difference is that Washington urged indi-vidual self-reliance to demonstrate personal achievement, accepting meekly what the whites might choose to acknowledge as the Negro's due. For Randolph, and now for Dr. King, collective self-reliance is crucial both for individual self-respect and the strategic strength of the organized protest.

Randolph sought to stimulate that sense of communal potency through the all-Negro policy of the March. To some extent this made a virtue of the need to make do without the support of white allies, and it reflected the lesson suffered in losing control of the National Negro Congress to the Communists. Does the united Negro movement of the present need a similar style of organization? If all that were meant by this is the advisability of maintaining an all-Negro membership there would be no real problem. The bulk of the NAACP's membership has always been Negro, as is the new Martin Luther King organization that grew out of the Montgomery, Alabama, bus boycott. The real question is whether an organization might not gain substantially from an emotional appeal of white-exclusion as a rallying cry. The dangers are the easy degeneration of the tactic into racial chauvinism, and the fact that such an appeal is bound to seem self-segregationist. Therefore, it is unlikely that white exclusion as an organizational rallying cry makes much sense today. Of course, appeals to self-reliance in terms of funds and leadership is another matter.

The NAACP and the neo-Gandhian movement of Dr. King appear to be in close harmony at present in terms of their objectives and the militancy with which their demands are made. But there is a fundamental source of friction which could erupt in the future. Dr. King's movement will yet have to meet the test of all mass movements. On the one hand, the specific objective which created the Montgomery boycott has been achieved. Can the fervor which sustained the group in its short-term struggle be maintained or will gradual apathy lead to its disintegration? Here the orthodox organizations stand ready to take over as in the past. Dr. King may well be content to let that happen, rationalizing the whole experience as a temporary and local affair with purely limited objectives.

Thus far the movement has been kept alive, and a conference in Montgomery of over five hundred Negroes recently considered the possibilities of further applying the passive resistance strategy. The taste of national prominence, the sense of personal charisma in his great success with the Negro masses may lead King to undertake a large-scale national organization "supplementary" to the existing groups. Inevitably, that would produce a hidden competition for funds and programatic priorities. Moreover, should any substantial violence erupt as a result of civil disobedience activities challenging jim-crow ordinances, the pressure on the NAACP leadership from some of its more conservative supporters might lead to an open schism.

There are no signs of this happening yet to any great extent. The activity of the NAACP is bound up in the effort to integrate the Southern public school system. That will be enough to solidify the forces on both sides of the racial dispute. Then too, the limits of the litigation method are fast approaching and the NAACP is likely to look for a new method capable of satisfying militants and conservatives within its supporting base. It seems very likely that a simple non-partisan get-out-the-vote campaign will keep the Negro leadership busy for the next several years. So long as this is resisted by any state governments, the campaign cannot fail to provide a source of cohesion around the established leaders. And in the North, where the main problem will be mass apathy, a substantial increase in Negro voting will surely provide great political strength. At the same time, the extreme reaction likely to be faced in the Southern school situation will contribute much propaganda material for over-coming apathy in the North.

There has been too great an inferiority complex among Negroes with respect to their leadership. A decided feeling persists that there is more schism in the Negro community than elsewhere. This reflects the view that there should be but one Negro organization leading the protest battle to which everyone can give wholehearted support, that anything less is but petty bickering. Presumably, if only *the* leader could be found to bring this about all would be well. Actually, the organized protest today is cast more in this image than at any previous time. But it is necessary to say that there is no more bickering in the Negro community than there is in other comparable groups, e.g., Jews and Catholics. Furthermore, the idea that there would neces-sarily be a gain from having a single organization is predicated on an assumption which is questionable. The assumption is that there is a single path to racial advancement.

Actually, the multiplicity of leaders and organizations (within limits, of course) provides a number of bases on which various strata of the population can be brought together. A single organization would be rather hard put to rally all classes of Negroes, not to mention the range of white sympathizers who can render useful support. Thus, a more efficient mobilization of the community can be brought about by a number of approaches around which segments of the total group can rally. True, some of their efforts will duplicate and there will be wasted energy expended in internecine strife. But there is no utopia in organizational life, any more than elsewhere, and the alternative is an organization which can appeal only to a part of the community leaving the rest unorganized. Efficient group organization is likely to be multiple-political rather than single-functional.

There are important differences between the 1941 situation and that prevailing at present. There is no world-wide shooting war against a totalitarian foe to reduce the national importance of the Negro problem. The white press is no longer "lily-white" to the degree it once was, and the country follows the news of Negro politics closely, as do the politicians. Nor is the problem of civil rights organization as complicated by the "left-wing" factionalism which sapped its strength during the Thirties and Forties. Negroes today are not without white allies who bring funds and organizational assistance to bolster their cause. And despite the rivalry which is as much the law of Negro organizational life as that found anywhere else, the Negro leadership seems as united today as at the peak of the March on Washington Movement.

Whether the Negro leadership will take action similar to that once threatened by the March is not a "slide-rule" question. It is true that they have rejected the term "gradualism" and that a Negro using it is likely to have the "handkerchief" knocked off his head. This has led to an unfortunate misunderstanding of the Negro position. What they have rejected is the use of the term "gradualism" to mean *no* motion rather than *slow* motion. Used as it has been, it became a noxious symbol of complete unwillingness to make significant headway.

The NAACP has moved slowly, through many years of litigation in a lengthy series of court tests. The Supreme Court too has moved slowly and broken with precedent, in recognition of the difficult social revolution involved, and ordered that its decree be effected with "deliberate speed." That is a form of gradualism which the Negro community shows itself willing to accept.

Dr. King spoke for all the Negro leaders when he said:

Now if moderation means pressing on for justice with wise restraint and calm reasonableness, then it is a virtue which all must seek to achieve in this tense period of transition. But if moderation means slowing up in the move toward freedom and capitulating to the whims and caprices of the guardians of a deadening *status quo*, then moderation is a tragic vice which all men of good will must condemn.

The pleas for "moderation" cannot be sincere if unaccompanied by measurable progress. The problem is not created by the Negro holding a political gun at the Nation's head and demanding the unjust or the impossible. The problem is "An American Dilemma" created out of our traditional ideals as inscribed in our fundamental law and upheld by a unanimous verdict of our highest tribunal.

Those who argue that politics and law cannot be the pathway to basic social change must descend from the level of moralistic platitudes to work vigorously on levels which produce tangible results. That is the task of opinion leaders from all walks of life and all sections of our Nation. Indeed it is true that salvation is not of Caesar —but political processes are inevitably the recourse of men who seek to balance power with justice. No less a religious voice than *Commonweal* has rebutted the argument that this is not a political problem:

On the whole, the history of the Negro in America makes clear that his lot has been improved by decisions and actions taken on the political and economic levels, rather than on the 'moral and spiritual plane.' . . . The Negro's most effective help has come from the court-house not the church.

The 'basic' element remains what it has always been—legislation aimed at interracial justice, and the vigilance of the courts over the execution of such legislation.

As the father of our Constitution, James Madison, well understood, liberty and faction are inseparable. Those who would discourage the excesses of national disunity latent in organizational politics over civil rights must indeed act morally; but, ineluctably, they will have to act.

Chronology of Major Events

January 1, 1863	President Lincoln's "Emancipation Proclamation" declared an end to slavery in rebel territory.
September 18, 1895	Booker T. Washington's "Atlanta Compromise" address.
May 18, 1896	The U.S. Supreme Court, in *Plessy v. Ferguson*, held racial segregation was not a violation of the Fourteenth Amendment if the facilities were equal.
June, 1905	Niagara conference of Negro leaders organized by Dr. W. E. B. Du Bois.
February 12, 1909	NAACP founded.
October, 1911	National Urban League formed by merger of three social work organizations concentrating on Negro problems.
Spring 1917	A. Philip Randolph and Chandler Owen began publishing *The Messenger*, "the only radical Negro magazine in America."
July, 28, 1917	NAACP protest parade on New York's Fifth Avenue.
August 2, 1920	Marcus Garvey's followers packed Madison Square Garden in New York.

August 25, 1925	Brotherhood of Sleeping Car Porters organized. Shortly thereafter Randolph became general organizer and in 1928 was elected president.
May 29, 1932	Bonus Army marched on Washington, D.C.
July 2, 1932	Franklin D. Roosevelt's acceptance speech as presidential nominee pledged " a new deal" to overcome the depression.
August, 1935	Seventh World Congress of the Communist International ushered in the era of the "Popular Front."
February, 1936	National Negro Congress formed with A. Philip Randolph as president.
April 9, 1939	Seventy-five thousand persons heard Marion Anderson sing at the Lincoln Memorial after the DAR refused to permit her to perform in Constitution Hall.
August 23, 1939	Nazi-Soviet neutrality pact ended the "Popular Front."
September 1, 1939	Nazi invasion of Poland triggered start of World War II.

1940

April 28	A. Philip Randolph resigned as president of the National Negro Congress charging Communist domination.
May	Committee on Participation of Negroes in the National Defense Program formed under *Pittsburgh Courier* sponsorship and headed by Dr. Rayford W. Logan.
May 26–June 4	Retreat from Dunkirk by the British Expeditionary Force.
September 27	President Roosevelt met with Negro leaders on military discrimination.
October 8	Anti-lynching bill failed in the U.S. Senate.
October 9	War Department policy in regard to Negroes released by White House declared that "the policy . . . is not to intermingle colored and white enlisted personnel in the same regimental organizations." It was implied that the Negro leaders endorsed this policy.

October 25   Negro spokesmen for the Committee on Partici-
                    pation of Negroes in the National Defense Pro-
                    gram met with President Roosevelt.
                    Benjamin O. Davis, Sr. appointed the first Negro
                    brigadier general in the Regular Army of the
                    United States.

November 5   Roosevelt reelected. Henry A. Wallace elected
                    Vice President.

December 29   President Roosevelt's "Arsenal of Democracy" ad-
                    dress pledged American industrial aid to Britain.

1941

January 25   A. Philip Randolph proposed that ten-thousand
                    Negroes march on Washington to demand an end
                    to racial discrimination in defense employment
                    and in the military services.

January 26   Designated National Defense Day by the NAACP
                    which organized protest meetings in twenty-three
                    states.

March 1   Randolph's union newspaper, The *Black Worker*,
                    published a call to march on Washington.

March 28–29   Negro Firemen's Conference organized by the
                    Brotherhood of Sleeping Car Porters.

April 11   Sidney Hillman, co-director of the Office of Pro-
                    duction Management (OPM), urged defense-con-
                    tractor employers to eliminate discriminatory hir-
                    ing practices.

April 12   Randolph announced that "plans for an all-out
                    march of ten thousand Negroes on Washington
                    are in the making and a call will be issued in
                    the next few weeks. . . ."

May 1   The March on Washington Committee issued a
                    formal call for Negroes to march on Washington
                    on July 1.

June 13   Conference in New York's City Hall between
                    Mayor LaGuardia, Mrs. Roosevelt and the lead-
                    ers of the March.
                        Randolph called to Washington to confer "on
                    your project."

June 15	President Roosevelt issued an official memorandum to the OPM that "I shall expect the Office of Production Management to take immediate steps to facilitate the full utilization of our productive manpower."
June 18	President Roosevelt and aids conferred with leaders of the March on Washington Committee. The President appointed a committee under Mayor LaGuardia to evolve a suitable plan.
June 22	Nazi Germany invaded the Soviet Union. American Communists shifted from opposition to support of the Allied cause in World War II.
June 24	Mayor LaGuardia conferred with MOWC leaders in New York City on the text of a proposed Presidential order.
June 24–29	National NAACP conference in Houston, Texas.
June 25	President Roosevelt issued Executive Order 8802 establishing the Presidents' Committee on Fair Employment Practices (FEPC).
June 28	Randolph broadcast a radio announcement "postponing" the march. The Youth Division of the Negro March Committee protested the decision to call off the July 1 march.
July 1	The date on which Negroes had been scheduled to march on Washington. A victory celebration replaced the march.
July 19	President Roosevelt named his appointees to the first FEPC.
October 20–21	FEPC staged first public hearing on employment discrimination in Los Angeles, California.
December 7	Pearl Harbor attacked by the Japanese and the United States became a belligerent in World War II.

1942

January 19–20	FEPC public hearings in Chicago, Illinois.
February 16–17	FEPC public hearings in New York City.

March 5   The Bureau of Employment Security revealed that in the period from September, 1941 to February, 1942 more than half of the available employment opportunities were closed to Negroes.

March 20   Fifty Negro organizations' delegates informed the Office of Facts and Figures' director, Archibald MacLeish, "that the Negro people were cool to the war effort" because of continuing racial discrimination.

April   The March planned a series of great rallies to demonstrate Negro strength and continuing dissatisfaction.

June 16   Eighteen-thousand Negroes packed New York's MOWM rally.

June 18–20   FEPC public hearings on employment discrimination in Birmingham, Alabama.

June 26   Twelve-thousand Negroes over-flow Chicago rally of the MOWM.

July 2   Odell Waller, Negro sharecropper, executed.

July 14–19   National NAACP convention. Randolph awarded the Spingarn medal as the outstanding Negro of 1941.

July 25   "Silent Parade" protesting the execution of Odell Waller held by the New York MOWM.

July 30   President Roosevelt placed FEPC under the jurisdiction of the War Manpower Commission.

August 4   MOWM plans are developed for a culminating mass-protest rally scheduled for September 4 in Washington, D.C.

August 6   The President's secretary, in a letter to Randolph, pleads "extreme pressure" on President Roosevelt's time precludes his meeting with a committee of Negro leaders.

August 14   A "giant" MOWM rally is held in St. Louis, Missouri.

August 31   Randolph advised Washington MOWM to "postpone" their plans for a large-scale rally.

September 26–27   Detroit Conference of the MOWM. Walter White and Lester Granger withdrew.

December 30   MOWM announced it was planning to employ
                       Gandhian civil-obedience tactics to break down
                       racial segregation.

1943

January 11   Paul McNutt, head of WMC, ordered FEPC to
                       "postpone" its scheduled public hearings on rail-
                       road employment discrimination.

February 15   "Save FEPC Conference" in Washington, D.C.

May 27   President Roosevelt's Executive Order 9346 re-
                       constituted the FEPC.

June 3–6   NAACP Emergency War Conference in Detroit,
                       Michigan.

June 7   "Left-wing" sponsored mass rally in Madison
                       Square Garden.

June 20   Race riot in Detroit, Michigan.

July 4   "We Are Americans Too" convention of the
                       MOWM.

August 1   Harlem race riot.

September 15   FEPC public hearings on railroad discrimination.

1944 to date

June 25–26, 1944   National MOWM "Non-Partisan Political Con-
                       ference."

November 7, 1944   Roosevelt reelected. Harry S. Truman elected
                       Vice President.

March 12, 1945   First state FEPC established in New York.

April 12, 1945   President Roosevelt died and Harry S. Truman
                       inaugurated President.

May 7, 1945   Germany surrendered.

January 18–
February 7, 1946   Senate filibuster killed Federal FEPC bill.

February 28, 1946   "Save FEPC Rally" in Madison Square Garden, New York.

August 14, 1946   President Truman announced the surrender of Japan.

October 19, 1946   Last national conference of the MOWM.

October 29, 1947   Report of President Truman's Committee on Civil Rights.

March 22, 1948   A. Philip Randolph and other Negro leaders conferred with President Truman.

March 31, 1948   Randolph and Grant Reynolds initiated a civil-disobedience campaign against military discrimination.

July 26, 1948   President Truman issued two executive orders 9980 and 9981 creating a Fair Employment Board to eliminate racial discrimination in Federal employment, and a Presidents' Committee on Equality of Treatment and Opportunity in the Armed Services.

November 2, 1948   Truman elected.

January 15–17, 1950   National Emergency Civil Rights Mobilization in Washington, D.C., initiated by the NAACP.

February 22, 1950   FEPC proponents were defeated in a crucial vote in U.S. House of Representatives.

March 8, 1950   The National Emergency Civil Rights Mobilization merged with the National Council for a Permanent FEPC.

May 19, 1950   FEPC proponents failed to overcome Senate filibuster. Another vote on cloture defeated on July 12.

June 25, 1950   Outbreak of Korean War.

February 2, 1951   President Truman issued Executive Order 10210 forbidding discrimination by government contractors.

December 3, 1951   President Truman's Executive Order 10308 created the Presidents' Committee on Government Contract Compliance.

August 13, 1953   President Eisenhower's Executive Order 10479 reconstituted the contract compliance agency, placing it under the chairmanship of the Vice President.

May 17, 1954   The U.S. Supreme Court ruled that racially segregated public schools are inherently unequal in violation of the Fourteenth Amendment. The *Plessy* (1896) "separate but equal" doctrine overruled.

January 18, 1955   President Eisenhower (Executive Order 10590) established the Presidents' Committee on Government Policy to enforce a non-discriminatory policy in Federal employment.

December 20, 1956   Year-long boycott of public buses by Negroes of Montgomery, Alabama ends in victory after U.S. Supreme Court orders an end to segregated seating.

May 17, 1957   Negro Prayer Pilgrimage to Washington, D.C.

September 9, 1957   First Federal civil rights bill in eighty-two years enacted.

September 24, 1957   President Eisenhower ordered Federal troops to Little Rock, Arkansas, to restore order after school integration rioting.

Notes

Notes to Chapter I

1. See H. L. Moon, *Balance of Power: The Negro Vote* (New York: Doubleday, 1948).

2. November, 1940, p. 343.

3. *State of the Union Message*, January 6, 1941.

4. *PM*, May 7, 1941, p. 18.

5. Lead editorial, *Pittsburgh Courier*, June 28, 1941, p. 6.

6. U.S. Federal Emergency Relief Administration, "Color or Race of Persons in Relief Families," *Unemployment Relief Census: October, 1933, U.S. Summary* (Washington, D.C., 1934), pp. 7–9.

7. *Ibid.*, adapted from Table C, p. 8.

8. U.S. Office of Administration of the Census of Partial Employment, Unemployment and Occupations, "Employment by Race," *Final Report on Total and Partial Unemployment*, Vol. IV (Washington, D.C., 1938), Ch. IV.

9. U.S. Department of Commerce, Bureau of the Census, *16th Census of the United States, 1940, Population, Characteristics of Persons in the Labor Force* (Washington, D.C., 1943), p. iii.

10. *Ibid.*, p. 5.

11. U.S. Federal Security Agency, Social Security Board, *Social Security Yearbook, 1941* (Washington, D.C., 1942), p. 184.

12. The disparity between the rate of placements of whites and non-whites (1941 vs. 1940) is explained by the *Social Security Yearbook* as probably due to "the more rapid turnover of employment in occupations in which most Negroes are placed." (*Ibid.*) An additional factor might be a greater overall use of public employment offices by Negroes, whites finding it as convenient, in times of full employment, to apply directly to factory personnel offices.

13. *Ibid.*

14. Herman Bronson, "The Training of Negroes For War Industries in World War II," *The Journal of Negro Education*, X (January, 1941), 121–132.

15. William H. Hastie, "The Negro in the Army Today," *The Annals*, 223 (September, 1942), 55–59; "The Negro in the U.S. Armed Forces in World Wars I and II," *The Journal of Negro Education*, Part I, XII (Summer, 1943).

16. As quoted by Sterling A. Brown, "Count Us In," in R. W. Logan (ed.), *What the Negro Wants* (Chapel Hill: University of North Carolina Press, 1944), p. 318.

17. March, 1941, p. 318.

18. "The Preservation of American Independence," address of December 29, 1940, *Vital Speeches of the Day*, VII (January 15, 1941), 196.

19. "The Negro's War," April, 1942, p. 164.

20. Cf. Walter White, "It's Our Country Too," *Saturday Evening Post*, December 11, 1940; Roi Ottley, "Negro Morale," *The New Republic*, November 10, 1941; "Editorial Comment: Negro Morale and World War II," *The Journal of Negro Education*, XI (January, 1942); "The Role of Morale Agencies Among Negroes in World Wars I and II," *The Journal of Negro Education*, XII (Summer, 1943).

21. "The Negro Wants Full Equality," in Logan (ed.), *op. cit.*, p. 130.

22. Sterling A. Brown, "Out of Their Mouths," *Survey Graphic*, (November, 1942), p. 482.

23. P. L. Prattis, "The Morale of the Negro in the Armed Forces of the United States," *The Journal of Negro Education*, XII (Summer, 1943), 355.

24. "The Negro's War," *op. cit.*, p. 78.

25. September, 1941, p. 279.

26. Earl Brown, "American Negroes and the War," April, 1942, p. 546.

27. "What the Negro Thinks of the Army," *Annals*, 223 (September, 1942), p. 67.

28. *Chicago Defender*, January 11, 1941.

29. Roi Ottley, "The Negro Press Today," in Sylvester C. Watkins (ed.), *Anthology of American Negro Literature* (New York: Modern Library, 1944), p. 96.

30. *New York Daily News*, December 12, 1940, p. 1. See the story on the *News*' handling of this affair in *Crisis*, January, 1941, p. 15.

31. *New York Amsterdam News*, November 15, 1941, p. 1.

32. Eleanor Roosevelt, "My Day," *New York World Telegram*, January

6, 1943. Cf. W. H. Brown, "A Negro Looks at the Negro Press," *Saturday Review of Literature*, December 19, 1942; V. V. Oak, "What About the Negro Press?" *Saturday Review of Literature*, March 6, 1943.

33. Walter White, *A Man Called White* (New York: Viking, 1948), Ch. 26. NAACP's *Crisis* was temporarily suspended at the end of World War I on similar grounds; see, Mary White Ovington, *Portraits in Color* (New York: Viking, 1927), p. 88.

34. E.g., Walter White in the *Saturday Evening Post*, *op. cit.*; and Earl Brown in *Harpers*, *op. cit.*

35. Roi Ottley, "Negro Morale" *op. cit.*, p. 614.

36. Lester Granger, as quoted by Kenneth B. Clark, in "Morale of the Negro on the Home Front; World Wars I and II," *Journal of Negro Education*, XII (Summer, 1943), 428.

37. *PM*, October 31, 1943, Magazine Section, p. 13. Cf., e.g., "England's Fight Our Cause, Randolph Says We Must Support Aid to Britain," *Pittsburgh Courier*, February 8, 1941, p. 13.

38. February, 1941, p. 35.

39. March 15, 1941.

40. XII (Summer, 1943), 264.

41. Quoted by Charles H. Wesley, "The Negro Has Always Wanted The Four Freedoms," in Logan, *op. cit.*, pp. 98–99.

42. Quoted by Samuel R. Spencer, Jr., in *Booker T. Washington and the Negro's Place in American Life* (Boston: Little, Brown and Co., 1955), p. 138.

43. Wesley, *op. cit.*, p. 99.

44. *An American Dilemma* (New York: Harper, 1944), p. 821.

45. Booker T. Washington and W. E. B. Du Bois, *The Negro Problem* (New York: James Pott & Co., 1903), p. 75.

46. Cf. E. D. Cronon, *Black Moses* (Madison: University of Wisconsin Press, 1955).

47. Cf. Walter White's account of

NAACP involvement in the 1941 Ford Motor Co. strike on the side of the United Automobile Workers union in *Man Called White, op. cit.*, ch. XXVII.

48. Cf. S. D. Spero and A. L. Harris, *The Black Worker* (New York: Columbia University Press, 1931), pp. 388 ff. This was published prior to Randolph's success in organizing the Pullman workers and is critical of his leadership. A more sympathetic and recent study is B. R. Brazeal, *The Brotherhood of Sleeping Car Porters* (New York: Harper, 1946).

49. Cf. Wilson Record, *The Negro and the Communist Party* (Chapel Hill: The University of North Carolina Press, 1951), pp. 153 ff. Communist involvement in the Negro protest is separately considered in the next chapter.

50. Roscoe E. Lewis, "The Role of Pressure Groups in Maintaining Morale Among Negroes," *The Journal of Negro Education*, XII (Summer, 1943), 472–473.

51. *Ibid.*, p. 465.

52. July, 1918, p. 111.

53. W.E.B. Du Bois, *Dusk of Dawn* (New York: Harcourt, Brace & Co., 1940), p. 245.

54. January, 1942, p. 7.

55. NAACP press release, December 12, 1941, quoted in Myrdal, *op. cit.*, p. 850.

56. Wesley, in Logan, *op. cit.*, p. 96.

57. W. E. B. Du Bois, (ed.), *An Appeal to the World!* (New York: NAACP, 1947).

58. Walter White, "Negroes," *The New International Yearbook for 1940* (New York: Funk & Wagnalls, 1941), p. 537.

59. *Crisis*, November 1940, p. 351.

60. *Ibid.*

61. *Ibid.*, p. 350.

62. *Ibid.*

63. The poem is by Esther Popel. This seems to be the only time that *Crisis* used a cover in this way. Ordinarily they tended toward popular-interest photography; planes, celebreties, pretty girls, etc.

Notes to Chapter II

1. "A. Philip Randolph," editorial, *Chicago Defender*, February 6, 1941.

2. *Man Called White, op. cit.*, p. 189.

3. Conference on the participation of the Negro in National Defense, *Findings and Principal Addresses* (Hampton, Va.: Normal and Agricultural Institute, 1940).

4. *Pittsburgh Courier*, November 30, 1940, p. 6.

5. *Ibid.*, January 25, 1941, p. 3.

6. February 8, 1941, p. 14.

7. In attendance, besides Randoph: Walter White, Secretary, NAACP; Dr. Channing Tobias, Senior Secretary of the National Council of the YMCA; Mary McCleod Bethune, President of the National Council of Negro Women; Dr. George E. Haynes, Executive Secretary of the Federal Council of Churches of Christ; and Lester Granger, Executive Secretary of the National Urban League.

8. "The President, The Negro and Defense," *Opportunity*, XIX (July, 1941), 204.

9. Letter to John Temple Graves, reproduced by Graves in "The Southern Negro and the War Crisis," *The Virginia Quarterly Review*, 18 (Autumn, 1942), 507–508.

10. Charley Cherokee, "National Grapevine," *Chicago Defender*, May 31, 1941.

11. "Houston Awaits Conference," June 1941, pp. 194–195, plus back cover. See May 1941 issue, p. 167, where arrangements for special trains to the Houston Conference are explained in detail.

12. Negro Congressman Arthur W. Mitchell attacked the March leadership in a commencement address, but White repudiated this counsel in his address to a Fisk University graduating class; "Walter White Urges End of Race Patience," *Pittsburgh Courier*, June 7, 1941, p. 3. Also, see *Chicago Defender*, June 28, 1941, p. 6, for Mitchell's attack on Randolph as the "most dangerous Negro in America."

13. *New York Times*, July 29, 1917, p. 12.

14. Dr. Du Bois, while declaring that "the present movement is more fundamental," comments on this parallel in his "Chronicle of Race Relations," *Phylon*, II (Third Quarter, 1941), 300.

15. A Communist leader declared: "Now the idea of a march on Washington for the rights of the Negro people is in itself a worthy idea. But it is only yesterday that these Negro reformist [sic] opposed such a type of struggle. They called this type of action 'radical,' 'lack of good taste,' and 'unintelligible.'" Henry Winston, "Negro Job March Must Be Made Real Fight For People's Demands," *Daily Worker*, June 16, 1941, p. 3.

16. For general discussion see Eric Hoffer, *The True Believer: Thoughts on the Nature of Mass Movements* (New York: Harper, 1951); and Georges Sorel, *Reflections on Violence* (Glencoe: Free Press, 1950). For a concrete example of how Communists have used a Negro issue in this way see the discussion of the Scottsboro case in Wilson Record, *The Negro and the Communist Party* (Chapel Hill: University of North Carolina Press, 1951), pp. 86. ff.

17. Cf. Philip Selznick, *The Organizational Weapon: A Study of Bolshevik Strategy and Tactics* (New York: McGraw-Hill, 1952). Communist policy toward the Negro leadership of the March on Washington followed this pattern exactly.

18. "Why This is Our War: An Editorial," July 8, 1941, p. 3.

19. James W. Ford, *The Negro and the Democratic Front* (New York: International Publishers, 1938), p. 83.

20. Cf. Record, *op. cit.*, pp. 86 ff. Also, Walter White, "The Negro and the Communists," *Harpers Magazine*, December 1931.

21. Communist Party of the United States, *Draft Resolution Proposed for the 8th Convention of the Communist Party of the United States* (New York: Workers Library Publishers, 1934), cited in Record, *op. cit.*, p. 92.

22. Cf. Ford, *op. cit.*, Ch. III.

23. *The Communist*, June 1941, p. 488.

24. February 10, 1941, p. 6.

25. March 3, 1941, p. 6.

26. Cf. the *Daily Worker*, March 12, 1941, p. 6, also May 30, 1941, p. 6 for continuing attacks on A. Philip Randolph and Walter White.

27. June 10, 1941, p. 6.

28. *Daily Worker*, June 11, 1941, p. 5.

29. Cf. A. Philip Randolph, "Why I Would Not Stand for Re-election as President of the National Negro Congress," *American Federationist*, July 1940.

30. Illustrations are plentiful. For example, one congressman from a Harlem district during the war was the late Vito Marcantonio.

31. Winston, *op. cit.*

32. *Daily Worker*, June 16, 1941, p. 1.

33. Winston, *op. cit.* For a "bigshot" business view of these same events see *Fortune*, "The Story of An Executive Order," June 1942, p. 80. *Fortune* maintained that the order

was "clearly the result of pressure" to which the Administration only grudgingly yielded. "It was a compromise between hard boiled pressure groups."

34. June 17, 1941, p. 1.

35. H. R. 3894.

36. June 19, 1941, p. 6.

37. From a leaflet in the Schomburg Collection, New York Public Library.

38. *Daily Worker*, June 17, 1941, p. 1.

39. June 26, 1941.

40. June 27, 1941, p. 6.

41. Theodore R. Bassett, *The Communist*, XX (September, 1941), p. 807.

42. *The Communist*, XX (December, 1941), p. 1072.

43. "Some Problems of the Negro People in the National Front to Destroy Hitler and Hitlerism," *The Communist*, XX (October, 1941), 888.

44. Record, *op. cit.*, p. 309.

45. See the *Daily Worker* for each of the following dates for calls to this mobilization: March 10, 11, 13, 24, 27, 29, April 1, 2, 3, 4, 5.

46. *Man Called White. op. cit.*, p. 192. Mr. Randolph told the writer that the President instigated an FBI investigation to determine the exent of Negro preparations to march.

47. *Ibid.*, pp. 191–192.

48. A. Philip Randolph, "March on Washington Movement Presents Program for the Negro," in Logan (ed.) *op. cit.*, p. 153.

49. Virginius Dabney, "Nearer and Nearer the Precipice," *Atlantic Monthly*, CLXXI (January, 1943), p. 94.

50. *New York Amsterdam News*, February 15, 1941, p. 13. Later the Chicago group chartered a train to take them to Washington for the march (interview with Mr. Theodore Brown, who was located in Chicago in 1941 and is now educational director of the BSCP.)

51. *Chicago Defender*, February 15, 1941, p. 1.

52. Louis Ruchames, *Race, Jobs and Politics* (New York: Columbia University Press, 1953), pp. 15–16.

53. April 19, 1941, p. 16.

54. *Chicago Defender*, April 12, 1941, p. 9.

55. The *Black Worker*, May 1941, p. 4. The "Call" was issued in the name of the Negroes' Committee to March on Washington for Equal Participation in National Defense, composed of Walter White, Rev. William Lloyd Innes, Lester B. Granger, Frank R. Crosswaith, Layle Lane, Richard Parrish, Dr. Rayford Logan, Henry K. Craft and A. Philip Randolph. At some later point, but prior to the "postponement" of the March, Rev. Adam Clayton Powell, Jr. must have been added to the Committee as he was one of those whom Randolph polled in deciding to call off the demonstration. Powell and the Youth Division delegates were the only ones opposed to the "postponement." See A. P. Randolph, "Why and How the March Was Postponed" (mimeographed), Schomburg Collection, New York Public Library.

56. The *Black Worker*, May 1941, p. 4.

57. *Ibid.*

58. May 31, 1941.

59. Charley Cherokee, "National Grapevine," 'Coxey's Army.' May 31, 1941.

60. XIX (July, 1941), 194.

61. Cherokee, *op. cit.*

62. *New York Amsterdam News*, June 28, 1941, p. 1.

63. *New World A-Coming* (Boston: Houghton Mifflin, 1943), p. 291.

64. The cities were: Kansas City, Mo.; Jacksonville, Fla.; Atlanta, Ga.; Savannah, Ga.; Cleveland, Ohio; Memphis, Tenn.; St. Louis, Mo.; Milwaukee, Wisc.; Richmond, Va.; Los Angeles, Cal.; Newark, N.J.; Balti-

more, Md.; Chicago, Ill.; Washington, D.C.; St. Paul, Minn.; Philadelphia, Pa. *Bulletin* (mimeoed), Vol. 1, No. 1, May 22, 1941, distributed by MOWM, BSCP files.

65. *New York Amsterdam News*, June 14, 1941, p. 10.

66. Interview, July 22, 1955.

67. The *Black Worker*, August 1941, p. 2. The previously cited *Bulletin* reported "over 15,000 buttons have been distributed in less than a week in the New York Metropolitan area."

68. *New York Amsterdam News*, June 7, 1941.

69. Quoted by Earl Brown, in "American Negroes and the War,"

op. cit., p. 549.

70. *New York Amsterdam News*, June 14, 1941, p. 1.

71. E.g., *New York Times*, June 16, 1941, p. 6.

72. June 21, 1941.

73. Murray, *The Negro Handbook 1942, op. cit.*, p. 84.

74. *New York Times*, June 26, 1941, p. 12. That same day the *New York Herald Tribune* gave the story front-page space.

75. The script, broadcast on June 28, was printed in The *Black Worker*, July 1941, p. 4.

76. Murray, *op. cit.*, p. 74.

Notes to Chapter III

1. *13 Against the Odds* (New York: Viking Press, 1944), p. 225.

2. Inscription on a huge photograph of Mr. Randolph displayed in the national headquarters of the Brotherhood of Sleeping Car Porters.

3. Embree, *13 Against the Odds, op. cit.*, title of chapter 12.

4. July 12, 1941, p. 14.

5. Roi Ottley, *Black Odyssey* (New York: Scribners, 1948), p. 279.

6. *New York Amsterdam News*, July 5, 1941, p. 4.

7. Cf. A. Philip Randolph, "Why And How The March Was Postponed," *Black Worker*, August, 1941, p. 1.

8. Editorial, May 28, 1941.

9. "The Negro's War," *Fortune*, April 1942, p. 80.

10. July 5, 1941, p. 1. For other press comment demonstrating specific emphasis on an executive order see the *New York Amsterdam News* editorials for June 21, 1941, p. 14 and June 28, 1941, p. 14.

11. *New York Amsterdam News*, July 5, 1941, p. 14.

12. Lester Granger, "The President, The Negro, and Defense," *op. cit.* p. 204.

13. *New York Amsterdam News*, August 2, 1941, p. 14.

14. *Chicago Defender*, July 5, 1941, p. 1.

15. The *Black Worker*, May 1941, p. 4 (italics supplied). The point is made in the resolutions of the NAACP Houston Conference; *Crisis*, September 1941, p. 296.

16. *Crisis*, September 1941, p. 296.

17. Roi Ottley, "Negro Morale," *New Republic*, November 10, 1941, p. 614.

18. *Ibid.* This was answered in the *Black Worker*, December 1941, p. 3.

19. Roi Ottley, *Black Odyssey, op. cit.*, p. 285.

20. BSCP files.

21. Letter to H.W., E.T. and R.P., July 18, 1941.

22. Cf. John Temple Graves, "The Southern Negro and the War Crisis," *Virginia Quarterly*, Autumn 1942; Virginius Dabney, "Nearer and Nearer the Precipice," *Atlantic*

Monthly, January 1943; David L. Cohn, "How the South Feels," *Atlantic Monthly*, January 1944.

23. The phrase is Pauli Murray's (outstanding Negro writer and attorney). Miss Murray explained that she did not mean to suggest that there could not have been a successful march but to characterize the poker game quality of the negotiations between Randolph and Roosevelt.

24. *Op. cit.*, p. 734.

25. Correspondence between Randolph and Anna Rosenberg (BSCP file).

26. *Ibid.*

27. Murray, *The Negro Handbook 1944, op. cit.*, p. 6.

28. September 1941, p. 291. Note the Association's self-applause with no mention of the MOWC.

29. Dickerson was regional director of the Democratic national campaign in 1928; see *Who's Who in Colored America*, 7th edition (Yonkers, N.Y.: Burckel, 1950), p. 152.

30. Executive Order 8823, July 18, 1941; U.S. President's Fair Employment Practice Committee, *First Report* (Washington: Government Printing Office, 1945), p. 9.

31. FEPC as the administration of public policy is dealt with in Louis Ruchames, *Race, Jobs, and Politics* (New York: Columbia University Press, 1953); also Cf. Malcolm Ross, *All Manner of Men* (New York: Reynal & Hitchcock, 1948). The official story is told in two reports issued by the U.S. President's Fair Employment Practice Committee, *First Report, op. cit.*; and *Final Report* (Washington: Government Printing Office, 1947).

32. October 18, 1941, pp. 2, 8. Note the phrase "under white supervision"; but this is a substantial improvement compared with the earlier statement by the North American Aviation Co. president, *supra*.

33. October 1941, p. 327.

34. *Supra.*

35. "It Must Not Fail," November 2, 1941, p. 8.

36. Interview, July 22, 1955.

37. *New York Amsterdam News*, July 12, 1941, p. 11.

38. *New York Amsterdam News*, December 27, 1941, p. 6.

39. Murray, *The Negro Handbook, 1944, op. cit.*, p. 1.

40. *Ibid.*, p. 3.

41. This slogan was popularized by the *Pittsburgh Courier*.

42. *New York Amsterdam News*, December 13, 1941, p. 9.

43. February 7, 1942, p. 14.

44. FEPC, *First Report, op. cit.*, p. 10.

45. *New York Amsterdam News*, July 12, 1941, p. 1.

46. *Ibid.*

47. BSCP files.

48. *New York Amsterdam News*, April 4, 1942, p. 1.

49. " 'Temper of Race Critical,' Says Urban League," *Pittsburgh Courier*, April 11, 1942, p. 4.

50. *New York Amsterdam News*, April 25, 1942, p. 7.

51. BSCP files undated but context indicates April, 1942.

52. *New York Times*, April 10, 1939, p. 19.

53. Letter from A. Philip Randolph to Harold Ickes, April 15, 1942 (BSCP files).

54. The reporter was J. Robert Smith. Cf. Julius L. Adams' column, *New York Amsterdam News*, July 31, 1943, p. 2.

55. Letter dated April 4, 1942 (BSCP files).

56. A. Philip Randolph, "Why Should We March?" *Survey Graphic*, November 1942, p. 489.

57. *New York Amsterdam News*, May 23, 1942, p. 13; *People's Voice*, May 30, 1942, p. 37. A financial report released by the March after the meetings (*People's Voice*, October 10, 1942, p. 10) listed total receipts from February through August as $12,781.-86. Total expenditures were $9,973.63.

58. June 17, 1942.

59. *New York Amsterdam News,* April 4, 1942, p. 5.

60. June 13, 1942, p. 21.

61. *Opportunity,* June 1942, p. 186 did run a brief item which failed to indicate Urban League sponsorship. *Crisis* carried nothing prior to the Madison Square Garden meeting. This may be contrasted with the buildup for later NAACP Madison Square Garden affairs. See *Crisis,* February 1952, p. 118; March 1952, p. 202; February 1953, p. 70; March 1953, p. 134.

62. Letter April 26, 1942.

63. Letter May 22, 1942.

64. May 28, 1942.

65. *New York Times,* August 3, 1920, p. 7.

66. *New York Amsterdam News,* April 18, 1942, p. 1.

67. *Ibid.,* June 27, 1942, p. 5.

68. Leaflet issued by MOWC, N.Y. Division.

69. August 1941, p. 1.

70. *New. York Times,* June 13, 1942, p. 21.

71. *New York Amsterdam News,* April 11, 1942, p. 21.

72. June 13, 1942, p. 21.

73. June 13, 1942, p. 1.

74. June 1942, p. 1.

75. *New York Amsterdam News,* June 13, 1942, p. 1.

76. *New York Amsterdam News,* June 20, 1949, p. 24.

77. Frank Crosswaith, "Above and Beyond," *New York Amsterdam News,* June 6, 1942, p. 7.

78. *New York Amsterdam News,* June 20, 1942, p. 1. Also, cartoon captioned "Here Lies Uncle Tom, Died June 16, 1942 at Madison Square Garden," and editorial, "Uncle Tom's Funeral," June 27, 1942, p. 6.

79. Theophilus Lewis, "Plays and a Point of View," *Interracial Review,* XV (July 1942), 111.

80. Estimates of attendance at Madison Square Garden vary between 18,000 (*New York Times,* June 17,

1942, p. 11), 20,000 (Randolph "Why Should We March?" *op. cit.*), and 25,000 (Murray, *Negro Handbook 1944, op. cit.,* p. 220). J. A. Rogers, in an article which enthused about the Garden rally, mentioned 6,000 empty seats (*Pittsburgh Courier,* June 27, 1942, p. 7). Rogers reported an attendance of 19,000. Randolph, *op. cit.,* claimed 16,000 attended the June 26, Chicago rally but the *New York Amsterdam News,* July 4, 1942, p. 2, claimed only "an overflow crowd of 12,000." Randolph, *op. cit.,* claimed 9,000 attended the St. Louis meeting.

81. Lewis, *op. cit.,* p. 111.

82. Myrdal, *op. cit.,* p. 702, generalizes: "As Negroes are commonly believed to be loud, ignorant, dirty, boisterous, and lax in sexual and all other morals, good manners and respectability become nearly an obsession in the Negro upper class."

83. Lewis, *op. cit.,* p. 111.

84. *New York Amsterdam News,* July 4, 1942, p. 2.

85. *New York Amsterdam News,* June 27, 1942, p. 7.

86. *Interracial Review,* July 1942, p. 100.

87. *Ibid.,* p. 109.

88. *New York Times,* June 17, 1942, p. 11. The *Times* based its story almost entirely on Crosswaith's appointment; there was no mention of the March as sponsor of the rally.

89. Ellen Tarry, *The Third Door: The Autobiography of an American Negro Woman* (New York: David McKay Co., 1955), p. 193. Also *The People's Voice,* June 20, 1942, p. 3 for Powell's interpretation of the Madison Square Garden rally (he was its editor). This issue, announcing his candidacy, was prepared in advance and sold outside the Garden.

90. *Interracial Review,* July 1942, p. 108. Channing Tobias, Director, Colored Division YMCA, similarly declared: "After this Niagara of eloquence which has preceded me, the only degree of distinction left for me

is to confine myself to the time limit." *Pittsburgh Courier*, June 27, 1942, p. 24.

91. Actually, the title is "Hold the Fort For We are Coming" but it was reported in the *Interracial Review* as we have recorded it. Perhaps the error reveals the idolization of Randolph so widespread in early 1942.

92. June 27, 1942, p. 4.

93. *Ibid.*, p. 24.

94. *Ibid.*, p. 12.

95. Embree, *op. cit.*, p. 225.

96. J. A. Rogers' column declared: "Not since the days of Marcus Garvey have I seen such a crowd." *Ibid.*, p. 7.

97. *Interracial Review*, July 1942, p. 102.

Notes to Chapter IV

1. *New York Amsterdam News*, February 8, 1941.

2. Tarry, *op. cit.*, p. 193.

3. July, 1942, p. 100.

4. *Pittsburgh Courier*, July 4, 1942, p. 14.

5. *Ibid.*, June 27, 1942, p. 22. A similar march on another plant was reported in the *Courier*, September 12, 1942, p. 22.

6. See Pauli Murray and Murray Kempton, "*All For Mr. Davis, The Story of Sharecropper Odell Waller*," (New York: Workers Defense League, undated pamphlet).

7. June 11, 1942, p. 22. Cf. the issue of June 19, 1942, p. 22 for an exchange between the presiding judge and the *Times*.

8. *Pittsburgh Courier*, June 27, 1942, p. 24. The entire back cover of the Madison Square Garden rally "Souvenir Program" had been devoted to the Waller case.

9. July 11, 1942, p. 1.

10. Murray, *Negro Handbook 1944, op. cit.*, p. 7. Ironically, this coincided with the appearance of a biography of Roland Hayes by McKinley Helm, *Angel Mo and Her Son Roland Hayes* (Boston: Little Brown, 1942). A prominent reviewer declared: "Well the color line is crumbling. Roland Hayes's career in itself is proof of this. The Negroes have

made greater gains in the last ten months of war than in the previous twenty years. . . ." Oswald G. Villard, *Saturday Review of Literature*, November 28, 1942, p. 6.

11. Minutes of Meeting of July 7, 1942 (New York MOWM Division).

12. *Ibid.*

13. *Ibid.*

14. Minutes of July 22, 1942, MOWM Meeting.

15. *Ibid.*

16. *Ibid.*

17. *The People's Voice*, July 25, 1942, p. 2, pictures a "poster walk" advertising the parade.

18. Minutes of July 7, 1942 meeting.

19. Minutes of July 22, 1942 meeting. A humorous sidelight documents the use of street meetings and, incidentally, illustrates the flavor of the March and its secondary leadership. The minutes record, "At this point, Colton Brown spoke very eloquently for approximately thirty minutes on the Negro and his problems. It was probably his street speech which he used to promote the plans for the parade." These minutes state that 300 persons were in attendance at the meeting.

20. *People's Voice*, August 1, 1942, p. 40. The entire back page is given over to a picture-story of the Waller parade.

21. "The demonstration was observed in strict silence and the faces of the marchers were impressive. A policeman who persisted in talking was soon made to realize the nature of the march." *Ibid.*

22. *Ibid.*

23. "Mr. Totten [International Secretary-Treasurer of the BSCP] stated that the idea of a silent parade probably started during the World War when a race riot occurred in East St. Louis." Minutes of "Call Meeting of the March on Washington Movement," July 7, 1942.

24. Murray, *Negro Handbook 1944, op. cit.,* p. 8.

25. *New York Amsterdam News,* September 5, 1942, p. 1 (a 1 column by 1 inch story); *People's Voice,* September 12, 1942, p. 23; *Pittsburgh Courier,* September 5, 1942, p. 4, a tiny item, "F.D.R. Too Busy To See Randolph's Group."

26. This sub-title owes an acknowledgment to John Beecher, "8802 Blues," *New Republic,* February 22, 1943, pp. 248 ff.

27. July 4, 1942, p. 20.

28. October 25, 1941, p. 1. Compare the attitude of aircraft companies prior to the FEPC, *Supra.*

29. Ruchames, *op. cit.,* p. 28.

30. *Ibid.*

31. *Pittsburgh Courier,* July 25, 1942, p. 4.

32. Ruchames, *op. cit.,* p. 29.

33. July 25, 1942, pp. 1, 3.

34. The *New York Amsterdam News* editorial was very mild contrasted with previous stands; July 18, 1942, p. 6.

35. Cf. Ruchames, *op. cit.,* p. 41. Note that Dickerson did not challenge Ethridge at the hearing itself but released his statement after the hearings were concluded.

36. Cf. B. Atkinson's review of Southern reaction to the Birmingham hearings in the *New York Times,* July 2, 1942, p. 44.

37. Beecher, *op. cit.,* p. 250.

38. Title of *New Republic* editorial, February 22, 1943, p. 240.

39. *New York Times,* July 24, 1942, p. 7.

40. September, 1942, p. 279.

41. *Pittsburgh Courier,* August 15, 1942, p. 4.

42. *Ibid.,* p. 1.

43. The *New York Times* reported a wire to the President signed by twenty-two organizations; August 18, 1942, p. 40.

44. August 7, 1942. The "inside" factors to which White refers may have concerned the jurisdictional conflict going on between Dr. Robert Weaver's Negro manpower service in the WMC and the FEPC group. Cf. *Pittsburgh Courier,* November 7, 1942, p. 6, which accused Weaver of trying to "completely sabotage the Committee."

45. A letter to Randolph from his St. Louis organizer stated, "We are reliably informed that the local office of the F.B.I. is trying to make a case against us charging sedition. . . ." August 22, 1942.

46. *New York Times,* August 18, 1942, p. 40.

47. *Pittsburgh Courier,* August 22, 1942, p. 4.

48. *Ibid.,* August 15, 1942, p. 1.

49. August 29, 1942, p. 6.

50. August 22, 1942, p. 1.

51. *Pittsburgh Courier,* August 15, 1942, p. 4.

52. *Ibid.,* August 1, 1942, p. 1.

53. *Ibid.,* August 29, 1942, p. 5.

54. March, 1942, p. 4. Cf., *Pittsburgh Courier,* March 28, 1942, p. 2.

55. August 4, 1942, to Mr. Thurman Dodson.

56. *Ibid.*

57. "Negroes began entering war jobs in large numbers in 1942, and continued through 1945 to make gains, both in the number of industries entered and in the recognition of skills." FEPC *Final Report, op. cit.,* pp. x–xii.

58. *Pittsburgh Courier*, July 18, 1942, p. 20.

59. Letter of August 31, 1942.

60. Letter to the writer, November 28, 1955.

61. *Interracial Review, op. cit.*, p. 106.

62. Letter to Randolph, June 2, 1942. Mrs. Bethune was, at the time, Director, Division of Negro Affairs, Federal Security Agency, National Youth Administration in Washington. The Treasury meetings referred to were war bond sales promotions.

63. Letter to Mrs. Bethune, June 8, 1942.

64. *Pittsburgh Courier*, October 3, 1942, p. 4.

65. "McNutt, MacLean Talk; FEPC Gets More Power," *ibid.*, October 31, 1942, p. 1.

66. *Ibid.*, November 7, 1942.

67. *Ibid.*, November 21, 1942.

68. Ruchames, *op. cit.*, p. 50.

69. *Ibid.*, p. 51. McNutt's action was the major news story of the week, and the FEPC situation received great attention for some time thereafter; e.g., *Pittsburgh Courier*, January 16, 1943, p. 1.

70. *An American Dilemma, op. cit.*, p. 852.

71. For the official report, see *Crisis*, August, 1942, pp. 264–265.

72. *Pittsburgh Courier*, July 25, 1942, p. 24.

73. A common distinction was made between "the intellectuals in the NAACP and the masses in the March on Washington committees." See Marjorie McKenzie's column in the *Pittsburgh Courier*, July 25, 1942, p. 7.

74. Horace Cayton, "NAACP Clings to Randolph's Coat-Tail," *Pittsburgh Courier*, July 25, 1942, p. 13. Mr. Cayton, a sociologist, is widely known as co-author (with St. Clair Drake) of *Black Metropolis* (New York: Harcourt Brace, 1945).

75. July 25, 1942, p. 1.

76. Cayton could obtain no "ex-planation from the [NAACP] officers." *Ibid.*, p. 4.

77. *Ibid.*

78. *Ibid.*

79. *Ibid.*

80. It was reported that Randolph's convention speech was delivered "with vehemence which reached a new high." *Pittsburgh Courier*, July 25, 1942, p. 1.

81. *Crisis*, August, 1942, p. 264.

82. *Pittsburgh Courier*, July 18, 1942, p. 13.

83. *Ibid.*, September 13, 1941, p. 13.

84. Letter dated June 15, 1942.

85. *The March*, Vol. 1, No. 1, October 17, 1942, 4 (mimeoed); in Schomburg Collection, N.Y. Public Library.

86. August 30, 1942.

87. September 2, 1942.

88. September 9, 1942, letter to fourteen members of Chicago Division, MOWM.

89. Cf. Robert Bierstedt, "The Problem of Authority," *Freedom and Control in Modern Society*, ed. by Morroe Berger, Theodore Abel, and Charles H. Page (New York: D. Van Nostrand Co., Inc., 1954), Ch. 3.

90. June 27, 1942, p. 6. Cf. Embree, *13 Against the Odds, op. cit.*, p. 228: "Critics say, 'He [Randolph] is just a dreamer.' They say, 'The March on Washington Movement is a symbol and a force, not a plan and a strategy.'"

91. Cf. "Program of the March on Washington Movement," *Survey Graphic*, November, 1942, p. 489.

92. The fifth point stated the "demand that the FEPC be made a permanent administrative agency of the U.S. Government. . . ."

93. Criticism had been directed at Randolph on similar grounds with respect to his early difficulties in organizing the Brotherhood. Sterling D. Spero and Abram L. Harris, *The Black Worker* (New York: Columbia University Press, 1931), p. 459, ac-

cused him of a "hunger for publicity." They maintained that "if it were his purpose to win recognition and gain concessions from the Pullman Company too much publicity was likely to strengthen the company's determination not to yield, because yielding in the glare of publicity would be a double defeat." But this is at minimum a dilemma, for "publicity" was surely crucial to creating a sense of cohesion among the unorganized porters. What sort of organizational apparatus could Randolph have wielded which might convince the Pullman executives to deal with him? At the outset there was no organization to wield. The practical situation would have made a mild-mannered organizer a company union man.

94. P. L. Prattis, *Pittsburgh Courier*, June 6, 1942, p. 13. This same article referred to June as "March on Washington Month."

95. George S. Schuyler, *Pittsburgh Courier*, August 1, 1942, p. 13. The subsequent shift to the right is clear in his "FEPC Is a Fraud," *The Freeman*, July 14, 1952, pp. 697 ff. Schuyler was once associated with Randolph on the *Messenger*. Some evidence reflecting on organizational ability may be found in Randolph's management of the MOWM 1942 rallies. The poor planning which overloaded the Madison Square Garden program was balanced by brilliant management of the propaganda buildup.

96. August 8, 1942, p. 6.

97. *New York Amsterdam News*, September 19, 1942, p. 7. Cf. J. Robert Smith, "It's the Truth," *ibid.*, October 24, 1942, p. 7.

98. *Interview*, July 22, 1955.

99. Letter dated September 25, 1942.

100. *Pittsburgh Courier*, October 10, 1942, p. 13.

101. September 1, 1942.

102. September 9, 1942.

103. The Credentials Committee reported that the delegates were distributed as follows: 12 from Illinois, 6 from Missouri, 4 from Washington, 8 from New York, 1 from Louisiana, 2 from Florida, and 33 from Michigan. "Proceedings of Conference Held in Detroit, September 26–27, 1942," p. 11.

104. "Memorandum on the National Policy Conference of the March on Washington Movement," undated.

105. "Proceedings," *op. cit.*, p. 18.

106. The NAACP at that time did not bind its Board of Directors to its national conference decisions.

Notes to Chapter V

1. *The True Believer: Thoughts on the Nature of Mass Movements*, *op. cit.*, pp. 155–6.

2. *New York Amsterdam News*, December 12, 1942, p. 4.

3. October 17, 1942.

4. "Proceedings," *op. cit.*, p. 27.

5. *Ibid.*, p. 39.

6. Quoted by Albert Parker, *Negroes March on Washington* (New York: Pioneer Publishers, undated pamphlet), p. 8.

7. *op. cit.*, p. 836.

8. *Ibid.*, p. 853 (italics in original text).

9. Cronon, *op. cit.*, pp. 106, 107, and 210.

10. Quoted in Embree, *op. cit.*, p. 227.

11. In Logan, *op. cit.*, p. 155.

12. C. B. Powell, then publisher of the *Amsterdam News*, wrote Randolph (October 15, 1942) that the Detroit conference white exclusion

"resolution is undemocratic and denotes segregation and elimination of whites who would help the course of Negro advancement." But after Randolph explained the reasons for the policy, Powell wrote again (November 3, 1942): "From the arguments put forward in your letter, the wisdom of your decision is apparent."

13. Randolph in Logan, *op. cit.*, p. 154.

14. Cronon, *op. cit.*, p. 200.

15. The *Black Worker*, December, 1948, p. 1.

16. White, *A Man Called White*, *op. cit.*, p. 61.

17. Randolph was active in many such organizations. Apart from the NAACP, he was head of the New York Citizens' Committee on Better Race Relations, an interracial committee; see Murray 1944, *op. cit.*, p. 275. Also, his union prided itself on the fact that "the Brotherhood has no color clause. . . . Its membership includes white barbers, Chinese maids, Filipino attendants and Mexican porters." *Black Worker*, June, 1941, p. 4.

18. Randolph, "Why Should We March?" *Op. cit.*, p. 489.

19. A. C. Powell, Jr., *Marching Blacks* (New York: Dial Press, 1945), p. 159.

20. Brazeal, *The Brotherhood of Sleeping Car Porters, op. cit.*, pp. 39–43.

21. See Myrdal, *op. cit.*, pp. 695–700. Cf. References to Mulattoes indexed in E. Franklin Frazier, *Black Bourgeoisie* (Glencoe: *Free Press*, 1957).

22. Southern Negroes were not ignored, but they were more vulnerable. For example, a church in Memphis was condemned for "fire code violations" immediately following an address by Randolph. The BSCP quickly donated $2,000 for repairs. See BSCP press release, (Schomburg Collection in New York Public Library), July 1, 1944.

23. Randolph told a Congressional Committee: "No white man here has felt the sting of discrimination and segregation, Jim Crowism. As a matter of fact, I believe anyone of you men would raise hell in America if you felt the indignities and injustices that are suffered in America. Right here in Washington, the Capital of the Nation, a Negro cannot go to a restaurant and get a sandwich, cannot go to a theater. Do you mean to say that a democracy is worth fighting for by black men which will treat them that way?" U.S. Senate, Eightieth Congress, Second Session, Committee on Armed Services, *Hearings on Universal Military Training* (Washington: Government Printing Office, 1948), p. 694.

24. Quoted in Mary White Ovington, *Portraits In Color* (New York: Viking Press, 1927), p. 83.

25. The *Black Worker*, May, 1940, p. 1. Randolph's concern for the sources of funds is also made clear in this article.

26. *New York Times*, July 18, 1943, p. 29.

27. A. Philip Randolph, "Government Sets Pattern of Jim-Crow," *Interracial Review*, July, 1942, p. 101.

28. *New York Amsterdam News*, June 21, 1941, p. 3.

29. "Proceedings," *op. cit.*, p. 5.

30. Some NAACP branches (particularly on the West Coast) were "captured" during the period (Record, *op. cit.*, p. 267) yet the Association could not take direct action against Communist infiltration until after 1949. See the account of relevant conference resolutions in Herbert Hill's, "The Communist Party—Enemy of Negro Equality," *Crisis*, June–July, 1951.

31. Powell, *op. cit.*, p. 69. A similar view was held by the editor of the *Chicago Defender*. See A. P. Randolph, "A Reply to Lucius C. Harper of the 'Chicago Defender,'" The *Black Worker*, May 1940, p. 4.

32. Cf. Roy Wilkins' column,

"Watchtower," *New York Amsterdam News*, April 4, 1942, p. 7. The Communists later confessed to this as a Browder fostered error. Cf. Record, *op. cit.*, p. 229.

33. L. D. Reddick, "The Negro in the United States Navy During World War II," *The Journal of Negro History*, April, 1947, p. 208.

34. Cf. J. Robert Smith's column, *New York Amsterdam News*, July 18, 1942, p. 7. He had previously defended the all-Negro policy of the March in his column of June 13, 1942, p. 7. For an exposition of the tactics of infiltration, see Philip Selznick's *Organizational Weapon, op. cit.*

35. Randolph's vigilance, and the need for it, are revealed in a letter he wrote his Washington MOWM chairman August 25, 1942: "You will note that according to this person, two Communists spoke on the program, and a third . . . was scheduled to speak. . . . I want to suggest that we keep the Communists out of our programs regardless of what the occasion may be."

36. October 23, 1942, p. 6.

37. *Pittsburgh Courier*, October 31, 1942, p. 23. This was a "mass prayer service" at the St. Louis Soldiers Memorial. The meeting had "the full cooperation of the Interdenominational alliance."

38. *People's Voice*, November 14, 1942, p. 8.

39. September 19, 1942.

40. Press release, December 5, 1942.

41. December 5, 1942, p. 8. Cf., e.g., Horace Cayton's column, "Leadership, An Articulate and Unified Mass Remains Leaderless Today," *Pittsburgh Courier*, January 2, 1943, p. 13.

42. *Pittsburgh Courier*, December 19, 1942, p. 24.

43. *Ibid.*, December 26, 1942.

44. *Ibid.*

45. "To March or Not to March," January 2, 1943, p. 6. Similarly, the executive secretary of the Atlanta, Georgia Urban League, an MOWM adherent, wrote Randolph (January 14, 1943): "I have wondered whether the name of the movement could not be changed . . . to something else which does not suggest that the sole activities . . . are limited to marching on Washington. It seems that many persons have not caught the significance of the movement as a technique of mass action which can be applied in any locality. They, therefore, think that the movement is failing if it does not live up to its name to march on Washington."

46. December 19, 1942.

47. D. G. Tendulkar, *Mahatma* Vol. I, (Bombay: Times of India Press, 1951), p. 109. Cf., M. K. Gandhi, *Satyagraha in South Africa* (Madras: S. Ganesan, 1928).

48. Richard B. Gregg, *The Power of Non-Violence* (Philadelphia: J. B. Lippincott Co., 1934).

49. *Gandhi's Autobiography* (Washington, D.C.: Public Affairs Press, 1948), p. 536.

50. Randolph was imprisoned for a short time for agitation against World War I. In 1948, he courted jail by publicly urging Negro youths not to register for selective service. This preceded President Truman's executive order of July 26, 1948 setting up a commission to end racial discrimination in the armed forces "as rapidly as possible."

51. Quoted in Spero and Harris, *op. cit.*, p. 387. Randolph often used such fighting poems for dramatic effect in his speeches.

52. BSCP press release, December 30, 1942 (Schomburg Collection in New York Public Library). Similarly, the *People's Voice* reported: "MOWM leaders stressed that it [civil disobedience campaign] was only under consideration and would not be discussed until a planned conference this Spring;" January 30, 1943, p. 6.

53. *Chicago Defender*, January 9,

1943, p. 4; *New York Amsterdam News*, January 9, 1943, p. 1.

54. January 23, 1943, p. 6. Later, April 24, 1943, p. 4, the *Courier* reported that a poll of Negroes rejected a "non-violent, civil disobedience campaign" as not likely to "help American Negroes"; 70.6% opposed the campaign, 25.3% were favorable, 4.1% were uncertain.

55. February 6, 1943, p. 6.

56. From the initial press release, "Program of Civil Disobedience and Non-Cooperation," December 30, 1942.

57. A separate press release from the one just cited but also dated December 30, 1942.

58. *Ibid.*

59. "THE MARCH ON WASHINGTON MOVEMENT AND THE WAR," Press release, January 29, 1943.

60. Press release, December 30, 1942.

61. Extract from Minutes of the Board of Directors, NAACP, meeting of February 8, 1943.

62. "*Proceedings*," *op. cit.*, p. 37.

63. January 11, 1943.

64. Murray, *Negro Handbook 1944*, *op. cit.*, p. 212.

65. Editorial, January 30, 1943, p. 14. The main story reporting McNutt's action, in the *Pittsburgh Courier*, was captioned, "McNutt Admits He Called Off Probe; No Resignations," January 16, 1943, p. 1.

66. Murray, *Negro Handbook 1944*, *op. cit.*, p. 105.

67. For Randolph's position arguing that the Negro FEPC members should "stay on and fight," see the *Black Worker*, February 1943, p. 4.

68. This cropped up regularly. The *Pittsburgh Courier*, September 27, 1941, p. 24, reported friction over colored locomotive firemen resolved by Townsend's withdrawal. However, the *Courier*, May 30, 1942, p. 1, reported, "UTSEA Plans Campaign on Rail Workers. . . . CIO Affiliation Adds Prestige to Campaign and May Make Inroads on Randolph's Car Porter's Brotherhood." Cf. *Black Worker*, February 1943, p. 2.

69. Miss Pauli Murray (letter of March 21, 1943) sought unsuccessfully to convince Randolph that "it is imperative that you and Townsend work in close unison" and complained that "it is also a matter of common knowledge that you do NOT work closely together." Townsend had written an article in his union paper very critical of the MOWM (*Bags and Baggage*, November 1942, p. 3). Randolph answered Miss Murray (April 16, 1943), "I don't consider a conference with him [Townsend] the key to the solution of any problem. There are other leaders in the labor movement like George E. Brown of the Hotel Workers' who represent a larger following than Mr. Townsend. I don't think that Mr. Townsend's connection with C.I.O. or being on the C.I.O.'s Board gives him any special strategic position so far as mobilizing Negro masses is concerned." However, ". . . we have no objection to his participating in the March On Washington, and he has always been invited. . . ." Later, Randolph and Townsend did co-operate in the National Council for a Permanent FEPC.

70. Cf. *Steele v. Louisville & Nashville Railroad Company*, 323 U.S. 192 (1944), and *Tunstall v. Brotherhood of Locomotive Firemen and Enginemen*, 323 U.S. 210 (1944).

71. The *Black Worker*, September, 1941, p. 4.

72. *Ibid.*, August, 1942, p. 1.

73. McNutt's Deputy "admitted that the 'postponement' resulted from pressure of 'big business,' the railroads, and the southern bloc in Congress. . . . " Ruchames, *op. cit.*, p. 51.

74. The *Black Worker*, January, 1943, p. 4.

75. Beecher, *op. cit.*, p. 248.

76. "Post Mortem on FEPC," edi-

torial in the *Pittsburgh Courier*, January 23, 1943, p. 6.

77. See The *Black Worker*, January, 1943, p. 1.

78. Following the MOWM Chicago convention, the *New York Amsterdam News* declared: "As it stands, other organizations have had more influence in determining the course of the FEPC than has the March on Washington Movement, and Randolph is further away from the White House than ever, when he should be closer"; August 4, 1943, p. 2. Actually, on August 2, Bishop Haas, the new chairman of FEPC requested Randolph and four other top Negro leaders to meet with him on August 7 (BSCP files). Behind the scenes, Randolph and Morris Milgram of WDL had conducted important negotiations with Attorney General Francis Biddle who handled the FEPC problem for the President at the time.

79. The publisher of the *New York Amsterdam News*, in an article strongly critical of Randolph's handling of the MOWM (July 31, 1943, p. 2), wrote concerning Randolph's experiences organizing the Pullman porters: "Personally I knew the Pullman set-up in Chicago . . . knew something of the activities of the company union. Moreover, I knew that Randolph could have just about written his own ticket if he had abandoned his fight for an independent organization for the porters. It would have meant selling out his friends and the men, and Randolph held fast. I was there! I know men who deserted him for a price! I knew newspapers that deserted him for a price, and I know Randolph merely wept and kept going forward."

80. The March sought to surround the Capitol with a picket line but Randolph was telegraphed, November 21, 1942, by the Washington MOWM chairman:
"UNABLE TO LAUNCH PICKET LINE FOR MONDAY. LEGAL BARRIERS PREVENT PICKETING OF SENATE WING OF CAPITOL OR OFFICE BUILDING. LINE WOULD HAVE TO EXTEND BEYOND CAPITOL RESERVATIONS; MAKING A LINE OF ONE MILE IN CIRCUMFERENCE WOULD REQUIRE BETWEEN 500 AND 1000 PERSONS TO BE EFFECTIVE. LOCAL COMMITTEE VOTED TO ESTABLISH LINE. PHYSICAL REQUIREMENTS PREVENT ESTABLISHMENT BEFORE WEEK OR TEN DAYS. NAACP AND ANTI POLL TAX LEAGUE OPPOSE PICKET IN TOTO."

81. E. Pauline Myers, *The March on Washington Movement Mobilizes A Gigantic Crusade For Freedom* (New York: MOWM, undated pamphlet), pp. 10 ff. Also, Dwight Macdonald, "The Novel Case of Winfred Lynn," *The Nation*, February 20, 1943.

82. Written by a well known white journalist and his wife, Nancy and Dwight Macdonald (New York: MOWM, undated but probably 1943). The authors were involved in an abortive effort to establish a white "Friends of the MOWM."

83. March 21, 1943. Randolph's reply (April 16, 1943) insisted that the decline was largely a press relations rather than a grass-roots loss. He pointed to Roosevelt's success in the face of a hostile press as well as his own experience in organizing the Brotherhood despite opposition from the Negro press. Furthermore, "it is no reflection upon the movement that there is internal strife and even dissension. We have it in the A. F. of L., the C. I. O., and even in Congress." But Randolph was on the defensive. See "A Reply To My Critics," which appeared in six weekly installments in the *Chicago Defender*, June 12, 19, 26; July 3, 10, 17, 1943; each on p. 13.

84. June 7, 1943; Murray, *Negro Handbook 1944, op. cit.,* p. 220.

85. *Crisis,* July 1943, p. 211.

86. *Pittsburgh Courier,* June 19, 1943, p. 13.

87. *Ibid.*

88. See Ruchames, *op. cit.,* pp. 55–56.

89. Executive Order 9346, May 27, 1943. The FEPC was removed from McNutt's jurisdiction and established as an independent agency within, but not subordinate to, the OPM.

90. Murray, *Negro Handbook 1944, op. cit.,* p. 220. On June 26, 1943, the *Pittsburgh Courier* front-paged the headline, 'RACE RIOTS SWEEP NATION, 16 Dead, Over 300 Hurt in Michigan, Texas, Mississippi." This was the issue immediately preceding the MOWM convention. On August 1, 1943, a riot broke out in Harlem, N.Y. See Murray, *op. cit.,* pp. 43–50. For a study of the Detroit riot see Alfred M. Lee and Norman D. Humphrey, *Race Riot* (New York: Dryden Press, 1943).

91. Murray, 1944, *op. cit.,* p. 45.

92. *Ibid.,* Had the MOWM conference not been postponed from May, any civil disobedience action launched by the Detroit MOWM might well have received the blame for setting off the riot.

93. *Pittsburgh Courier,* July 10, 1943, p. 12.

94. Later the Committee on Racial Equality (CORE) of the Fellowship of Reconciliation (a Christian pacifist group) and the Howard University chapter of the NAACP waged successful forays into Jim Crow territory. Cf., George M. Hauser, *Erasing The Color Line* (New York: Fellowship Publications, 1947), a pamphlet with a foreword by A. Philip Randolph. Randolph's 1948 civil disobedience campaign aganst discrimination in the military services has been noted previously. The bus boycotts in Montgomery, Alabama and Tallahassee, Florida provide recent examples of political "non-cooperation" by Negroes.

95. By now the Negro press regularly carried full page advertisements offering war jobs. Cf., the *New York Age,* July 17, 1943, p. 12; the *People's Voice,* September 25, 1943, p. 7. This unquestionably reduced rank and file militancy.

96. July 4, 1943, p. 12. The *New York Amsterdam News* all but ignored the MOWM convention. The issue of July 3 contained nothing; on July 10, they ran a front page captioned picture of Randolph but no story; on July 17, S. W. I. Garlington wrote what amounted to an obituary of the March in his column "Generally Speaking," p. 11. The *Chicago Defender* ran a small p. 1 story, July 10, 1943.

97. *Pittsburgh Courier,* July 10, 1943, p. 12.

98. July 10, 1943.

99. See the detailed account of these panels in the *Pittsburgh Courier,* July 10, 1943, p. 12.

100. The attendance can be inferred from the size of the vote to retain the important Negroes-only membership policy (102 to 2); *New York Times,* July 4, 1943, p. 12. Randolph had previously declared that "a conference of five hundred delegates is a good conference." Letter to Pauli Murray, April 16, 1943.

101. The National Executive Secretary was let go a few months after the convention. Some question had been raised of incompetency, but the primary reason (she was not replaced) was financial. The treasurer's report of October 30, 1943 revealed an indebtedness of $2,091.15 with but $86.85 on hand. By now the BSCP had poured close to $50,000 into the March.

102. A. Philip Randolph, "March On Washington Movement Presents Program For the Negro," in Logan (ed.), *op. cit.,* p. 145.

103. *The Black Worker,* July 1944, p. 3.

104. A vice-president of the BSCP

answered our question concerning why the name of the MOWM had been retained; it ". . . was not changed because it kind of dissolved into the Council for a permanent FEPC." Another MOWM leader actually declared: "the name of the organization WAS changed," so strong was his recollection that "the National Council for a Permanent FEPC . . . was the successor to the MOWM." He even named a white lawyer, active in the National Council, as the man who "was elected Chairman . . . after the name was changed." Of course he was trying to recall happenings of thirteen years ago and specifically warned, "of this I am not certain," but it is revealing of when the March died as a matter of perception by its active leaders. Randolph, too, now stresses the "temporary and limited purpose" of the March primarily in terms of the FEPC.

105. Report by A. Philip Randolph, National Director; National Conference, March on Washington Movement, (Chicago, Illinois, October 19, 1946).

106. Letter of February 24, 1944; BSCP files.

107. January 23, 1947.

Notes to Chapter VI

1. *All Manner of Men* (New York: Reynal and Hitchcock, 1948), p. 83.

2. Executive Order 9346, May 27, 1943. The railroad hearings began the following September 15.

3. U.S. Congress, House, *To Investigate Executive Agencies:* Hearings before the Special Committee to Investigate Executive Agencies, House of Representatives, 78th Cong., 1st and 2nd Sess., on H. Res. 102 (Washington: Government Printing Office, 1944), Part 2.

4. Will Maslow, "FEPC—A Case History in Parliamentary Maneuver," *University of Chicago Law Review,* XIII (June, 1946), pp. 412–414.

5. Kesselman, *op. cit.,* p. 39.

6. *Ibid.,* pp. 38–39.

7. The position of Jews during the war is described by H. M. Kallen, "National Solidarity and the Jewish Minority," *Annals* 223 (September, 1942). On "defense" organizations, see R. M. MacIver *et al., Report on the Jewish Community Relations Agencies* (New York: National Community Relations Advisory Council, 1951).

8. Direct intervention was not advocated by organizational leaders. A 1940 statement declared: "The disastrous effects of the war on the Jews of Central and Eastern Europe, intensely tragic as it is, is a part of a calamity almost world-wide in scope. Happily, our country is not a party in this conflict. Convinced as we are of the futility of war, knowing as we do its incalculable material and moral costs, we hope and pray it may be possible for our country to remain at peace." Executive Committee of the American Jewish Committee, "Annual Report," *The American Jewish Year Book 5701,* Vol. 42, (Harry Schneiderman (ed.) [Philadelphia: Jewish Publication Society of America, 1940]), p. 643.

9. The rise of "hate groups" in this country during the post-World War I era is well known; e.g., The Coughlin, German-American Bund, Silver Shirt movements, and the campaign of Henry Ford's *Dearborn Independent.* See Donald S. Strong, *Organized Anti-Semitism In America* (Washington: American Council on

Public Affairs, 1941). In Britain, the Mosley group was much weaker than its counterparts in the U.S. (*ibid.*, pp. 11–12). Indeed Gunnar Myrdal observed: "It is the present writer's impression that anti-Semitism, as he observed it in America during the last years before the Second World War, probably was somewhat stronger than in Germany before the Nazi regime." (*An American Dilemma, op. cit.*, p. 1186.) Public opinion polls showed substantial anti-Jewish prejudice during the period prior to and during World War II. See Hadley Cantril and Mildred Strunk (eds.), *Public Opinion 1935–1946* (Princeton: Princeton University Press, 1951), pp. 381–388; a Fortune poll of July, 1939 (*ibid.*, p. 383) found 10.8% of its sample believed Jews "make respected and useful citizens so long as they don't try to mingle socially where they are not wanted"; 31.8% thought "some measures should be taken to prevent Jews from getting too much power in the business world"; 10.1% wanted to "make it a policy to deport Jews from this country to some new homeland as fast as it can be done without inhumanity"; 38.9% felt "Jews have the same standing as any other peoples and they should be treated in all ways exactly as any other Americans"; 9.5% "don't know" or "refused to answer."

10. Joseph C. Hyman, Twenty-Five Years of American Aid to Jews Overseas: A Record of the Joint Distribution Committee," *The American Jewish Year Book 5700*, Vol. 41 (1939–1940), 141.

11. *The Role of the American Jew* (New York: American Jewish Congress, undated pamphlet), p. 9.

12. Cf. "The Mirage of the Economic Jew," in Graeber and Britt, *op. cit.*, Part Six; U.S. President, Fair Employment Practice Committee, *First Report, op. cit.*, and *Final Report, op. cit.*; Arnold Aronson, *Post-war Employment Discrimination*

Against Jews (report of National Community Relations Advisory Council, undated); J. X. Cohen, *Who Discriminates and How?* (American Jewish Congress, undated); and, Albert J. Weiss, "Post-war Employment Discrimination," *Jewish Social Service Quarterly*, XXIII (June, 1947), 396–405.

13. This is readily established by contrasting attention to the issue in Negro and Jewish yearbooks. Frequent references have been made herein to Murray's *Negro Handbook*. Cf. *American Jewish Year Book*, Harry Schneiderman (ed.), succeeded by Morris Fine with Vol. 51, *op. cit.*, during war and post-war years. The first substantial reference is in Geraldine Rosenfield, "Combating Anti-Semitism," *ibid.*, 47 (1945–1946), 280, 281, 284, 285. Two important national conferences of major Jewish organizations during the war failed to mention FEPC in their proceedings; see Alexander S. Kohanski (ed.), *The American Jewish Conference, Its Organization and Proceedings of the First Session, August 29 to September 2, 1943, New York, N.Y.* (New York: American Jewish Conference, 1944); *ibid., Proceedings of the Second Session, December 3–5, 1944, Pittsburgh, Pa.* (New York: American Jewish Conference, 1945).

14. Kesselman, *op. cit.*, p. 102.

15. Maurice J. Karpf, *Jewish Community Organization in the United States* (New York: Bloch Publishing Company, 1938), p. 64.

16. Bureau on Jewish Employment Problems, *What Price Employment Barriers: Report of Activity, 1938–1940* (Chicago: undated pamphlet), p. 2.

17. "Memorandum; Subject:. President's Committee on Fair Employment Practice," January 22, 1943 (dittoed copy).

18. August 22, 1942, p. 6.

19. *Ibid.* Cf. "Negroes and Jews," editorial, *New York Amsterdam News*, August 22, 1942, p. 6; and

Kenneth B. Clark, "Candor About Negro-Jewish Relations," *Commentary*, I (February, 1946), 8.

20. FEPC, *Final Report, op. cit.*, p. vi.

21. Maslow, *op. cit.*, provides a thorough analysis of the parliamentary battle in the Seventy-ninth Congress. See also Ruchames, *op. cit.*, pp. 199–206.

22. *People's Voice*, December 1, 1945, p. 18; February 16, 1946, p. 20; March 2, 1946, p. 16. Cf. *Manuscript*, No. 36 (November 19, 1945), p. 3.

23. Kesselman, *op. cit.*, pp. 158–160.

24. Arthur Krock characterized it as "A Filibuster That Kept Banker's Hours" and claimed: "The advocates of the disputed measure [FEPC] are merely making a show of their advocacy to relieve themselves of immediate political pressure and are quite willing to blame the Senate rules for their failure." *New York Times*, February 14, 1946, p. 24.

25. *The New York Times* (March 1, 1946, p. 23) estimated 15,000 persons attended the Madison Square Garden rally held February 28, 1946. Cf. R. G. Martin, "FEPC Rally," *New Republic*, CIV (March 18, 1946), 379.

26. Telegram from Allen Knight Chalmers and A. Philip Randolph, co-chairmen, to constituent organizations composing the National Council for a Permanent FEPC, March 22, 1946. The NAACP participated in the February 22 conference but it is not clear whether they endorsed the plan for a new march; see *Crisis*, March, 1946, p. 74.

27. The importance of the postwar employment concern is revealed in the enactment of the "Full Employment Bill" a few days after the FEPC filibuster ended. See Stephen K. Bailey, *Congress Makes a Law: The Story Behind the Employment Act of 1946* (New York: Columbia University Press, 1950).

28. "When the proponents of FEPC plans its proposed new March on Washington, all segments of the population will be urged to join—not just Negroes as the original movement provided." *Manuscript*, No. 50 (February 26, 1946), p. 5.

29. Full-page ad for the Madison Square Garden "Negro Freedom Rally," *Peoples Voice*, June 14, 1947, p. 20.

30. "A. Philip Randolph's proposed MARCH ON WASHINGTON as a strategy in the FEPC fight has run afoul of the National CIO Committee to Abolish Discrimination, which has addressed him a 2-page letter of objections." *Manuscript*, No. 56 (April 9, 1946), p. 5. On electoral reprisal activity, see Henry Lee Moon, "The Negro Vote In 1946," *Crisis*, LIII (October, 1946), 306–308.

31. "FEPC Foe Defeated," *Crisis*, LIII (September, 1946), 265.

32. *New York Times*, April 13, 1944, p. 11; and April 19, 1944, p. 15.

33. Press release, October 25, 1944.

34. A. P. Randolph *et al.*, "Ideas For A New Party: A Symposium," *Antioch Review*, VI (December, 1946), 602–624. James A. Wechsler declared that "some of the ablest figures in labor's top echelons. . . ." were involved in the new-party move; "The Liberal's Vote and '48," *Commentary*, IV (September, 1947), 217.

35. "A. Philip Randolph," *New York Times Index, 1946*, p. 1959. This was in reaction to Truman's plan to draft strikers in key industries.

36. A. Philip Randolph, "Why I Voted For Norman Thomas," *Black Worker*, November, 1948, p. 2.

37. *Crisis* declared Truman's speech "the most comprehensive and forthright statement on the rights of minorities in a democracy, and on the duty of the government to secure and safeguard them that has ever been made by a President of the United States" in editorial, LIV (August, 1947), 233. Also, see U.S. President's

Committee on Civil Rights, *To Secure These Rights* (Washington: Government Printing Office, 1947), and comments thereon in *Crisis*, LIV (December, 1947), 361, and LV (January, 1948), 10–11.

38. See the editorial analyses in *Crisis*, LV (January, 1948), 9; and LV (September, 1948), 361.

39. In the 1946 CIO convention, a "left-right" split was assiduously avoided, though with difficulty. The big break came in 1948 and was completed by 1949. See Robert Bendiner's series of articles in the *Nation*, "CIO Tightrope Act," CLXIII (November 30, 1946), 601; "Murray's Limited Purge," CLXVII (December 15, 1949), 361–363; "Surgery in the CIO," CLXIX (November 12, 1949), 458–459. Cf. Max Kampleman, *The Communist Party vs The CIO* (New York: Praeger, 195). On the NAACP and the Urban League, see Record, *op. cit.*, and editorials in *Crisis*, "Keep An Eye On The Communists," LIX (April, 1948), 105, "The NAACP and the Communists," LX (March, 1949), 72. American Jewish Congress actions date from 1948; two constituent "left-wing" groups, the American Jewish Labor Council and the Jewish People's Fraternal Order, and the metropolitan Detroit chapter were finally ousted in 1949; *New York Times*, June 8, 1949, p. 12, and November 11, 1949, p. 22. Also at this time, Congressman Powell removed the editor of his newspaper and changed its political orientation; see *The People's Voice*, December 27, 1947, p. 3.

40. Her original resignation, July 15, 1946, cited only the financial crisis. At the August 2 National Council Board of Directors meeting, Mrs. Hedgeman submitted a second statement declaring, "I do not believe that the National Council for a Permanent FEPC as presently constituted is utilizing effectively the established political affiliations necessary to enactment of such legislation." Mrs. Hedge-

man was urged to separate her criticisms from her resignation since it "contained the inference of an indictment of the Council which might impair the future welfare of the FEPC movement." Though she would not accede to this request, the Board accepted her resignation "with gratitude for the significant contribution she has made to the cause of fair employment practice." Minutes of meeting; BSCP files.

41. Letter to Mr. Roy Wilkins, January 7, 1948.

42. A close associate of Randolph confidentially attacked the election of Wilkins as a "Trojan Horse." There was less rivalry with the Urban League (its exclusive social-service function made it less competitive for program than the NAACP), and Randolph had to urge Lester Granger to come on the reorganized Board of Directors.

43. White wrote Randolph and Chalmers asking to "disassociate myself" from a Council wire to Senator Taft which asked priority of FEPC over anti-lynching and anti-poll tax bills. He argued that "despite its record of more than a quarter of a century in support of anti-lynching legislation, the NAACP has abstemiously refrained from asking priority for that legislation." White was a member of the Council's strategy committee. (February 27, 1948; BSCP files.) In 1950 Roy Wilkins, as chairman of the Council's executive committee, wrote to Senators: "Major religious, labor, civic, veterans, racial and ethnic organizations have declared FEPC to be 'the most fundamental' of all pending civil rights bills." (January 4, 1950; BSCP files.) In June, 1949, AFL, CIO, NAACP and NCRAC spokesmen "united in urging that top priority be given to FEP among all civil rights measures." Arnold Aronson, "Employment," *American Jewish Year Book 1950*, Vol. 51, *op. cit.*, 101.

44. From 1948 to 1953 the American Jewish Congress and NAACP issued a joint annual report, *Civil Rights in the United States: A Balance Sheet of Group Relations.* Jewish organizations have also submitted briefs to support Negro cases as "friends of the court." This activity was not entirely new; Rabbis Emil G. Hirsch and Stephen S. Wise were among the signers of the 1909 Lincoln birthday call for the conference which established the NAACP.

45. "Organized anti-Semitic activity, which began to decline after the war, continued at a low ebb during the year under review [1949]." George Kellman, "Anti-Jewish Agitation," *American Jewish Year Book 1950,* Vol. 51, *op. cit.,* p. 110. Cf. Arnold Forster and Benjamin R. Epstein, *Cross-Currents* (Garden City: Doubleday & Co., 1956).

46. NCRAC was established after the war to co-ordinate the work of Jewish agencies engaged in community relations activities. Aronson, who earlier came from the Chicago Bureau on Jewish Employment Problems, was in charge of employment work for NCRAC. See MacIver, *op. cit.,* for an interesting example of the conflict between organizational sovereignty and functional allocation of programs which led to the 1952 withdrawal of the American Jewish Committee and the Anti-Defamation League from NCRAC. Cf. Selma G. Hirsh, "Jewish Community Relations," *American Jewish Year Book 1953,* Vol. 54, *op. cit.,* 162 ff.

47. See the sketch of BSCP leaders in Murray Kempton, *Part of Our Time: Some Ruins and Monuments of the Thirties* (New York: Simon & Schuster, 1955), ch. 8.

48. *Manuscript* reported a "rivalry of Negro leadership"; "According to some NAACP officials, the independent efforts of that organization were not too welcome in the FEPC fight. Randolph, it is claimed, wanted to prove he was big enough to do the job without Walter White. This was discussed in the recent NAACP Board meeting where a resolution was adopted to set up a new FEPC committee to carry on the fight on the ground that Randolph's group had been given its chance without interference."

The report further stressed that Walter White, Roy Wilkins, and other NAACP representatives at the February 22 strategy conference following the filibuster absented themselves when a resolution was adopted "extending a vote of confidence to the leadership of Randolph and Anne Hedgeman . . . and condemning any move on the part of any other organization to set up a competing committee." No. 60 (February 26, 1946), p. 1.

49. Letter to Wilkins, *op. cit.*

50. Ruchames, *op. cit.,* p. 206. Cf. Arnold Aronson and Samuel Spiegler, "Does the Republican Party Want the Negro Vote?" *Crisis,* LVI (December, 1949), 364; editorial, "Democrats Fail on FEPC," *Crisis,* LVII (June, 1950), 374; and Alan Barth, "The Democrats And FEPC," *Reporter,* VII (August 5, 1952), 13.

51. July 26, 1948; Executive Order 9980 established what the *New York Times* referred to as a "little FEPC" (July 27, 1948, p. 1), a Fair Employment Board was charged with enforcing the President's order to eliminate bias in Federal employment. Executive Order 9981, issued simultaneously, established the President's Committee on Equality of Treatment and Opportunity in the Armed Service to implement the order to end military discrimination "as rapidly as possible, having due regard to the time required to effectuate any necessary changes without impairing efficiency or morale." (*New York Times, ibid.*) On the significance of Executive Order 9980, see Arnold Aronson, "Employment" *American*

Jewish Year Book 1950, op. cit., Vol. 51, pp. 106–108.

52. *New York Times,* July 27, 1948.

53. Grant Reynolds, "A Triumph For Civil Disobedience," *Nation,* CLXVII (August 28, 1948), 228.

54. *New York Times,* April 1, 1948, p. 1.

55. *Ibid.* Cf. U.S. Congress, *Congressional Record,* Eightieth Congress, Second Session, Vol. 94, Part 4, (April 12, 1948, Senate) 4312–4318.

56. *New York Times,* July 18, 1948, p. 36.

57. "Fighting The Jim Crow Army," *Crisis,* LV (May, 1948), 136. This article referred to Randolph as manifesting "his usual eloquence and sincerity." The same issue reprinted a *PM* editorial by Max Lerner containing the significant statement, "Randolph and Reynolds come closer to the true feelings of the masses of American Negroes . . . than their more cautious and circumspect colleagues." (p. 154.)

58. *New York Times,* June 5, 1948, p. 16.

59. *Ibid,* April 27, 1948, p. 17.

60. *Ibid,* April 2, 1948, p. 18.

61. *Ibid,* June 27, 1948, p. 35. There was some question as to whether the executive order issued by Truman precluded "segregation" —the term used in the order was "discrimination." The Negro leaders regarded segregation as prima-facie evidence of discrimination and welcomed the order as "courageous." Their view was later accepted by the Supreme Court in the school segregation cases which reversed the "separate but equal" doctrine. Cf. Oliver Brown *et al. v.* Board of Education of Topeka, Shawnee County, Kansas, *et al.* 347 U.S. 483 (1954). Randolph regarded the executive orders as a victory and called off the civil disobedience campaign. Cf. Grant Reynolds, *op. cit.*

62. U.S. Congress, Senate, *Universal Military Training,* Hearings be-

fore Committee on Armed Services, U.S. Senate, 80th Congress, 2nd Sess. (Washington: Government Printing Office, 1948), p. 686.

63. To be sure, this is a comparative statement. Given sufficient intensity of a crisis in public morale, Congress could not remain aloof. However, it seems a sound generalization that the pressures would have to be more intense and involve a broader range of interests to move the legislative branch compared with the executive. The sheer number of individuals, with differently based power positions who would have to be made vulnerable, produces an important difference. Also important is the seniority system of selecting powerful heads of committees. Thus, the Congress is a more conservative institution than is the office of President. Cf. Stephen K. Bailey, *op. cit.,* ch. XII.

64. *Black Worker,* February, 1950, p. 1.

65. National Emergency Civil Rights Mobilization, "To All Sponsoring Organizations," BSCP files March 8, 1950. This report reveals that "a total of 410 persons was not accredited because credentials were found not to be in order." It is likely that this represented the "left-wing" groups which sought to participate in the Mobilization; see Roy Wilkins' report that Communists had tried to "infiltrate and control the mobilization," *Crisis,* LVII (August–September, 1950), 512–513. The March 8, 1950 report provided the following breakdown of delegates: NAACP, 2891; CIO 383; American Jewish Congress, 185; B'nai B'rith, 350; National Baptist Convention, 53; AFL, 119; AMEZ and other church organizations, 41; National Alliance of Postal Employees, 23; Committee for a Permanent FEPC, 11; Greek Letter Fraternities, 12; Americans for Democratic Action and SDA, 60; Elks, Masons and other fraternal

organizations, 17; Catholic Interracial Council, 5.

66. National Emergency Civil Rights Mobilization, *op. cit.*

67. Arnold Aronson, "Employment," *American Jewish Year Book 1951*, Vol. 52, *op. cit.*, 29. The delegation to the President included A. Philip Randolph, though Roy Wilkins was spokesman. *Crisis*, LVII (February, 1950), 108.

68. During this period, there was talk of formalizing the Republican-Dixiecrat alliance. Cf. "Should the G.O.P. Merge with the Dixiecrats?" "Yes," by Senator Karl E. Mundt (R.-S. Dak.), "No," by Representative Clifford P. Case (R.-N.J.), *Colliers*, CXVIII (July 28, 1951), 20 ff.

69. From the report of the Illinois delegation to the Mobilization.

70. The FEPC campaign in the Eighty-first Congress is described in Ruchames, *op. cit.*, pp. 206–212; and Arnold Aronson, "Employment," *American Jewish Year Book 1951*, Vol. 52, *op. cit.*, 29–31.

71. National Emergency Civil Rights Mobilization, *op. cit.*

72. *Ibid.*

73. *Ibid.*

74. Ruchames, *op. cit.*, p. 209.

75. *New York Times*, April 12, 1950, p. 18.

76. May 16, 1950, p. 3.

77. This rule was adopted March 17, 1949. It changed the previous situation, where two-thirds of those present and voting could impose cloture. Then, it had been theoretically possible to invoke cloture with 33 votes (two-thirds of a quorum). Now it was necessary to have 64 irrespective of how many Senators were voting on the proposition. The rule was jointly offered by Carl Hayden (D.-Ariz.) and Kenneth Wherry (R.-Neb.) as a "compromise" to solve the impasse created by reversal of a ruling by Vice-President Barkley (March 10, 1949) that cloture applied to any business before the Senate, to pro-cedural as well as substantive matters. The Hayden-Wherry rule was a compromise between no cloture at all on procedural matters (in effect, no cloture) and the majority-rule principle demanded by civil rights proponents. See "SENATE GIVES FILIBUSTERS GREEN LIGHT," *Crisis*, LVI (April, 1949), 105. Cf. George B. Galloway, *The Legislative Process in Congress* (New York: Thomas Y. Crowell Co., 1953), pp. 559–570.

78. *Crisis*, LVII (June, 1950), 374–375.

79. Democrats, however, claimed Vice-President Barkley's ruling as a Truman Administration effort for civil rights (Galloway, *op. cit.*, p. 562). Twenty-five Democrats and sixteen Republicans voted to sustain the Chair, twenty-three Democrats and twenty-three Republicans overruled the Chair. The NAACP used this vote as an important item in appraising the voting records of senators; "The NAACP Legislative Scoreboard," *Crisis*, LVII (Ocober, 1950), 549 ff. (The statistics in *Crisis*, however, are not accurate with respect to the vote on the McConnell substitute. Their table seems to be based on that in the *Congressional Quarterly Almanac*, VI (1950), 550–51 which contains errors.)

80. "There will be a second cloture vote, probably while this editorial is in the press. Additional votes will be picked up from among absentees." *Crisis*, LVII (June, 1950), 375.

81. *Ibid.*

82. *Ibid.*, p. 374.

83. See the efforts made by each side in Senate debate to pin the onus for defeating FEPC on the other party. Only the Southerners claimed credit for the defeat. U.S. Eighty-first Congress, second session, *Congressional Record*, Vol. 96, Part 6 (May 19, 1950), 7300–7307; *ibid.*, Vol. 96, Part 8 (July 12, 1950), 9982–9985.

84. The 1948 Republican platform declared: "This right of equal opportunity to work and to advance in life should never be limited in any individual because of race, religion, color, or country of origin. We favor the enactment and just enforcement of such Federal legislation as may be necessary to maintain this right at all times in every part of this Republic."

The 1948 Democratic platform declared: "We call upon the Congress to support our President in guaranteeing these basic and fundamental rights: . . . the right to equal opportunity of employment. . . ."

Congressman Claire E. Hoffman (R.-Mich.) told the House that the Democrats had paid no attention to items in their own platform and thus had no right to point to the Republican FEPC plank. Bluntly, he stated, "Platforms, as many people know, are made to garner votes, not to guide the party after the election." U.S. Eighty-first Congress, second session, *Congressional Record*, Vol. 96, Part 2 (February 22, 1950), 2184.

85. The NAACP advised its members, *"Any Congressman who voted for the McConnell substitute on February 22 was voting against a major part of the Association's program.* Remember that." *Crisis*, LVII (October, 1950), 549–550.

86. Cf. Arnold Aronson, "Employment," *American Jewish Year Book 1951*, vol. 52, p. 30.

87. Arthur Krock, "Has Mr. Rayburn a Senior (Silent) Partner?" *New York Times*, January 26, 1950, p. 26.

88. Cf. American Political Science Association, Committee on Political Parties, *Toward A More Responsible Two-Party System* (New York: Rinehart, 1950).

89. National Council for a Permanent FEPC in cooperation with the National Emergency Civil Rights Mobilization, Minutes of Executive Committee Meeting, July 20, 1950.

90. Nine hundred delegates met in Washington, February 17–18, 1952. *Crisis*, LIX (March, 1952), 170. "Rule 22" specifies the procedure for invoking cloture.

91. It proved very difficult to separate the problem of Senate rules from the substantive issues. See Clarence Mitchell, "These Are the Issues," *Crisis*, LIX (October, 1952), 485.

92. Arnold Aronson, "Discrimination in Employment," *American Jewish Year Book 1953*, Vol. 54, *op. cit.*, 51.

93. "During the Depression and the war, fair employment practices had been their [race relations organizations] key objective. . . . Then, in the middle forties, there was a change in opinion about race relations. Job discrimination was no longer quite so important when there were jobs for all." Martin Meyerson and Edward C. Banfield, *Politics, Planning and the Public Interest: The Case of Public Housing in Chicago* (Glencoe: Free Press, 1955), p. 21. Actually, FEPC had top priority throughout the forties.

94. This was strikingly illustrated to the writer at a "Workshop Conference on Human Relations" sponsored by District 31, United Steel Workers of America, CIO (April 21, 1951), in Chicago. The participants, many of whom were Negroes, reported "no" employment discrimination in their plants. Close questioning revealed that this was scarcely the case, but employment "discrimination" to them did not refer to upgrading or employment in all departments of a firm. Their perception of "job discrimination" was clearly restricted to whether the plant was "lily-white" or not.

95. The thirteen states are Colorado, Connecticut, Massachusetts, Michigan, Minnesota, New Jersey, New Mexico, New York, Oregon, Pennsylvania, Rhode Island, Washington and Wisconsin. Alaska also

has a mandatory law. Kansas and Indiana have "educational" FEPC programs. Arizona recently established criminal penalties for discrimination in public employment. There are also municipal ordinances, thirty-six of the "enforceable" type and two without penalties for violations. Cf. W. Brooke Graves, *Fair Employment Practice Legislation in the United States, Federal–State–Municipal*, Public Affairs Bulletin No. 93 (Washington: Library of Congress Legislative Reference Service, 1951); Pauli Murray (ed.), *States' Laws On Race and Color* (Cincinnati: Woman's Division of Christian Service, Board of Missions and Church Extension, Methodist Church, 1950), and *ibid., Supplement* (1955); U.S. Eighty-third Congress, Senate (Document No. 15), *State and Municipal Fair Employment Legislation*, Staff Report to the Subcommittee on Labor and Labor-Management Relations of the Committee on Labor and Public Welfare (Washington: Government Printing Office, 1953); the series of reports on employment and civil rights in the *American Jewish Year Book* 1945–1946, Vol. 47 to date; and the FEPC report of the American Jewish Congress, December, 1957.

96. Letter of January 7, 1948. Cf. Kesselman, *op. cit.*, pp. 57–58.

97. Randolph did try to broaden the base of his operations in preparation for the 1945–46 campaign. He wired Mr. Burton, chairman of the Chicago MOWM: "URGE YOU MAKE EVERY EFFORT TO ENLIST ALL JEWISH ORGANIZATIONS, CATHOLIC GROUPS, AND WHITE PROTESTANTS. THEY ARE READY TO COOPERATE AND FORMIDABLE OPPOSITION TO FEPC AS WELL AS PRINCIPLE OF UNITY AMONG ALL MINORITIES MAKE IT NECESSARY FOR US TO UNITE THEM. . . ." November 13, 1945.

98. Cf. Bernard Goldstein, *The*

Dynamics of State Campaigns for Fair Employment Practices Legislation (Chicago: Committee on Education, Training and Research in Race Relations of the University of Chicago, 1950), (mimeographed). Not all of the factors noted are attributable to Mr. Goldstein; some are based upon personal observations in Illinois and Michigan.

99. Cf. Robert Michels, *Political Parties: A Sociological Study of the Oligarchical Tendencies of Modern Democracy*, trans. Eden and Cedar Paul (Glencoe: Free Press, 1949).

100. Herbert H. Stroup, *Community Welfare Organization* (New York: Harper & Bros., 1952), p. 116. Cf. Herman D. Stein, "Jewish Social Work in the United States, 1654–1954," *American Jewish Year Book* 1956, Vol. 57, section on "the Growth of Professionalism," 51–56.

101. This raises a serious matter for consideration by those who would evaluate the relative resources available to various forces seeking to influence governmental policy. What is the tax-exempt status of so-called institutional advertising by business organizations or the funds raised by the American Medical Association to defeat "socialized" medicine? Are reform-protest groups at a government-fostered disadvantage?

102. Cf. B. R. Berelson, P. F. Lazarsfeld, and W. N. McPhee, *Voting: A Study of Opinion Formation in a Presidential Campaign* (Chicago: University of Chicago Press, 1954), pp. 209–212.

103. Theodore Leskes, "Civil Rights," *American Jewish Year Book* 1956, Vol. 57, 156.

104. Cf. Gus Tyler, 'The House of Un-Representatives," *New Republic*, CXXX (June 21, 1954), 8; *ibid.*, Part II (June 28, 1954), 14; *ibid.*, Part III, CXXXI (July 5, 1954), 13.

105. Cf. Goldstein, *op. cit.*, pp. 8–9.

106. "An Illinois FEPC Law came within one vote of final passage. That victory was so near is a tribute to the courageous leadership of Governor Stevenson and his Administration. . . ." Illinois Fair Employment Practice Committee, "Report to the Illinois Community," June 30, 1949.

107. Cf. Samuel Lubell, *The Future of American Politics.* (New York: Harper & Bros., 1952), chaps. 1, 5, 6.

108. Public Law 1881, Seventy-sixth Congress, Third Session, Title II, Section 3E.

109. Arnold Aronson, "Employment," *American Jewish Year Book* 1952, Vol. 53, 95.

110. Theodore Leskes. "Discrimination in Employment," *American Jewish Year Book* 1954, Vol. 55, 27.

111. Based on a confidential interview; see the favorable report by Theodore Leskes, "Civil Rights," *American Jewish Year Book* 1956, Vol. 56, 208.

Index

Atheneum Paperbacks

HISTORY—AMERICAN

Atheneum Paperbacks

HISTORY

HISTORY—ASIA

THE NEW YORK TIMES BYLINE BOOKS

Atheneum Paperbacks

STUDIES IN AMERICAN NEGRO LIFE

LAW AND GOVERNMENT

Atheneum Paperbacks

DIPLOMACY AND INTERNATIONAL RELATIONS

ECONOMICS AND BUSINESS

PSYCHOLOGY AND SOCIOLOGY

Atheneum Paperbacks